Beyond the wire

This publication is based on research funded by the European Union Programme for Peace and Reconciliation in Northern Ireland and the Border Region of Ireland under Measure 2.1, Reconciliation for Sustainable Peace, as administered by the Northern Ireland Community Relations Council.

Project part financed
by the European Union
Peace and Reconciliation Programme

Community Relations Council

Beyond the Wire

Former Prisoners and Conflict Transformation in Northern Ireland

PETER SHIRLOW and KIERAN McEVOY

Pluto 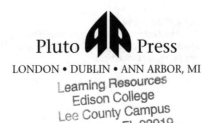 Press

LONDON • DUBLIN • ANN ARBOR, MI

First published 2008 by Pluto Press
345 Archway Road, London N6 5AA
and 839 Greene Street, Ann Arbor, MI 48106

Distributed in the Republic of Ireland and Northern Ireland by
Gill & Macmillan Distribution, Hume Avenue, Park West, Dublin 12, Ireland.
Phone +353 1 500 9500. Fax +353 1 500 9599. E-Mail: sales@gillmacmillan.ie

www.plutobooks.com

Copyright © Peter Shirlow and Kieran McEvoy 2008

The right of Peter Shirlow and Kieran McEvoy to be identified as the authors of
this work has been asserted by them in accordance with the Copyright, Designs
and Patents Act 1988.

British Library Cataloguing in Publication Data
A catalogue record for this book is available from the British Library

Hardback
ISBN   978 0 7453 2632 0

Paperback
ISBN   978 0 7453 2631 3

Library of Congress Cataloging in Publication Data applied for

Designed and produced for Pluto Press by
Chase Publishing Services Ltd, Fortescue, Sidmouth, EX10 9QG, England
Typeset from disk by Stanford DTP Services, Northampton, England
Printed and bound in the European Union by
CPI Antony Rowe Ltd, Chippenham and Eastbourne, England

Contents

List of Tables

Preface

Pat McGuigan, author of the lyrics to the well-known Irish Republican song 'The Men Behind the Wire', was interned in 1972 because those lyrics were deemed inflammatory and prejudicial to peace in Northern Ireland. A less well-known Loyalist version of the song also exists, which like its Republican namesake demands community support for those imprisoned. Both songs present political prisoners as individuals of principle, and speaks to the notion of communities which 'stand behind' such men and women. Imprisonment – those years 'behind the wire' – are a sacrifice before a 'triumphant' return to family, friends and community, that is, the period of being 'beyond the wire'.

Such songs, with their narratives of sacrifice and loss, are deeply embedded within Loyalism and Republicanism. Of course, the realities of relationships between former Loyalist and Republican prisoners and their respective communities are more intricate than such eulogies suggest. Certainly there are clear differences between Republican and Loyalist former prisoners and the communities from which they emanate. That said, the reality of a nearly thirty-year-long conflict in Northern Ireland is that the experience of political imprisonment is a relatively 'normal' element of working-class family and community life in both Republican and Loyalist areas. Moreover, former prisoners remain as an organic part of such communities, prominent in many aspects of civil and social life. Yet the role that they have played in the reconstruction of a damaged society is relatively unexplored and at times purposefully ignored. This lacuna in the research on post-conflict transformation is somewhat peculiar given that former prisoners have been linked to the development of some of the most notable models of conflict transformation. It is less peculiar when we consider that there remains a desire, by some, to continue to demonise those who can be most easily 'blamed' for the conflict. Such a perspective is challenged within this book in order to pinpoint a more meaningful and appreciative understanding of the complexities of conflict and post-conflict recovery and the particular role which former combatants can play in such processes.

This book represents the first sustained academic effort to explore the lives of such former prisoners and their families and the roles that they have played and continue to play in the transition from conflict. Of course, former prisoners were amongst those who signed the Belfast Agreement in 1998 and more recently, Ian Paisley and Martin McGuiness, both themselves former prisoners, have rightly received international plaudits for their peacemaking efforts in reaching the power-sharing accommodation of 2007. However, such an elite-led peace process as that achieved in 2007 requires a concurrent focus upon transitional work that has taken place 'on the ground'. Even less evident is any significant deliberation on the role that former prisoners have operationalised in the provision of leadership in grass-roots conflict transformation within and between communities. Such exertions are often demanding, unglamorous and unrewarding, but absolutely crucial in embedding the peace process in places that have suffered significant harm and violation.

Our work is based upon extensive interviews, focus groups and survey work with former Ulster Volunteer Force/Red Hand Commando and Provisional Irish Republican Army prisoners in North and West Belfast over a two-year period. It builds upon the authors' cumulative experience of almost twenty years working with and researching politically motivated prisoners in Northern Ireland and elsewhere.

We believe that the Northern Ireland experience provides a useful corrective to those assumptions prevalent in the international literature on how to 'deal' with former prisoners and ex-combatants in a transition from conflict. In many other contexts it appears that such individuals are viewed as a managerial headache, portrayed as largely passive recipients to whom measures such as Disarmament, Demobilisation and Reintegration should be applied to remove them from the transitional equation as quickly as possible lest they prove a destabilising influence. The Northern Ireland experience suggests a much more dynamic role for former prisoners, ex-combatants and the organisations which they formed. Indeed it is precisely because of their violent pasts that such individuals have been amongst the voices with greatest credibility in promoting messages of peacemaking. Despite continued structural obstacles, and what many would argue was a lack of adequate financial support, many former prisoners have none the less become key agents of conflict transformation in the transition of Northern Ireland to peace.

There are many people who aided this project and provided support in various forms, in particular, Professor Brian Graham, who made a very significant contribution to this project and the arguments and analysis that we promote. We wish to record special thanks to Dawn Purvis, MLA and Dr Feilim Ó hAdmhaill who provided excellent research assistance during the fieldwork. Libby Smitt at the Community Relations Council helpfully administered the research grant upon which this project was largely based. Advice and help regarding the conduction of the survey work and also attendance at various workshops was supplied by Tom Roberts, Tommy Quigley, Michael Culberth, Martin Snoddon, Rab Jackson, Eddie Kinner, Padraic McCotter, William Smyth, Rosie McCorley, Rosena Brown, Joe Doherty, Paul O'Neill, Leo Morgan, Robert McCallan, Sean Campbell, Joseph Barnes, Tony Catney and Mike Ritchie.

We would also like to thanks the staff of Tar Isteach, EPIC, REACT Armagh, REACT North West and Coiste na n-Iarchimí. The deaths of Billy Mitchell and David Ervine, both of whom supported our efforts and were prime examples of former prisoners giving their all in seeking to transform conflict, are deeply regretted. Our colleagues at Queen's are also due thanks. Shadd Maruna, Clare Dwyer and Ruth Jamieson all provided support and sensible advice. Kirsten McConnachie did the same as well as providing additional research assistance. Also thanks to the support provided by the ever-interested and enthusiastic staff in the peerless Northern Ireland Political Collection at the Linenhall Library.

In addition, members of civic society presented themselves for interviews which helped us locate this body of work beyond the former prisoner community. We would like to thank the hundreds of people who took the time to attend focus groups and who completed the questionnaires. Finally Kieran McEvoy owes thanks to Lesley and Órlaith for putting up with more time spent at the computer when there were dinosaurs that needed tending and Peter Shirlow thanks/ apologises (yet again) to Oonagh, Aoife and Ruairi. We hope that this project has also been worthwhile for those who supported us.

Introduction

Between 1969 and the restoration of the devolved Northern Ireland Assembly in 2007, the conflict (colloquially termed 'the Troubles') cost the lives of some 3,700 people. The death toll, combined with significant levels of physical and psychological injuries, are but the most striking reminders of a violent past. The peace process during the last two decades has seen no diminution in the importance of the competing political ideologies of Nationalism or Unionism and minor evidence of a 'moderate' shared identity. Instead, the process has witnessed a series of compromises which appear broadly to have squared the circle of retaining core political objectives, managing political constituencies and an incremental acceptance of the need for pragmatic and non-violent accommodations over issues previously considered unsolvable. Despite all its bumps and dips, the Northern Ireland peace process is in our view rightly considered a relative success in terms of contemporary peacemaking.

The particular focus of this book is upon the role that former prisoners have played in conflict transformation. We will argue that the lack of visibility of former prisoners in the delivery of peace in the jurisdiction, particularly on the ground in communities most affected by violence, is a significant deficit in understanding the transition from conflict. For some commentators, the primary attention given to former prisoners appears to either evoke past acts of violence or assume that the conspicuous involvement of some in contemporary acts of criminality or thuggery is emblematic of the behaviour of the entire former prisoner community. As is detailed below, we are not naïve and do not believe that all former prisoners are beyond reproach or admonishment. None the less, we do argue that perpetual negative labelling undermines a more reasoned consideration of both individuals and groups of former prisoners. Evidently, unconstructive stereotyping significantly undersells the importance of former prisoners in sustaining and indeed nourishing the peace process to date.

Ultimately, the transition of Northern Ireland from violent conflict to peace has been a tortuous but enduring process. It has involved the renegotiation of relations between Britain and Ireland, as well as establishing a complex architecture for the governance of Northern

Ireland. It has required sustained efforts to manage deeply contested issues of cultural identity and re-evaluate claims to territory that are, in themselves, at the very root of political disagreements and cultural atavism (Shirlow et al., 2005). The creation of a post-conflict society has also witnessed significant changes to the police and criminal justice system, legislative changes and institutions designed to oversee and deliver human rights and equality of treatment and intricate processes intended to effect the decommissioning of weaponry, the dismantling of armed groups and the normalisation of security (Aughey, 2005; Cox et al., 2006). Finally, as in other conflicts, amongst the most controversial element to the process of conflict transforma-tion has been the release and reintegration of politically motivated prisoners (McEvoy, 1998, 1999; Von Tangen Page, 1998).

Under the terms of the 1998 Agreement (henceforth 'the Agreement'), all qualifying paramilitary prisoners belonging to organisations on ceasefire were to be released from prison within two years. Although the numbers released under these provisions constituted only a small percentage of 'activists' imprisoned as a result of the conflict, the decision remains controversial. To date, 449 prisoners have been released (196 Loyalist, 241 Republican and 12 non-aligned) under the provisions of the 1998 Agreement. These men and women joined thousands of other former prisoners who had already served prison sentences related to the Northern Ireland conflict. While it is notoriously difficult to estimate the total number imprisoned, some sources suggest approximate totals of 15,000 Republicans and somewhere between 5,000 and 10,000 Loyalists (McEvoy, 2001). The overall aim of this book is to examine the ways in which groups of politically motivated former prisoners (a term discussed fully in Chapter 1) are involved in peace-building and societal transition and to evaluate the constraints and impediments placed upon their activities by the effects of the imprisonment process and their continued structural exclusion from aspects of civic and social life.

THE 1998 AGREEMENT AND ITS AFTERMATH

Conflict transformation refers to methods that alter the nature of the conflict from violent to non-violent strategies (Lederach, 1995, 1997). While the armed combat stage of the Troubles is complete, conflict is maintained consciously through other means, including contestation over housing, education, delivery of services and disparate interpretations of the past (Healing Through Remembering, 2006). In particular, the sustained contestation over 'the past' reflects the continuation of unreconciled narratives regarding the nature and meaning of the conflict.

Republicans interpret and narrate their conflict as one against the British state, a conflict which contains elements of territorial self-determination, assertion of civil rights and reactionary violence against torture, imprisonment and the violation of human rights (Adams, 1997; Moloney, 2003; English, 2004). For Republicans, the British state has been engaged as an active and aggressive party at all stages in the conflict while simultaneously trying to portray itself as an unwilling but committed umpire between two warring 'tribes'. Thus Republicans recount their 'war' as an anti-imperialist rather than civil conflict.

Loyalists, in contrast, construct their conflict as primarily one of defence: defence of their communities from Republican violence, and defence of the constitutional Union (Bruce, 1992). Although the British state has not shown unqualified appreciation for these activities, arresting and imprisoning Loyalist paramilitaries for 'taking on' the enemies of the state (Shirlow and McGovern, 1996, 1998; Graham and Shirlow, 2002; Shirlow and Monaghan, 2004; Gallaher and Shirlow, 2006), the Loyalists' enemy was clearly defined as Republicans (who were seeking to 'bomb' northern Protestants into a united Ireland) and, by extension, the Catholic civilian community (Shirlow, 2003a, 2003b; Graham, 2004). As one Loyalist participant in the research carried out for this book commented:

I seen it as a civil war and still see it as a civil war. When Republicans say the war was with the British but most of the military action was directed against the Protestant community in the terms that 'our war might be against the Brits but if Prods [Protestants] are killed or injured and they are regarded as collateral damage – so what.' 'If people are incinerated at La Mon in our economic war – so what – the Prods don't count.'[1] I think the idea was that while Republicans looked at the Brits as the enemy they were sort of discounting the Unionist population as irrelevant, 'they don't matter, if we can bomb the Brits out these people will do as they're told,' and that was when our reaction set in saying 'hold on we won't do as we are told'. In the early stages we did look at every Nationalist as an enemy, and at the same time Republicans looked at the Protestant community as people who could be killed because they were irrelevant, they weren't part of the situation, they could be killed and no one would care about it. That's where we seen the conflict as being between two sets of people. [Loyalist: workshop]

In 1998, and for some years thereafter, it appeared that a necessary set of processes to achieve conflict transformation had been codified in the Agreement and the subsequent Northern Ireland Act. This was very much a consociational accord, a form of government that seeks to hold together divided societies by accommodation at the elite level (Tonge, 2005). In general, consociational agreements are 'often the equilibrium outcomes of bargains or pacts between the political leaders of ethnic or religious communities' (O'Leary, 1999: 68) to which end, they 'avoid the compulsory integration of peoples: instead they seek to manage differences equally and justly' (ibid.: 76). Bi-nationalism lies at the core of the Agreement. Some critics contend that the approach taken institutionalises and freezes national and sectarian identities (Dixon, 2004). Such critics have argued that parity of esteem could cement the existing blocs and thus become a charter for social and spatial apartheid rather than transition. In response, we would argue that strong and secure identities (such as those evident amongst many of the former prisoners interviewed for this research) can also serve as the basis for political generosity and explicit efforts at conflict transformation which challenge sectarianised attitudes and practices.

While the work of the former prisoners discussed below offers considerable comfort to supporters of the Agreement, few would contend that it magically resolved the political problems of Northern Ireland. The decommissioning of paramilitary weaponry, the demobilisation of paramilitary organisations, state demilitarisation, police reform, and the focus of this particular book, prisoner release – these and other issues presented substantial obstacles during the transition from violence. Although the Agreement addressed the constitutional status of Northern Ireland, it is clear that at the local level, especially within communities most affected by conflict, the construction and reproduction of identity remains embedded within notions of territoriality and ethnically defined allegiance (Graham, 1997; Shirlow and Murtagh, 2006).

The provisions of the Agreement were democratically endorsed by political representatives and via referendums in Northern Ireland and the Republic of Ireland. The devolved Assembly was suspended on several occasions due in the main to Unionist demands concerning Provisional Irish Republican Army (IRA) decommissioning and allegations concerning a Republican spy-ring. In the elections that have taken place since 1998 there has been a significant growth in the political power-base of Sinn Féin, with its historical legacy of 'physical-force' Republicanism, and the Democratic Unionist Party (DUP), who operated an anti-Agreement stance. The more 'moderate' pro-Agreement political parties such as the Social Democratic and Labour Party (SDLP), the Ulster Unionist Party (UUP) and the Alliance Party have each lost votes. Both the SDLP and UUP have shifted from being the mainstays of Irish Nationalism and Unionism to positions of secondary importance within each of these political blocs. The main emphasis in political negotiations since the suspension of the Assembly in 2002 has been upon encouraging the DUP to share power with Sinn Féin. Some rewriting of the Agreement via the 2006–07 St Andrews Agreement and complete IRA decommissioning led to the restoration of devolution through what had appeared as the improbable scenario of a DUP/Sinn Féin power-sharing Executive. The subsequent image of Martin McGuinness (Sinn Féin) and Ian Paisley (DUP), men who had been at the forefront of political contestation in Northern Ireland since the 1960s, sharing power at Stormont has been widely lauded locally and internationally as confirmation *par excellence* of political conflict transformation in action.

Notwithstanding the considerable achievements of such 'top-down' peacemaking, the focus of this book is upon the concurrent need for conflict transformation at the 'grass-roots' level. As former UN Secretary General Kofi Annan (2004) has argued when discussing the lessons of peace-building, such work must be 'deeply rooted in local communities'. As is developed further below, we argue that much of the 'heavy lifting' in conflict transformation in those highly polarised communities which have been most affected by violence in Northern Ireland, has in fact been undertaken by former combatants and former prisoners. It is they who have played a fundamental role in embedding the peace process through conspicuous demonstrations of leadership 'on the ground'.

The organic nature of such leadership and related modes of conflict transformation are somewhat distant from 'official' community relations discourse which has until recently been the dominant framework for inter-community reconciliation in Northern Ireland (McEvoy et al., 2006). In fact, we would argue that the experience of former prisoners in conflict transformation work offers a powerful and timely critique to such a framework.

By way of background, since the early 1970s, government policy in Northern Ireland has placed significant emphasis upon 'reconciliation' between the 'two communities' (Porter, 2003). Alongside the more recent political negotiations, devolved and direct rule administrations have pursued their statutory responsibilities in this area under a number of guises including 'community relations', 'good relations' and at present 'A Shared Future' (Harbinson, 2002). Inter-communal division has been 'addressed' through the funding, policy-making and advisory functions of the Central Community Relations Unit (CCRU), Community Relations Council (CRC) and District Councils Community Relations Programme. In addition, educational policy initiatives include the cross-community contact schemes for schools and sports, youth, community groups, support for integrated education, and curriculum attention to education for mutual understanding and cultural heritage. Such programmes are not without controversy (McVeigh, 2002).

Republicans accuse the CRC and associated 'community relations industry' of perpetuating the idea that the conflict was between 'two traditions' whereas the British state was a full party to the 'war' and remains committed to attacking Republicanism by other means including the 'active reproduction of sectarianism' (Sinn Féin, 2003: n.p.). Unionists and Loyalists are critical of the CRC for funding groups antagonistic to the state and, in particular, to what they take as the tenet of CRC policy which supports Republican claims for 'equality'. Loyalists also castigate the community relations tradition for demonising working-class Loyalism and associated aspects of Protestant culture (Shirlow et al., 2005). Below, we explore further the attitudes of former political prisoners towards the vexed notion of reconciliation more generally. Before doing so, we provide a background to 'A Shared Future' and some critical reflections regarding its relevance to the style of reconciliation work identified herein.

FORMER PRISONERS, RECONCILIATION AND THE 'SHARED FUTURE' FRAMEWORK

The complexities of the term 'reconciliation' in Northern Ireland are explored in considerable detail elsewhere (Hamber and Kelly, 2005). Former prisoners have expressed considerable misgivings about its usage, primarily because of its association with the community relations tradition (McEvoy et al., 2006). The most recent official iteration of that tradition is the framework discussed in 'A Shared

Future'. Although the complexities and nuances of this agenda are beyond the scope of this book,[2] its particular significance for the work of former prisoners is worth exploring in some additional detail.

Between 2003 and 2006, following an extensive consultation process, the Direct Rule administration oversaw the unveiling of the 'Shared Future' strategy. Written by civil servants and other prominent figures associated with the community relations tradition, the policy has a stated aim of establishing 'a peaceful, inclusive, prosperous, stable and fair society firmly founded on the achievement of reconciliation, tolerance, and mutual trust and the protection and vindication of human rights for all' (OFM/DFM, 2005: 3). It continues that Northern Ireland's difficulties are not ones of inequality but rather because of 'a culture of intolerance' (OFM/DFM, 2005: 9). It sets out a range of measures designed to give effect to the government's vision of reconciliation with considerable emphasis on the sharing of resources, the encouragement of 'good relations' and 'building upon' the success of the equality agenda in Northern Ireland.

Although the need to tackle sectarianism, racism and other discriminatory practices and attitudes in Northern Ireland is self-evident, the experiences of former prisoners highlight a number of important flaws in this evermore dominant concept of reconciliation. These include the likely continuance (at least for the foreseeable future) of communities that are both socially excluded and segregated, an arguable astructural bias of the 'Shared Future' framework which is manifested most obviously in its ambivalence towards substantive equality and the tendency to eulogise an illusory 'middle ground'.

In Northern Ireland, particularly in working-class areas, identity remains vested in traditional principles of ethno-nationalism that locate cultural belonging and citizenship in a 'living space' defined by clearly demarcated boundaries (Shirlow and Murtagh, 2006). Senses of belonging correspond to contested issues of territoriality that are the basis of essentialised group identities and the potent focus of national mobilisation (Ignatieff, 1999; Yiftachel, 2002). In many such working-class communities, levels of poverty and social exclusion remain formidable despite the apparent post-conflict economic boom. Northern Ireland currently has a historically low level of unemployment (approximately 5 per cent) which is close to the UK average (DTZ, 2005). However, its percentage of 'economically inactive' individuals (which includes people claiming other types of welfare benefits) remains amongst the highest in the UK, and the numbers of 'workless' households (after correcting for those in retirement) has remained broadly stable since 1997 (Kenway et al., 2006). As local human rights group the Committee on the Administration of Justice highlighted recently: 'A particularly stark fact ... is that people who live in workless households, whether Catholic or Protestant, have not benefited from the economic up-turn that others have experienced' (CAJ, 2006: 65).

In particular, the areas of North and West Belfast (where most of the former prisoners interviewed for this book lived) remain stubbornly at the top of Northern Ireland's 'poverty chart', as they did throughout much of the conflict. It is in these communities where territorial and identity tensions are at their most visible that the challenge to sectarian asperity, anti-social activity and the promotion of alternative and meaningful inter-community contact is being prominently constructed, aided and delivered, either by former prisoner groups or by individual former prisoners who work in other areas of the community and civil society sector (McShane, 1998). The range of work in which former prisoners are involved within such areas includes capacity-building, anti-poverty work, anti-racist work, resolving disputes at interface areas and concerning contested marches, community-based restorative justice, youth diversionary work, initiatives on dealing with the past, equality and human rights campaigning, and a host of other related activities. Such efforts are often grinding, difficult and unglamorous.

Some of it involves direct negotiation and accommodation with 'the other side'. Other efforts entail former prisoners working predominantly *within* the communities from which they emanate. In either case, such work moves beyond the rhetoric of reconciliation to pragmatic and engaged efforts at peacemaking in the communities where it is most needed. Real reconciliation within and between such communities requires more than platitudes concerning 'cultures of intolerance'. Rather, it requires an appreciation of the particular contribution of the work of ex-combatants and former prisoners (completely omitted from the 'Shared Future' framework), a recognition of the continued realities of segregated and excluded communities and an acknowledgement of the responsibilities of government to ameliorate the structural conditions of poverty and social exclusion which feed prejudicial attitudes and behaviour in the first instance.

To this end, the work of former prisoners also provides a useful corrective to the evident misgivings concerning equality which apparently underpin the 'Shared Future' framework. As is detailed elsewhere, the notion that the human rights and equality frameworks in particular are 'divisive' is often either explicit or implicit in much community relations discourse (McEvoy et al., 2006).[3] Although the 'Shared Future' framework makes reference to the importance of human rights, it sets its stall out clearly as 'building on the success' of the equality agenda – in effect an argument that long-standing equality legislation has served its purpose in reducing the most egregious practices of discrimination against Catholics – and arguing that policy should now be directed by 'good relations' between communities. It also emphasises that rights should be framed as individual rather than group or community rights and equates the assertion of rights with 'a perpetual and sterile battle for ethnic power' (OFM/DFM, 2005: 9). The vacuity of these arguments and the approaches that emerge from them is both highlighted and confronted by the examples of former prisoners.

As is discussed in further detail below, the individual rights of former prisoners receive insignificant protection under existing human rights legislation. As a group, they do not receive specific protection under Northern Ireland's equality legislation. In fact, as is discussed further in Chapter 5, at the time of writing, existing fair employment legislation explicitly upholds their disbarment and exclusion from protection on the basis of their previous support for political violence. Continual efforts by Republican and Loyalist former prisoner groups to challenge such obvious structural exclusions is hardly a 'sterile battle for ethnic power'. Former politically motivated prisoners have lodged legal challenges, lobbied for greater legislative protections for former prisoners and maintained a constant pressure on bodies such as the Human Rights Commission and Equality Commission to ensure that the rights of their constituencies remained firmly on their respective agendas. As McEvoy notes (2000), when one considers that IRA prisoners used to refuse to recognise the courts in the 1970s, the increased recourse by serving prisoners and their political allies to the use of law was a key element of the broader critical reappraisal of the use of political violence which preceded the IRA ceasefires in particular. Engagement in rights talk inevitably entails a process described by Habermas (1975: 108) as 'communicative sharing', a dialogical exchange which entails the rational articulation of a position that not only renders it open to objective analysis but also inevitably entails an acknowledgement of the rights of the 'other' involved in such a dialogue. Historically, both Loyalists and

Republicans viewed violence as the logical response to the denial of their respective rights. Put simply, their current recourse to a rights and equality discourse as part of broader strategies of non-violent mobilisation is, for us, proof positive that the peace process is actually taking root and embedding.

Finally we would argue that the 'Shared Future' approach to reconciliation and much of the community relations tradition in which it is firmly located appears locked into a world-view that sees the breaking-down of prejudice between the two principal traditions as synonymous with developing a 'middle ground' in Northern Ireland politics devoid of the 'extremism' of either side (McEvoy et al., 2006). In a context where Sinn Féin and the DUP have – at least temporarily – triumphed over more moderate expressions of Irish Nationalism and Ulster Unionism, such a perspective would appear to encourage a politics of despair and nihilism. However, it is our contention that self-confessed 'extremists' among the former prisoner and former combatant communities have shown identifiable leadership in transforming cultures of violence in Northern Ireland. As is argued below, it is precisely because of their 'extreme' pasts that they have had the credibility to demonstrate such leadership both within and between the communities which were most marked by the conflict. A key lesson which emerges from Northern Ireland is that the political generosity required for conflict transformation is to be found not only among self-defined 'moderates' but, more significantly, within those political 'extremists' who are most secure and confident in their identities.

POLITICAL ATTITUDES TO FORMER PRISONERS

As is discussed in considerable detail below, much of the conflict concerning prisoners in Northern Ireland concerned their status as politically motivated rather than criminal actors. We would argue that the *de facto* acceptance of the political motivation of paramilitaries, as evidenced by the early release programme and other measures, did not imply either approval or appeasement. Rather, they were indicative of an understanding that 'unpalatable' measures such as prisoner release were necessary in the process of conflict transformation. The logic of such an understanding also requires a recognition that the removal of certain structural obstacles to successful prisoner reintegration is a prerequisite foundation for a new society. As stated by a prominent member of civic society in Northern Ireland:

if you are saying to people that we want you to desist from a path of struggle, you must also be saying that here is an alternative path and it's not simply an alternative political path, cause you can't separate politics and economics in that neat way. It's a question of an alternative path, which of course, for those who are politically motivated and active, must include being able to earn an income. The alternative path, which integrates them fully into society, is one that goes hand in hand, in other words not just politically but economically too. [interview: member of civic society, 8 February 2005]

In a similar fashion to political imprisonment during the conflict, debates concerning the fate of serving and former prisoners were a useful prism through which to view other elements of the body politic beyond the state. Certainly the issue of prisoner release was the most significant obstacle to pro-Agreement Unionism during the referendum debates (McEvoy, 2001; Von Tangen Page, 2006). Nationalists of whatever hue appeared by and large to accept that prisoner release was a necessary part of the broad conflict transformation process, regardless of the largely indiscriminate nature of the Loyalist campaign of violence.[4] Few politicians or commentators from that community ever posited the likelihood of a 'security' or military solution to the conflict. For many Unionists, on the other hand, decades of discourses which pathologised violence and obfuscated the broader political causes of conflict appeared at times to have been internalised and actually 'believed' (Robinson, 1980; Cochrane, 1997). This refusal to recognise political motivation insulated Unionism from what Republicans, Nationalists and some Loyalists would view as a moral culpability in the reproduction of conflict and provided a bulwark against the need for significant political change. The perspective of the DUP on the early releases is instructive: 'All decent people recoil with moral contempt at the prospect of the mass release of those who have murdered and maimed the innocent' (DUP, 1998).

Similarly, the MP for Lagan Valley, Jeffrey Donaldson (then a member of the UUP, now DUP) has indicated that it was the prisoner release issue together with decommissioning which prevented him from supporting the Agreement. As Gormally has argued, for Unionists in particular, 'prisoners and former prisoners are the most obvious ex-combatants, the visible concentration of everything people feel about the conflict … they are the perpetrators of numerous atrocities, the enemies of democracy and civilisation incarnate' (2001: 5).

The reality is that the *de facto* acceptance (by the British government at least) of political motivation heralded through the prisoner releases represented a betrayal of the Unionist 'fiction of blamelessness' (McEvoy, 2001: 352). Further investment of whatever scale in the process of prisoner reintegration only appeared to further inflame Unionist opposition. Prisoner release and resettlement became emblematic of the broader process of unpalatable change.

One prominent feature of the attitude towards prisoners articulated by the UUP and DUP has been a consistent linkage of the question of prisoner release and resettlement with the treatment of victims of violence. Thus, a persistent theme in the campaigns against the early releases was that of Unionist politicians framing their position as 'speaking on behalf of the victims of violence'. Of course, many victims of violence were indeed opposed to the early releases. However, their views were not monolithic. Other victims felt they could not take a position on the issue whilst others argued in favour of the early release programme (McEvoy, 1998). Amongst the most high-profile supporters of the early release programme as part of the broader process of reconciliation were Mrs Joan Wilson, mother of Marie Wilson, killed by the IRA in the 1987 Enniskillen 'Poppy Day' bombing, and Mr Colin Parry, whose son Tim was killed in 1993 by an IRA bomb in Warrington, Lancashire.[5] The generosity of these and other victims who have suffered most egregiously at the hands of paramilitary and state actors (see also Hamber, 2003, 2005) appeared to have little impact. Neither indeed did the fact that many of the communities from which prisoners had emerged (which were also amongst the most victimised places in Northern Ireland) also contained victims who were wholly supportive of release.

Unionist politicians also gave prominent support to legal challenges mounted to test the provisions of the early release programme (Morgan, 2000). In the wake of the releases, a number of Unionist politicians have also consistently criticised the resources allocated to the resettlement of prisoners, often juxtaposing such expenditure with the amount allocated to victims. While some victims and victims' organisations have become increasingly disillusioned with politicians who 'speak in their name' (McBride, 2004), the debate concerning former prisoners amongst mainstream Unionists in Northern Ireland has lost little of its vituperative tone.

A central concern of this book is therefore to encourage more measured and reasoned analysis of the role of former prisoners in the transition beyond stereotypical perceptions of tattooed thugs imposing their will on cowed and passive communities. With colleagues, we have explored elsewhere the complexities of the dialectical power relationships between paramilitaries, former para-militaries and their respective communities (Shirlow and McGovern, 1996; McEvoy and Mika, 2002). Below, we also discuss recidivism rates of prisoners released under the Agreement and the differences between the various paramilitary groupings in their attitudes to criminality and commitment to the transition from violence (see Chapters 2 and 7). Those cold-eyed assessments aside, the research findings within this book point to former prisoners as effective peacemaking agents, particularly at the micro-scale level within and between local communities. Given the misgivings outlined above concerning the utilisation of the term 'reconciliation', we have instead sought to examine such activities under the rubric of the phrase largely used by former prisoners themselves: conflict transformation.

CONFLICT TRANSFORMATION

By way of background, in recent years, three main schools of thought have developed in relation to how conflict should be handled. These are often classified under the broad (and occasionally overlapping) headings of conflict resolution, conflict management, and conflict transformation. All three not only articulate varying approaches to conflict intervention, but also reflect different conceptualisa-tions of conflict itself. Even within these three broad approaches differing perspectives exist. It is also the case that many theorists and practitioners interchange the terms, adding to the confusion.

For the sake of brevity, conflict resolution approaches have tended to be the traditional response to conflicts which have not been able to 'resolve' themselves satisfactorily through violence or other means (McEvoy and Newburn, 2003). Proponents of these approaches, such as Burton (1993), argue that it is possible to transcend conflicts if parties can be helped to explore, analyse, question and reframe their positions and interests. Conflict resolution, therefore, usually emphasises intervention by skilled third parties working with political and military leaders to cultivate new thinking and novel relationships and thus involves aiming to move parties from zero-sum destructive patterns of conflict to positive-sum constructive outcomes (Deutsch et al., 2006). Different types of intervention may be appropriate at different times; for example, facilitation may be appropriate at the early stages of conflict but power-based mediation (or even coercion) is required when a conflict has reached a high stage of polarisation and there is considerable emphasis on the 'ripening of conflict' in order to secure the most effective results (Kleiboer, 1994).

Conflict management approaches emerged in the context of conflicts which did not appear to have a readily available solution (Tidwell, 1998; Ramsbotham et al., 2005). Advocates of these approaches tend to view violent conflicts as the result of differences of values, interests and power within and between communities (Bloomfield and Reilly, 1998). Resolving such conflicts is viewed as unrealistic: the best that can be done is to manage and contain them, and occasionally to reach a historic compromise in which violence may be laid aside in order that normal politics is resumed (Bar-Siman-Tov, 2007; Zartman, 2007). Conflict management is usually concerned with making appropriate interventions to achieve political settlements, particularly by the most powerful actors who possess the authority and resources to bring pressure on the conflicting parties in order to induce them to settle.

More relevant for current purposes are those scholars and practitioners who advocate the pursuit of 'conflict transformation', as opposed to 'conflict resolution' or 'conflict management' (Francis, 2002). While conflict and conflict transformation has been defined both broadly and narrowly, we have found the approach offered by Ho-Won Jeong most useful for our purposes:

Enduring and mutually assured outcomes will not be attained without taking into account power imbalances and equitable social and economic relations. Self esteem and identity as well as physical well-being are key elements to be considered in conflict resolution and peace building. The nature of relations between adversaries needs to be examined in terms of looking for transformative possibilities. In rebuilding communal relations, long-term hostile relationships have to be overcome to prevent future occurrences of violent conflict. [Jeong, 1999: 3]

Probably the best-known proponent of this approach is John Paul Lederach (1995, 1997) who has argued that conflict transformation differs because it reflects a better understanding of the nature of conflict itself. For him, a 'conflict resolution' approach suggests that conflict is destructive and thus something that should be ended. It also suggests that conflict can be 'resolved' permanently through mediation or other intervention processes. Lederach contends that it is incorrect to ignore the fact that many conflicts occur as a result of endemic injustices or inequalities and that 'resolution' does not require substantial long-term structural changes. Moreover, while 'conflict management' may represent an improvement because it accepts that conflicts often cannot be resolved quickly, it too has limitations including an emphasis that violence is the primary predicament or cause of conflict – an approach which may divert attention away from an appreciation of the more meaningful *causes* of violence and inter-community atavism.

Conflict transformation thus recognises that when social conflict occurs it transforms the nature of the relationships which engender conflict (Ryan, 2007). Conflict transformation approaches can, however, reduce the potential for such conflicts to materialise by operating at a number of levels to help transform the relationships, interests and discourses which support the continuation of violence. It can operate at the personal level, where beliefs and perceptions are challenged and where non-violent advocacy methods are evoked and rationalised. Crucially, however, in the Northern Ireland context, it can lead to an acknowledgment that transformation also involves structural changes with regard to injustice and the perpetuation of structural inequalities. Conflict transformation thus involves a focus not only upon the relationships between individuals, groups and communities involved in conflict but also upon structural issues including ending oppression, guaranteeing rights protection and ensuring a more equitable sharing of resources (Francis, 2002; Mertus and Helsing, 2006). Conflict transformation thus represents the most secure means of conceptually grounding this study of politically motivated former prisoners at the individual, communal and societal levels. As one Loyalist respondent summed up:

Our interpretation of conflict transformation is not only transforming the nature of the conflict, from violence through dialogue to something else through the democratic process, but it's transforming the nature of relationships between key people in conflict and that has to start with me and with you. To transform the nature of the conflict depends on transforming the nature of relationships. That's why, right from our prison experience, we realised that unless I can change the attitude towards Republicans, no matter who the enemy is then the nature of the conflict is not going to change. It is about transformation rather than resolution because we can't resolve the constitutional issue without one becoming the other [Unionist becoming Republican or vice versa]. A resolution of the 'Irish Problem' means we're all British or all Irish. Governments talk about conflict management so we focus on transformation. It's about transforming politics, transforming community action, transforming restorative justice

– everything is about transforming. It has to start with the individual. If it doesn't change the individual then it's not going to change anything. [Loyalist: focus group]

STUDYING POLITICALLY MOTIVATED FORMER PRISONERS

While the centrality of prisoner release to the process of conflict transformation has been widely acknowledged in writing on the Northern Ireland peace process (for example, Mitchell, 2000), the fate of politically motivated prisoners after release has received comparatively little attention. Indeed, much of the research on released prisoners has been conducted by former prisoner groupings themselves (see, for example, An Tus Nua, 1998; Tar Anall, 2000; Ó hAdhmaill, 2001; Tar Isteach, 2004), or in cooperation with academics (see, for example, Shirlow, 2001a; Grounds and Jamieson, 2003; McEvoy et al., 2004; Gormally et al., 2007). The field research for this present study, which took place in 2004–05, represents the first sustained quantitative and qualitative attempt to involve both Republicans and Loyalists in an investigation of the impact of imprisonment and the role of politically motivated former prisoners in the process of conflict transformation in Northern Ireland.[6]

More widely, this is one of the few large-scale studies of politically motivated former prisoners, from both Republican and Loyalist backgrounds, in any recent conflict of which the authors are aware. While the political landscape has changed in Northern Ireland since the re-establishment of devolution under the DUP/Sinn Féin-led administration, the fate of former prisoners has remained largely unchanged. More broadly, we would argue that some of the key themes concerning the role of former prisoners and ex-combatants in processes of conflict transformation may be of direct relevance to other societies seeking to emerge from conflict (McEvoy et al., 2008).

For former Republican and Loyalist combatants, it is readily apparent that the dialogue accompanying that transition has been informed and articulated through their common prison and post-imprisonment experiences. While there are significant differences in ideologies, capacities and relations with their respective communities, both sets of former prisoners have delivered identifiable and important conflict transformation practices on the ground.

We are concerned with Republican and Loyalist former prisoner groups 'working within and working between' their respective communities. This refers to their involvement in dialogue and various forms of practical community work, both within their own communities and with the 'other' community. As is discussed extensively elsewhere, the term 'community' itself has multiple meanings and is often used loosely in the Northern Ireland context to define socio-territorial units that extend from the scale of small inner-city micro-societies to the ethnic group as a whole (Shirlow and Murtagh, 2006). Conflict transformation may entail working with former prisoners themselves, developing programmes within and for the communities within which former groups are located, and relationship-building and engaging in practical activities with the historically estranged communities.

The research was conducted in parts of North Belfast and the Greater Shankill area of West Belfast. Participants in the study generally originated from the highly segregated, interfaced and socially deprived inner-city communities within which former prisoner groups operate. The effects of the conflict were magnified in such areas and they remain the arenas of political groups 'seeking to mobilise political discourse through territorial control' (Shirlow and Murtagh, 2006: 18). As was noted above, some of the communities involved are ranked in the top 10 per cent of the most deprived communities in Northern Ireland. Around 60 per cent of the households within the study areas are in receipt of housing benefit compared to an average of 24.9 per cent for Northern Ireland. Thus the majority of the participants in this study live within areas that are targeted with regard to social need as well as policies that aim to dilute the impact of cultural and political tension (Shirlow, 2001a).

Two politically motivated former prisoner groups facilitated the research for this book (see Chapter 3). The Ex-Prisoners' Interpretive Centre (EPIC) was established on Belfast's Shankill Road in 1995 while Tar Isteach (meaning 'come in') was launched in 1999 and is based in the New Lodge area of inner North Belfast. It is part of a larger network of Republican former prisoner groups that come under the umbrella organisation Coiste na n-Iarchimí (Coiste), which functions at an all-island of Ireland level. Both EPIC and Tar Istaech are involved in campaigning work on behalf of politically motivated former prisoners as well as direct service provision in areas such as counselling, training and welfare rights for former prisoners and their families. The groups also operate a series of schemes concerned with conflict transformation, social capital and community development.

In its examination of the contribution of politically motivated former prisoners to conflict transformation in Northern Ireland, the research from which this book is drawn had seven specific objectives:

- to trace the evolution and development of former prisoner groups;
- to evaluate the impacts of imprisonment and release on the personal lives of former prisoners;
- to assess the constraints imposed on former prisoners as agents of change in conflict transformation by the residual criminalisation arising from their status;
- to determine the potential of the former prisoner community in challenging intra-community tensions and evaluate their potential and actual contribution to conflict transformation at the inter-community level;
- to compare and contrast the differing capacities of Loyalist and Republican former prisoners to act as agents of change within their own communities;
- to explore the concept of reintegration through which former prisoners can act as agents of social and communal transformation within the broader political and civic processes of negotiating conflict transformation in Northern Ireland; and
- to examine the broader international and legal context of this study of politically motivated former prisoners in one particular process of conflict transformation.

The research for the book was coordinated by a steering group.[7] Understanding the position, vulnerabilities and future of the former prisoner community in the context of conflict transformation creates important research challenges and requires a diverse and interlinked empirical design. There is an extensive research tradition into the effects of the conflict in the island of Ireland and, in particular, the experiences of spatially segregated communities (see, for example, Shirlow and Murtagh, 2006). Hargie and Dickson (2003) have described the range of research conducted on community relations in Northern Ireland and identified the need for sensitivity, objectivity and rigour in researching the impact of ethno-social division, whilst Connolly and Healy (2002) argue that quantitative techniques alone fail to unpack the processes at work in divided communities. They believe, as do we, that qualitative approaches are essential to capture fully the lived experiences of divided cultures and uncover the causal relationships which explain why groups act in certain ways.

The integrated research methodology incorporated a questionnaire survey, a workshop, focus-group meetings and semi-structured interviews.

A *questionnaire survey* of former prisoners and their relatives was employed to help determine:

- the impact of imprisonment on family life, the effect and nature of release upon self-esteem and other social relationships, and the relevance of these processes to resistance and post-conflict transition;
- the extent and importance of residual criminalisation; and
- attitudes to and impediments in conflict transformation and peace-building at the community scale.

The sample included 150 Republican and 150 Loyalist former prisoners and their relatives (75 from each community). Interviewing was carried out during 2004. It was important to include family members, who have been under-investigated in earlier studies, an omission that undermines the meaning of the impact of imprisonment upon communities and also obscures a series of complex intra-community relationships. The survey aimed at obtaining a range of responses from former prisoners, both in terms of their age and the nature of the regimes under which they were imprisoned. Republican respondents came from the New Lodge, Antrim Road, Bone and Ardoyne districts of North Belfast. Although the bulk of the Republican former prisoners were connected to the IRA, some respondents had been involved in other Republican organisations and a few had no connection with any particular group but had been imprisoned for politically motivated activities. The Loyalist respondents originated in the Greater Shankill area and were drawn from within the Ulster Volunteer Force (UVF) and Red Hand Commando (RHC) groups.

The qualitative dimension to the research comprised three elements. First, a one-day *workshop*, jointly involving both Republican and Loyalist former prisoners, was held to explore their sometimes different and sometimes shared key concerns in terms of the impacts of imprisonment and residual criminalisation and also their abilities to deliver on conflict transformation.[8] Second, in order to provide a discursive and informed context for the results of the questionnaire survey, two *focus-group meetings* were held separately with Loyalist and Republican former prisoners.[9] Finally, *semi-structured interviews* were conducted with a number of key former prisoners and representatives of former prisoner groups and also members of 'civic society' during 2005. All meetings and interviews were taped with the permission of participants and interviewees and subsequently were transcribed: verbatim quotations cited in this book are, of course, anonymous (with the exception of the historical account of prisoner groups in Chapter 3 where names are used with permission), and retain the original, often colloquial, language.

STRUCTURE OF THE BOOK

The remainder of this book is divided into eight chapters. In Chapter 1, we outline the international and local context of political imprisonment. Chapter 2 examines prisoner release, reintegration and respective relationships to conflict transformation. In Chapter 3, we analyse the evolution of former prisoner groups within the historical context of the prison regimes, drawing upon qualitative data to differentiate between Republican and Loyalist experiences. Chapters 4–6 are based on the three core themes: transition, residual criminalisation, and conflict transformation in the communities. In Chapter 4, the personal dimension of politically motivated former prisoners is examined through an analysis of family life, self-esteem and other social relationships. The focus in Chapter 5 is on residual criminalisation and the ways in which this set of processes can act as an impediment in the ability of former prisoners to work both within and between their communities. Chapter 6 is concerned with the contribution of former prisoners in their communities, a theme which is further developed in Chapter 7, which employs qualitative evidence drawn from the focus groups and the workshop to elaborate on the contrasting experiences of both Republican and Loyalist politically motivated former prisoners at working within and between their respective communities. Finally, Chapter 8 considers some of the broader lessons which may be learned from the Northern Ireland experience concerning the reintegration of politically motivated former prisoners and ex-combatants.

1

Understanding Political Imprisonment: Northern Ireland and the International Context

The 'post-imprisonment' experience of former prisoners in Northern Ireland cannot be fully understood without some background to the history of political imprisonment within the jurisdiction. Much of that history has been dominated by the struggle between the prisoners and their gaolers concerning the status of the inmates. To that end, this chapter provides an overview to some of the key themes and events which have shaped political imprisonment in Northern Ireland. The chapter begins with a brief discussion on the definition of political imprisonment. It then explores the different styles of prison management deployed by the prison authorities in dealing with the prisoners in their charge. We then examine various 'resistance' techniques utilised by the inmates themselves to assert their status as 'political' rather than 'criminal' prisoners. Where appropriate, the discussion is informed by the international context of political imprisonment, including inevitable resonances with the contemporary 'War on Terror', now morphed into the 'Long War' (Greenberg et al., 2005).[1] In making such comparisons, we do not imply that the experiences of one jurisdiction can be transposed mechanistically onto another. Rather, to paraphrase Nelken (1994), we would argue that certain key themes are universalisable from such a comparative gaze, which may in turn act as an incentive to 'sharpen the awkward questions' about our own context.

DEFINITIONS OF POLITICAL IMPRISONMENT

Definitional questions concerning prisoners and former prisoners incarcerated as a result of the Northern Ireland conflict have long been highly contested. The practical and symbolic nature of the prison conditions in Northern Ireland, the Republic of Ireland and Great Britain were represented as something of a microcosm of the broader 'conflict about the conflict' (McKeown, 2001; McEvoy, 2001; Corcoran,

2006). As was noted above, much of the violence and political strife concerning the prisons focused on the struggle between the prisoners' assertion of their status as political prisoners and attempts by the prison authorities to resist, undermine, or manage that assertion. Whether or not former prisoners are 'politically motivated' lies at the heart of the interpretation of conflict. Such a contest, between what constitutes a 'political' rather than a purely 'criminal' act or actor is not, however, unique to this particular context.

For example, there is an extensive tradition within critical criminology that places particular emphasis on the ways in which acts which are defined as 'criminal' are inevitably politically constructed (Quinney, 1970; Hagan, 1997). From such a perspective, any analysis of political imprisonment must take as its starting-point the power of the state to criminalise particular behaviour (usually the 'crimes' of the weak and the poor) while condoning or even, in some instances, encouraging the 'crimes' of the powerful and the rich (Buck, 2000). Imprisonment, together with law, warfare and policing, is central to the state's broader process of social ordering. It embeds hegemonic definitions of right and wrong and helps to reproduce existing social order and dominant forms of class and race relations (Rodriguez, 2006). Since this entire process is heavily politicised, for some critical criminologists, almost all of those imprisoned as a result of the criminal justice process may be regarded in some sense as political prisoners.

Notwithstanding the political and ideological forces at work in the process of crime control, such a sweeping assessment is open to a number of obvious critiques. Historically, some variants of this style of critical scholarship appeared to view criminals as 'outlaw heroes' while simultaneously ignoring the suffering of the victims of crime who were often themselves the poor, women, or other vulnerable groups. As Cohen (1996) has argued, the imputing of political motives to criminal offenders who were assumed to be fighting the capitalist system gave the whole endeavour (of exploring the politics/crime axis) a bad name. In addition, such a broad catch-all definition of political crime is of limited analytical utility in places such as Northern Ireland where disputes concerning the motivations of inmates were contested literally to the point of death.

Of more direct relevance is the range of circumstances in which different types of prisoners are described, managed, or indeed self-assert or 'resist' as *political* prisoners. McEvoy et al. (2007) have formulated a detailed framework around which to discuss such dynamics regarding the contemporary 'War on Terror/Long War' which proposes five definitional categories of political imprisonment: prisoners of war, prisoners of conscience, conscientious objectors, radicalised 'ordinary' prisoners, and politically motivated prisoners. The most pertinent of these definitional categories for current purposes is that of politically motivated prisoners.

POLITICALLY MOTIVATED PRISONERS

The term 'politically motivated prisoners' appears to have evolved most explicitly within the Northern Ireland context. It can be utilised to describe prisoners who are otherwise referred to as 'terrorists' by either the state which incarcerates them or by other actors who oppose their methods or political ideology. However, given the long-standing lack of conceptual precision associated with the term 'terrorism' (Schafer, 1974; Primoratz, 1990; Schmid et al., 1990; Gearty, 1996; Gearty and Tomkins, 1996; Guillaume, 2004) and its undoubted pejorative connotations (Goodwin, 2006), the more neutral terminology of politically motivated prisoners became increasingly used from the mid-1990s onwards by those who were then working on issues concerning the possibility of early release (Gormally and McEvoy, 1995; McEvoy, 1998).[2] While 'politically motivated prisoner' does not have the specific legal significance of a term such as 'prisoner of war', it does, however, offer a more objective lens through which to view the actions of both state and prisoners (McEvoy et al., 2007).

The utilisation of the term in Northern Ireland occurred in a context where the acknowledgement of political motivation as an element in terrorist violence has been enshrined in legislation almost since the outbreak of the conflict. From 1972, 'terrorism' was defined in successive pieces of Emergency Legislation (relating both to Northern Ireland and Britain) as 'the use of violence for political ends and includes any use of violence for the purpose of putting the public or any section of the public in fear'. A terrorist was defined as 'a person who is or has been concerned in the commission or attempted commission of any act of terrorism or in directing, organising or training persons for the purpose of terrorism'.[3] From 1973 onwards in Northern Ireland, any person charged with a suspected terrorist offence (a 'scheduled offence') has had their case heard before a single judge in a special juryless court with amended rules of evidence (Jackson and Doran, 1995).[4] The obvious political characteristics of such trials had comparatively little effect on the authorities' response to defendants' assertion of their status as political defendants taking part in a political trial (McEvoy, 2000).

This instrumentalist view of terrorism was a classically British state response to the challenges of responding to political violence.[5] It meant that successive British governments could hold a public position that while individuals might be engaged in acts of violence 'for political ends' as defined in the legislation, such acts remained 'criminal' in nature. Individuals apprehended for such crimes could be tried in a bespoke criminal justice process with significantly amended rules of procedure and admissibility of evidence but, if convicted, there was no onus on the government to treat them any differently than ordinary prisoners tried and convicted by the regular courts. Unlike many other European jurisdictions where there are legislative and, in some instances, constitutional requirements to treat politically motivated offenders differently (Radzinowicz and Hood, 1979), the British tradition has always been to resist strongly any suggestion of 'special' treatment for such prisoners. If anything, the political nature of terrorist actions would sometimes appear to be viewed more heinously than ordinary criminality since such acts represent a more explicit attack on societal values (Wilkinson, 1986).

The utilisation of the term 'politically motivated prisoners' in Northern Ireland, since it drew from the definition set down in the Emergency legislation, thus emerged as an attempt at a 'value-neutral' phrase designed to circumnavigate some of the obvious difficulties associated with the other categories of political prisoners noted above. The straightforward phrase 'political prisoner' immediately encourages an ultimately circular debate as to what – or who – constitutes a political prisoner. Since the government had always strongly resisted acknowledging the political character of the Northern Ireland conflict at any level, there was little likelihood of recognising politically motivated prisoners as 'prisoners of war'. The use of armed violence excluded Republican and Loyalist prisoners from categorisation as conscientious objectors or (with the possible exception of some internees) as prisoners of conscience. The mechanism chosen to effect early releases ultimately proved capable of determining the bona fides of those few cases of 'radicalised ordinaries' who claimed political status. 'Politically motivated prisoners' was a term which, while neither the state nor indeed the prisoners nor their respective organisations would have eulogised, did at least provide a language for a range of pragmatic conversations to take place.

The years which preceded the ultimate accommodation around this phrase were characterised by a sustained conflict between the prisoners and those tasked with managing them. McEvoy (2001) and others (McKeown, 2001; Corcoran, 2006) have analysed the contours of that relationship between the incarcerated and their gaolers in considerable detail. For those less familiar with the history of political imprisonment associated with the conflict in Northern Ireland, this is a useful juncture at which to draw out some of the principal themes which characterised that history and to locate such themes within the broader international context of political imprisonment.

THE MANAGEMENT OF POLITICAL PRISONERS

There is a wealth of literature on the challenges of managing different types of prisons and prisoners (Dilulio, 1987; Ditchfield, 1990; Sparks et al., 1996; Freeman, 1999; Philips and McConnell, 2004). The more thoughtful styles of such scholarship regard prison organisation as more than the technical exercise of *running* a prison. Rather, prison management is best viewed as a process which involves organisations and staff working through the challenges of holding (sometimes extremely dangerous and resourceful) people against their will. Such work is often complicated by a range of external political, social, legal and ideological factors. In the case of politically motivated prisoners, often the fact that they are imprisoned as a result of a violent conflict on the outside even further complicates the managerial task. The media, political supporters and opponents, the international community, and a wide array of other external actors may take a vocal and often contradictory interest in the ways in which such prisoners are treated. Even within and between state institutions themselves, different departments (such as defence, intelligence, policing) apart from those normally tasked with prison oversight may stake a claim on policy formulation concerning such prisoners. Finally, given the public prominence of those who are imprisoned, political leaders up to and including cabinet members, prime ministers and presidents may well interfere in policy and practical management issues concerning such inmates on matters of detail that might never normally reach such upper echelons. Dealing with political prisoners, particularly in the context of an ongoing conflict outside and indeed within the prisons, is a hugely challenging professional task.

Despite the historical and contemporary significance of those challenges, comparatively little has been written about the particular demands of managing such prisoners. Notwithstanding the immense variety of contexts of and responses to political violence, there are broad commonalities in penal policy which remain detectable. For current purposes, these can be divided into three broad styles of prison management. These styles or 'models' of prison management were derived from different phases of the Northern Ireland conflict (Gormally et al., 1993; McEvoy, 2001; McEvoy et al., 2007). They are 'reaction, containment and negotiation' (1969–75); 'criminalisation, repression and the denial of political motivation' (1976–81); and 'managerialism, bureaucratisation and political prisoners as a "scientific" challenge' (1981 onwards).

REACTION, CONTAINMENT AND NEGOTIATION

Elements of the reaction, containment and negotiation model may be seen in the colonial experiences of the British in places such as Cyprus, Kenya, Malaysia as well as Northern Ireland (Dewar, 1985; Kitson, 1991), the French in Algeria (Maran, 1989), the Israeli and Turkish response to Palestinian and Kurdish political violence respectively (Bornstein, 2001: Gunter, 1997; Greenwood, 1989), some civil war or interstate conflicts,[6] and a range of jurisdictions in Latin America which have faced violent internal insurrections. While there is occasional evidence of an awareness of tried and tested methods elsewhere,[7] the deployment of this model is usually characterised by immediate, localised and largely ahistorical security concerns.

In Northern Ireland, the period of reactive containment saw the prisons as but one element of an overall counter-insurgency strategy (for example, Greer, 1995). It was characterised by the primacy of the state's need to react to the outbreak of political violence, to contain those perceived to be involved in that violence, and to suppress such actors and their supportive constituencies until a negotiated settlement could be achieved. Such a model was characterised largely by what could generally be described as a militaristic and securocratic mindset. Due process and human rights concerns were viewed as, at best, irritating impediments which undermined the effectiveness of the state's response to political violence. Thus the model entailed considerable energies being devoted to methods of circumnavigating, co-opting, or otherwise undermining legal protections afforded to politically motivated defendants and prisoners. It was certainly not a strategy designed to win over the hearts and minds of those who were opposed to the state. That said, in its least repressive guise, the focus upon 'getting the enemy off the streets' did arguably lead to a diminution of attention to the behaviour of prisoners once they were locked up behind the prison walls. Since its primary focus was security related to the conflict on the outside, such an approach did arguably lead to a fairly sanguine attitude to the political character of the conflict and thus some pragmatic accommodations with the prison inmates once they were incarcerated.

In the Northern Ireland context this era (extending broadly between 1969 and 1975) witnessed the granting of 'special category status' to convicted paramilitary prisoners. Such prisoners were held in the Long Kesh 'compound' which was segregated on the basis of paramilitary allegiance. They operated within paramilitary command structures through which all negotiations with the prison system were channelled. Military and political lectures were permitted, prisoners were allowed to wear their own clothes and indeed on occasion to march or drill in military-style uniforms for special occasions. In effect, in all but name, these prisoners enjoyed *de facto* prisoner-of-war status (Adams, 1992; Crawford, 1979, 1999).

In addition, from 1971 until 1975, suspected 'terrorists' were interned without trial (Farrell, 1976). Internees were held in camps similar to but separated from the sentenced prisoners, and segregated by perceived paramilitary affiliation (Fields, 1973). The legal process to intern such suspects was fairly rudimentary. An internment order was issued by the Minister for Home Affairs in the Stormont era (later the Secretary of State for Northern Ireland). Defendants were often excluded from the administrative hearings, limitations were routinely placed on cross-examination by defence counsel, witnesses (usually police officers) gave evidence from behind a screen and an expression that they 'believed' an individual to be involved in acts of terrorism was normally sufficient to warrant granting or extension of a detention order. Such orders could be renewed for up to a year and there was little practical grounds for a legal challenge other than 'bad faith' (Spujt, 1986). Internment was a measure directed largely against the Catholic/Nationalist community. In total, 2,060 suspected Republicans were detained, compared to 109 suspected Loyalists (Hogan and Walker, 1989: 94). The Gardiner Committee Report, which was established by the government, concluded that internment had 'brought the law into contempt', 'fanned a widespread sense of grievance and injustice' (Gardiner, 1975: 38–43) and recommended its phasing-out.

The application of this model to Northern Ireland also saw significant changes to the ways in which paramilitary suspects were arrested and tried. In 1972, following the recommendations of the Diplock Committee (1972), a number of legislative changes were introduced. These included an extension of the army and police powers of stop, search, arrest and detain. The law governing the admissibility of confessional evidence was also relaxed to permit convictions based solely upon confessions. In addition, as noted above, a system was introduced wherein offences connected to political violence would be deemed 'scheduled offences' and thus be tried in specially designed juryless 'Diplock' courts (Dickson, 1992; Jackson and Doran, 1995). Finally, throughout this period the army had a prominent role in the oversight of security at Northern Ireland's prisons as the prison system struggled to cope with the exponential growth in prison numbers from approximately 600 in 1969 to 2,687 by 1975.

Under this model it was perfectly compatible to countenance simultaneously any number of unpleasant strategies and tactics to deal with political prisoners (up to and including extra-judicial killings and torture), to negotiate with the prisoners' leadership during their incarceration,[8] and ultimately, if the political conditions on the outside required it, to release such prisoners without momentous soul-searching on the legal or ideological implications of such a move. In effect, it allowed those tasked with prison management to make pragmatic judgements on security grounds (for good and ill) as to how to best engage with political prisoners, while not losing sight of the political character of the conflict in which both they and the prisoners were inevitably constituent parts.

CRIMINALISATION, REPRESSION AND THE DENIAL OF POLITICAL MOTIVATION

The second broad model for the management of political prisoners, which again was drawn from the Northern Ireland context, is one which places greater emphasis upon imprisonment as a central element in the broader political and ideological conflict. Criminalisation is a perspective which views prisons as more than simply places to contain, interrogate and imprison combatants while conflict is ongoing on the outside. Rather, they become key sites in efforts to 'break' prisoners. Denying their status as political and presenting them as criminal actors is, by extension, to deny the broader political character of the struggle in which they are engaged.

Implementing a criminalisation policy in the prisons requires a contingent and partial attitude to law and legality. On the one hand, rigid rule enforcement is adopted as a means to harass and repress prisoners. On the other, law offers only a very limited check on the behaviour of staff towards inmates – the need to 'break' the prisoners' morale and, at times, physical or mental capacity has primacy. This model cannot countenance the trappings associated with political rather than ordinary offending. Thus, issues such as recognition of and negotiations with prisoner command structures, segregation by paramilitary faction, the prisoners' refusal to do prison work or wear the uniform of ordinary felons – these and related issues inevitably become battlegrounds between the prisoners and the system. An uncompromising construction of prisoners as 'terrorists' or 'criminals' places prisons on the front line of a broader ideological battle which frames the conflict exclusively in security terms, holds out the possibility of a military 'victory', and finds it difficult to consider negotiations with prisoners or their compatriots on the outside as anything other than capitulation. Again while many states deploy the rhetoric of criminalisation in responding to political violence (including the current 'War on Terror/Long War'), Northern Ireland is the place where the strategy has arguably been most rigorously implemented.[9]

Although the period of reactive containment in the early 1970s in Northern Ireland was marked by a period of enforced pragmatism, the coordinated attempts at criminalisation from 1976 until around 1981 arguably resonated more closely with British legal and political culture (McEvoy, 2001). Following the Gardiner Report of 1975, the strategy of criminalisation began to be implemented in earnest. Internment without trial was abandoned and any prisoner convicted of a 'terrorist' offence was to be treated in exactly the same fashion as an ordinary prisoner, including being forced to wear a prison uniform and do prison work. Attempts were made to integrate such prisoners with ordinary prisoners and those from opposing factions and the prison system refused to recognise the prisoners' paramilitary command structure (Campbell et al., 1994; Stevenson, 1997; McKeown, 2001). In the prisons, the strategy was characterised by a rigid enforcement of rules and assertion of the powers of staff, the internalisation of what were essentially propagandist positions by staff and managers, a prison culture of brutality, violence and dehumanisation, and constant political 'interference' from senior politicians, including the then prime minister, in the micro-management of the prisons. As Margaret Thatcher summed up: 'There is no such thing as political murder, political bombing or political violence. There is only criminal murder, criminal bombing and criminal violence. We will not compromise on this. There will be no political status.'[10]

Throughout the criminalisation period, prison managers and their political masters were involved in formulating policies which deliberately sought to obfuscate the political character of the prisoners, and placed the prisons front and centre in the broader political and ideological battles of the conflict. As is discussed below, these policies provoked considerable resistance from politically motivated prisoners. Although ultimately pragmatism prevailed in the Northern Ireland context, for a time it appeared that individuals charged with policy formulation and delivery in the prisons had actually internalised such discourses and believed that the imprisonment of such activists could be divorced from the politics that motivated them in the first place.

MANAGERIALISM, BUREAUCRATISATION AND POLITICAL PRISONERS AS A 'SCIENTIFIC' CHALLENGE

A third era for the management of political prisoners in Northern Ireland was what can be broadly described as 'managerialism'. This style of management privileges managerial and bureaucratic discourses over ideological and political rhetoric. It is characterised by a view of prisons not so much as a vehicle for the 'defeat' of political violence but rather as places which can at best manage the consequences of such violence, or at least seek to avoid mismanagement which will in turn provoke further violence or social unrest. It tends to regard the management of such potentially highly difficult prisoners as one further 'scientific' or technical challenge which, while it requires a discrete set of skills and techniques, is comparable to other 'specialised' forms of prison management such as that of long-term prisoners, women prisoners, or sex offenders.

Drawing in particular from prison and criminal justice management experience which has seen the elevation of such technicist discourses over the last two decades (Feeley and Simon, 1992; Newburn, 2003), this version of managing political prisoners seeks, where feasible, to rationalise the policy-making process, make decisions based on the objective calculation of risk and avoid conflict with prisoners by imbuing the mundane aspects of running a prison with unnecessary political or ideological baggage. It is certainly not a 'politics free' approach to management which simply capitulates to each and every demand of the prisoners. Indeed, one of the guiding principles of managerialism may be to seek to quarantine, where possible, the power and influence of political prisoners. Neither is it necessarily a deliberately benign form of prison management. However, much of the certainty and rationality of the managerialist model requires greater deference to legality, an acceptance that the power of staff is inevitably checked by international human rights standards and an acknowledgement that such safeguards are 'in the final analysis' useful in preventing prison mismanagement. Managerialism in this context is informed by a small 'p' political awareness which requires more subtle forms of engagement, as well as a large 'P' political awareness that once conflict is provoked in the prisons it can have quite disastrous consequences on the outside.

The particular style of managerialism which developed in the Northern Ireland context in the 1980s and 1990s is undoubtedly quite jurisdiction-specific.[11] Certainly the combination of the disastrous consequences of the Republican hunger strikes against criminalisation (discussed below), the ensuing reduction in political 'interference' from cabinet level, the change in tactics by the prisoners themselves away from overt conflict, and the 'slow read-across' of managerialist discourses from the public sector and criminal justice system in Britain, all combined with other factors to produce a particular style of managerialist discourse which characterised the prisons for well over a decade (McEvoy, 2001).

In some senses, there was undoubtedly a scientific 'celebration-ist' aspect to the managerialist model. Thus, for example, Northern Ireland operated a highly successful home-leave scheme for long-term prisoners from the mid-1980s onwards under which large numbers of prisoners were released for up to ten days in the course of a year in the summer and Christmas periods. Many of those who benefited were politically motivated prisoners convicted of the most serious of offences. All such prisoners returned (since to have absconded would have been to scupper the scheme for their comrades), in the case of Republicans, sometimes literally to resume escape efforts which had been underway before their temporary furlough (Gormally and McEvoy, 1993). The scheme was continuously (and justifiably) trumpeted as a success by the Northern Ireland Prison Service (NIPS). Similarly, and perhaps even more notoriously, in 1990 the BBC was permitted to film a documentary, 'Inside the Maze' (also referred to as Long Kesh), which included interviews with prominent Loyalists and Republicans. One of those interviewed was Raymond McCartney, IRA Officer Commanding in the prison at the time and now a Sinn Féin Member of the Legislative Assembly. McCartney was filmed in negotiations with a prison governor discussing the size of the sausage rolls. He had been one of the prisoners who had taken part in the first IRA hunger strike in 1980 for precisely this kind of political recognition. Clearly, however, the prison authorities were willing to permit the filming of such discussion, whatever their ideological misgivings, because this underlined how pragmatic and well managed the prisons had become compared to ten years previously.

Although it was sometimes characterised as outright capitulation to the power of the paramilitaries in the prisons (particularly by the Northern Ireland Prison Officers Association), such a perspective is an oversimplification of the managerialist model. Rather, it is more accurate to say that lines were drawn in the sand to seek to limit paramilitary influence (for example, the long-standing policy of resistance towards the segregation of remand paramilitary prisoners) and these positions were defended vigorously until they became untenable, and then the lines were redrawn. That said, as the peace process emerged from the mid-1990s onwards, and the prisoner issue became gradually more important in future political negotiations, the impetus not to destabilise the political process through events in the prisons did arguably formalise a considerably altered power relationship in favour of the prisoners.[12]

In sum, the Northern Ireland conflict saw three styles of prison management of political prisoners which correspond broadly with management practices in various other jurisdictions. They were, however, uniquely shaped by external and internal factors. The conduct of the armed groups to which the prisoners belonged as well as the broader political developments in which these models arose had a direct impact upon the management models. It was inside the prisons, however, that the models were shaped, refined and contorted around the actions of the prisoners. Those actions are best understood as techniques and strategies of resistance.

POLITICAL IMPRISONMENT AND RESISTANCE

Political prisoners often do more than simply cope with imprisonment. Many engage in acts of individual or indeed coordinated and strategic resistance (Buntman, 1998, 2003). As noted above, given the sporadic efforts of the prison managers and staff which are designed explicitly to 'break' the prisoners, political prisoners frequently and self-consciously regard the prison as a further political and ideological site of contest, a different battleground to the struggle on the outside to which they are still affiliated (Kaminski, 2004).

The anthropological use of the term 'resistance' (Scott, 1985, 1990; Sluka, 1995) tends to offer very broad definitions. Within that framework, resistance is normally understood as being characterised by purpose, either implicit or explicit, manifesting itself in opposition to, or taunting, undermining and attacking the exercise of power (Foucault, 1983; Pile, 1997). For political prisoners, resistant actions are often deliberate, calculated and, to varying degrees, explicitly politicised. Some of the most thoughtful writings on resistance have focused on power relationships and, in particular, on notions of resistance as ways of examining the 'weapons of the weak' (Scott, 1990). However, one important feature of political prisoners is that, in some instances, they may be in a more powerful position *vis-à-vis* the institution than ordinary prisoners (Sparks et al., 1996). They may be able to organise collectively within the prison; they may have amongst their ranks inmates with considerable organisational, military, or intellectual gifts; they may have supportive political constituencies, willing lawyers and, of course, organisations upon whose assistance they can call.

The nature of the prison regime and the political system in which it is located will inevitably shape the nature of the prisoners' resistance (Mathiesen, 1965). Amongst the prisoner groupings themselves, in addition to individual factors such as age and gender, styles of resistance will be fashioned by variables such as political ideology, prevalence of a political history within the prisoner culture, the calibre of recruits and leadership, and organisational capacity. Resistance may be expressed in a wide number of ways, ranging from the dramatic (escape, hunger strike or self-harm, legal challenge) to the routine (smuggled contraband, illicit communications, organisational discipline, political education). However, the essential similarity of prison structures worldwide ensures that a number of avenues of resistance are commonly employed. These include formation of a prison community, escape (resistance as ridicule), law (resistance as legal challenge), hunger strike (resistance as sacrifice), and violence (resistance as infliction). These were also the styles of resistance most readily identifiable within the Northern Ireland context.

COMMUNITY AS RESISTANCE

Prison sociologists have long understood that a collectively experienced 'prison community' (Clemmer, 1940) or 'inmate society' (Sykes, 1958; Sykes and Messinger, 1960) is one of the key bulwarks against the power of the prison staff and management. For political prisoners who have belonged to some form of collective organisation or cellular structure on the outside, re-forming such a community is often a key priority when imprisoned. It is precisely because of the capacity of such collectives to alter power relationships within the prison that management and staff often try to disrupt them. Prisoner collectives may vary from an unwritten code of honour, to an intricate subculture, to a full formal military or paramilitary command structure (Buntman, 2003; Kaminski, 2004). For political prisoners, the organisation's ideology will unsurprisingly shape the collective. Thus, for example, both the African National Congress (ANC) in South Africa and the Republican prisoners in Northern Ireland placed considerable emphasis on the 'communal' nature of their imprisonment, putting into practice their broadly socialist leanings by, for example, pooling resources (McKeown, 2001; Buntman, 2003). Loyalist prisoners in Northern Ireland, on the other hand, while part of a larger organisation, tended to have a much more individualistic approach to imprisonment with more fluid command structures, less emphasis on the collective and a relatively disorganised approach to resistance strategies and tactics (Stevenson, 1996; Shirlow, 2001b).

Finally, collective resistance requires a 'site' in that it needs to 'take place' in a geographical location, hence the continued importance of 'Long Kesh', most particularly in the Republican psyche. Even temporary, partial, or contingent prisoner control over a physical location within the prison offers opportunities for techniques of resistance (such as escapes) but also suggests a fundamental critique of the primary feature of imprisonment, the control of space (Hennessey, 1984; Dunne, 1998; Narey, 1998; Pile, 1997; Shirlow and Murtagh, 2006). In order to affect forms of resistance, resistors must establish (however temporarily) spaces and networks which reduce the effectiveness of such control and surveillance (Routledge, 1997; Graham and Shirlow, 2002). They must determine some sovereignty over space in order that a sense of community can be properly 'imagined', organised and realised.[13]

ESCAPE AS RESISTANCE

The classic expression of resistance for political prisoners is escape. As noted above, many political prisoners view themselves as 'prisoners of war' with a resultant 'duty' to escape. Escapes may facilitate rejoining the military struggle on the outside, boost morale for comrades and supporters, and strike a symbolic blow against their gaolers. Escapes from imprisonment speak to key ideological and political struggles between political prisoners and the state. In Northern Ireland, Republicans in particular were willing to commit disproportionate resources to supporting and securing escapes well beyond what would have normally been sanctioned for regular 'military operations' (Bishop and Mallie, 1987). Republicans escaped from custody throughout the conflict. They dug tunnels, scaled prison walls, hijacked helicopters, escaped by swimming, drove out of prison, escaped disguised as staff, legal teams and even female visitors. In short, escape was a defining characteristic of the Republican prison experience. With less obviously supportive constituencies to escape to (many Republicans appeared to go to the Irish Republic or the United States), less interest in directly challenging the legitimacy of the state and (arguably) less organisational capacity, Loyalist prisoners did not appear to consider it their 'duty' to escape from incarceration as acutely as their Republican counterparts, although some did and others tried.

For its part, the state in Northern Ireland appeared to view escape as the ultimate in ideological and political effrontery, also expanding enormous resources in, for example, seeking to extradite successful escapers back to the jurisdiction, regardless of the costs (McEvoy, 2001). If, besides death, imprisonment is the greatest sanction which a state can impose upon its enemies, then escape from custody is the most direct of challenges to the exercise of state power.

RESISTANCE AS LEGAL CHALLENGE

The notion of law as a key weapon in the armoury of the state in times of violent conflict is well established (Fuller, 1958; Hart, 1983; Dyzenaus, 1991). However, even in settings which are highly unsympathetic to political prisoners, legal hearings – whether to determine guilt or innocence, or in challenges related to the nature of a political prisoner's detention – may offer some basis for political claim-making despite the trappings of legal formalism (Kirchheimer,

1961; Mandela, 1994). The courts in such instances may also serve as further sites of practical and symbolic resistance.

Some political prisoners may seek to use the opportunity to attempt to make a speech from the dock, to have 'written into the record' their motives and views on the system which tries them (Benson, 1981). For others, such as Republican prisoners in Northern Ireland during the 1970s who often used to refuse to recognise the legitimacy of the courts as tangible symbol of British rule in 'Ireland', their protest was primarily symbolic, a communicative action aimed primarily at the Republican constituency (McEvoy, 2001). From the 1980s onwards, many paramilitary prisoners attempted a more practical utilisation of the courts to challenge state authority in applications to international human rights courts and for habeas corpus, judicial review and extradition hearings (Hain, 1984; Campbell, 1989; Hadfield and Weaver, 1994). Within Republicanism, the 'line' was transformed from a stance wherein members used to refuse to recognise the legitimacy of the courts to one wherein every case was fought regardless of the chance for success. Indeed, this litigiousness amongst Republicans and some Loyalists led to a range of judicial review challenges to the disciplinary apparatus in the prisons which rendered implementation of the Prison Rules all but impossible (McEvoy, 2000).[14]

HUNGER STRIKE AND DEATH: RESISTANCE AS SELF-SACRIFICE

The use of hunger strike as a strategy of resistance or protest in political, ethnic and social conflicts is well documented. It has been used by suffragettes (Christensen-Nelson, 2004), students, pacifists and human rights activists (Bennett, 2003; Zhao, 2004), veterans protesting against war (Nicosia, 2004), as well as doctors protesting over conditions for themselves or their patients (Kenyon, 1999). While 'ordinary' prisoners also utilise hunger strikes to draw attention to conditions or indeed claims of innocence (Williams, 2001), organised protests to the death are more associated with politically motivated inmates. In South Africa (Buntman, 2003), Israel (Healy, 1984; Bornstein, 2001), the former Soviet Union (Borneman, 1997; Applebaum, 2003), West Germany (Becker, 1989; Schubert, 1986), Turkey (Anderson, 2004), the contemporary context of the 'War on Terror/Long War' (Center for Constitutional Rights, 2005, 2006) and, of course, Ireland North and South (Beresford, 1987; O'Malley, 1990), political prisoners have long resorted to hunger strike as a key strategy for staking their claim (Mulcahy, 1995).

Hunger strike is a resistance strategy deployed against a seemingly more powerful foe. Through the symbolically charged process of denial, self-sacrifice and endurance, the body is itself transformed into a symbolic site of struggle (Feldman, 1991). Indeed, in some cases, the body may become a literal site of struggle as the prison authorities may seek to force-feed prisoners. The symbolism of such struggles in a hunger strike in part derive from the juxtaposition of the state's power which is challenged by the willed process of decay of a striking prisoner. Hunger strikes often elicit widespread support and sympathy beyond the naturally supportive constituency of the prisoners. They speak to the commitment and sense of purpose of political prisoners and they undermine the state's claim to rationality and proportionality (Aretexaga, 1995). In some contexts (including Northern Ireland), all of the complexities of a political conflict may, for a time, become narrowed to a prisoner's capacity for endurance as those inside and outside wait for his or her death and the inevitable political and social reactions thereafter. In others, such as Turkey where 107 prisoners died on hunger strike between 2000 and 2003 (Anderson, 2004), political conflicts appear to continue without significant change to their innate rhythm despite events in the prison.

Self-sacrifice is of course a high-risk strategy for prisoners and one in which they must carefully calculate the likely costs, benefits and outcomes. Most crucially, they must accurately assess the durability and resolve of the strikers, the length of time it may take them to die, the resultant political pressure that can be built in such a period, and the likely state response to such pressures (Beresford, 1987; Anderson, 2004). Hunger strikers rely on the fact that their death will provoke a reaction which will in turn pressurise the state towards meeting at least some of their demands. When national or international public opinion is successfully mobilised in favour of hunger strikers, as it eventually was in the Irish hunger strikes of 1980–81, then their actions can be symbolically and strategically powerful. However, while public opinion is usually a state's Achilles' heel, prison policy is a particular arena where politicians and officials are generally applauded for a hard-line approach.

The Republican hunger strikes emerged largely as a strategy of desperation on the part of the prisoners at the perceived failure of the long-running blanket and 'no wash' protest which had ultimately come to be regarded as self-defeating (McKeown, 2001).[15] Between 1976 and the beginning of the first hunger strike in 1980, hundreds of protesting Republican prisoners refused to wear a prison uniform in protest at the removal of 'special category status' (discussed above). Prisoners instead chose to wear their prison-issue blankets. This 'blanket protest' ultimately became a no-wash and then a 'dirty protest' wherein prisoners smeared the walls of their cells with their own excrement (Coogan, 1980, 1987). The actions of the prisoners was met with violence from the staff, intrusive body searches, beatings and other abuses and, with prison officers being assassinated by the IRA on the outside, inmate/staff relations spiralled downwards during this period. By April 1978 there were 300–400 prisoners engaged in this form of protest. A decision in 1979 by the prison authorities to remove all of the leaders from the blocks and place them in one location (designed to weaken the will of the remaining men) had the effect of facilitating a reappraisal of a strategy which was clearly not working (Campbell et al., 1994). The prisoners began to pressurise the IRA leadership on the outside to give permission for a hunger strike. The outside leadership, who were 'tactically, strategically, physically and morally opposed to the strike' (Whyte, 1984: 219), ultimately relented when it appeared such a strike might begin without their permission (Taylor, 1997). The first hunger strike began in October 1980.

During the first hunger strike, seven prisoners went on hunger strike demanding political status, a claim which had been refined to five practical demands in 1979.[16] These seven prisoners went on hunger strike at the same time, a tactical error (since staggered prisoners approaching death at different times built more political momentum) which was not repeated in the second hunger strike (Clarke, 1987). As one of the initial prisoners, Sean McKenna, neared death, a further 27 prisoners went on strike on 15 December and a further seven on 16 December 1980. The first hunger strike ended when Secretary of State Humphrey Atkins provided the prisoners with a document which offered various concessions on issues such as 'civilian-style' clothes, food, parcels, visits, association and other issues (McEvoy, 2001). As far as the prisoners were concerned, the government ultimately reneged on that document (Beresford, 1987; O'Malley, 1990; Campbell et al., 1994).

The second hunger strike began in March 1981, led by the then prison Officer Commanding Bobby Sands. The day after Sands' strike began the prisoners called off their no-wash protest, having concluded that it had run its course. In the second hunger strike, prisoners were to join the strike in stages. While initially it had been difficult to garner public support, even amongst the Republican constituency (Beresford, 1987), that changed when Sands was elected as Member of Parliament for Fermanagh and South Tyrone. Mrs Thatcher announced that the result changed nothing: 'A crime is a crime is a crime ... It is not political, it is a crime' (O'Malley, 1990: 60). Bobby Sands died on 5 May 1981, on the 66th day of his hunger strike. His funeral was attended by over 100,000 people and his death produced a massive (and largely negative) international reaction to perceived British intransigence (Taylor, 1997, 1980). Despite a range of efforts by mediators (Collins, 1986), and direct channels of communication to the British government through the Foreign Office, ten hunger strikers were to die before this second hunger strike was called off in October 1981. Under intense pressure, families began to give permission for medical intervention once their sons slipped into comas, and the hunger strike was abandoned in October 1981 (O'Malley, 1990). While the hunger strikes were widely viewed by the prisoners as a failure, the five demands were eventually granted in full in the ensuing years. More broadly, the strikes led directly to the political development of Sinn Féin and this was ultimately to transform the nature of Irish Republicanism and the political landscape of Northern Ireland more generally.

VIOLENCE AND RESISTANCE AS INFLICTION

In some ways the use of hunger strike can be construed as a method of violence, albeit directed against the self. However, prisoners can of course also engage in acts of violence against staff and other inmates. There is a rich literature on violence as a means of resistance (Burton, 1997; Muller and Weede, 1990). For political prisoners who resort to acts of violence, this may result from viewing prison as a site for the continuance of the armed struggle in which they were engaged on the outside. It may also be a response to material conditions or a result of poor (as well as strategic) leadership within the prison. Violence may even be a rational calculation in which its efficacy is compared to other strategies of resistance.

Prisons are places which are well known for their capacity to produce violence from both staff and inmates. Studies of prison violence usually entail an analysis of the individual and/or structural reasons why prisoners resort to violence while incarcerated (Edgar et al., 2003). Apart from individual factors which may motivate particular offenders towards violence, more generic structural factors include the nature of the prison regime, levels of fear among inmates, cultures of violence, impunity in particular institutions, poor training or educational facilities, and poor training of and/or a propensity towards violence from prison staff. The reality is that in understanding the relationship between political prisoners and violence in prisons, such individual and structural factors must be considered in light of an overlay of politics pervading violent incidents.

As noted above, such violence may be directed against staff, against prisoners from rival factions, or indeed ordinary prisoners (who may be regarded as a threat to security or the objects of a 'forced integration' strategy where they are being utilised to break up the cohesion of groups of 'politicals' such as occurred in Northern Ireland), or against the property of the prison. On occasion, prisoners in Northern Ireland were able to enlist the support of their comrades on the outside to carry out armed acts in support of their prison struggle. For example, in the Northern Ireland context, 29 prison officers were killed by paramilitary groups, all but two of them by Republicans in support of prisoner campaigns such as the 'no-wash' protest, hunger strikes and anti-prisoner integration. Loyalist organisations also carried out attacks on prison officers, not only in the prisons but also in the communities in which they lived, a process made easier by the fact that the vast majority of prison officers lived in or at least were originally from similar working-class Protestant communities as the Loyalist prisoners in their charge.[17]

While violence has its attraction in any prison setting as a break from the monotonous regime (Carrabine, 2005: 902), for political prisoners, the use of violence, like going on hunger strike, is a high-risk strategy. It can be counter-productive, encouraging an even harsher reaction from the regime and damage to relations with prison management and staff. Such damage can also have adverse consequences for the broader political struggle to which the prisoners belong. One of the key resources for political prisoners is their potential to illicit sympathy in the face of a powerful and often repressive regime. Violence may jeopardise the reserve of good will in provoking a possible adverse public reaction. It is therefore arguably most effective when it is well calibrated. While violence from Loyalist prisoners was always somewhat unpredictable, violence against staff by Republicans from the late 1980s onwards became less frequent and apparently much more strategic. Republicans appeared to become more conscious that violence as a strategy of resistance was arguably most effective as a constant threat, often unspoken and rarely used, but none the less sufficiently real to maximise the conditioning of staff and to progress the demands of prisoners while only requiring actual recourse to violence as last resort.

CONCLUSION

The prisons in the Northern Ireland were a key site of the conflict as whole. The various styles of prison management detailed above were the out-workings of different ideological, political and practical attitudes within the state structures towards Republican and Loyalist violence. The strategies adopted by the prisoners, all of which centred upon their collective assertion of their status as political offenders in a political conflict, offer important insights into the ways in which their respective organisations 'thought' at different junctures over the past thirty years.[18] Debate as to what should be done with the Maze prison site underlines its iconic status as a symbol of the conflict. A cross-party committee which included representatives from Republicanism and the DUP has recommended that the Maze site should become a new international sports stadium with associated hotel and leisure facilities. This report also recommends that a number of elements of the prison be maintained, including the prison hospital where the hunger strikers died, and these will form part of a Centre for Conflict Transformation at which the respective histories of the staff, Loyalists and Republicans would be detailed. As that report suggests: 'The overriding objective is to provide an internationally recognisable physical expression of the ongoing transformation from conflict to peace and to provide an inclusive, shared resource for the people of the region and beyond, reflecting the broad range of aspirations expressed during the work undertaken by the Maze Consultation Panel' (Maze Consultation Panel, 2006: 121).

Central to this conflict transformation has been the early release and reintegration of politically motivated prisoners as a result of the Agreement. Before we begin to explore in greater detail the work of former prisoners in the communities to which they have returned, it is important first to examine the process of release and reintegration itself.

2

Prisoner Release and Reintegration in the Northern Ireland Context

Having examined the context of political imprisonment in Northern Ireland more generally, this chapter now explores issues related to the release and reintegration of politically motivated prisoners. Given its local prominence, the inevitable focus of much of the discussion below concerns the decision to release early those politically motivated prisoners who were deemed 'qualifying prisoners' under the terms of the Agreement. Together with the measures designed to facilitate the reintegration of such prisoners, this process remains for many commentators what Von Tangen Page (2006: 201) has described as 'a most difficult and unpalatable' aspect of the entire Northern Ireland peace process. In light of that controversy, we have chosen in this chapter in particular to illustrate the themes from the Northern Ireland experience of prisoner release and reintegration with relevant international experiences and analogies.

However, before exploring these most recent releases in more detail, it is important to acknowledge that politically motivated prisoners were of course released from gaol throughout the Northern Ireland conflict. For example, internees were released in large numbers both before and after internment was phased out in early 1975 (Gardiner, 1975). From the mid-1970s onwards, other than during the period of the dirty protest and hunger strikes when remission was lost due to the protests, prisoners who had received fixed-term sentences were released once they had served 50 per cent of their original sentence.[1] From the early 1980s, in partial response to political pressure concerning 'SOSPs' (Secretary of State's Pleasure, that is, prisoners under 18 at the time of the sentence but given the equivalent of a life sentence), a new mechanism was devised to oversee the release of lifers and SOSPs (NIACRO, 1984; NIPS, 1985, 1987). As a consequence, the Life Sentence Review Board continued to release lifers and SOSPs right up until the post-Agreement early releases. As well as those 'permanently' released on license, from 1985 onwards, long-term prisoners were also afforded periods of temporary release prior to their final discharge from incarceration. As noted in

Chapter 1, the success of these schemes was marked by the reality that prisoners did not by and large reoffend or otherwise abuse the trust of the authorities while benefiting from such furloughs. In short, although the early release provisions of the Agreement may have appeared exceptional and out of the ordinary, for prison managers at least, there was in fact considerable evidence to suggest that it would be a viable process.

In any jurisdiction where the question of prisoner release becomes relevant, a number of generic themes are likely to arise. The first relates to the social and political conditions which are required before an early release process may be considered. Second, as also discussed in Chapter 1, definitional issues will inevitably emerge as to who is or is not a political prisoner and therefore might benefit from such a release process. A third and related matter is the practical mechanism adopted by which such releases may be brought about. Finally, as with the release of ordinary prisoners, questions relating to prisoner 'reintegration' should certainly feature in the minds of policy-makers taking such decisions. Together with the issue of prisoner reintegration, each of these themes featured prominently in the Northern Ireland debate. Again, drawing on relevant international analogies where appropriate, we discuss each in turn.

THE SOCIAL AND POLITICAL CONTEXT FOR EARLY RELEASE

The release of combatants from prison after a conflict has a long tradition. Processes of prisoner release or pardon are entirely in keeping with the common-law legal tradition which has permitted the sovereign exercise of power to mitigate punishment for individual offenders or classes of offenders since at least the seventh century (Bresler, 1965; Moore, 1989). Between 1310 and 1800 the British Parliament enacted 110 Acts of general pardon or amnesty for various classes of offenders (Kirchheimer, 1961). More recently, that historical tradition in the British and indeed Continental legal systems was incorporated into Additional Protocol II (1977) to the Geneva Conventions which calls for 'the widest amnesty possible' following hostilities. Given its centrality to most conflicts wherein combatants have been incarcerated, it is perhaps surprising that prisoner release does not feature significantly in either the academic or policy literature on conflict transformation (McEvoy, 1998).

In reviewing the limited research on a range of jurisdictions wherein prisoner release has been part of conflict transformation efforts (Gormally and McEvoy, 1995; Fealy, 1995; McEvoy, 1998; Von Tangen Page, 1998), we would argue that four broad preconditions determine whether or not prisoner release will feature as a part of a 'peace process'.

First, there are prisoners incarcerated who represent a significant constituency for an armed group (or their political allies) and for whom such releases were a key demand in moving away from political violence. Second, there is an acknowledgement, no matter how grudging, that violent conflict has been, in some sense, *political* and that it is moving towards some form of *political* resolution to which prisoner release may contribute. Third, the process which entails prisoner release will contribute to (at the very least) a partial cessation of violence. Certainly, few governments are willing to risk releasing prisoners to have them simply rejoin a fully fledged armed campaign. Finally, at a political level, it will be possible to devise some form of 'workable consensus', both that early release should take place and the method(s) by which it should be achieved.

With regard to the significance of prisoners for armed groups and the political parties associated with those groups, prisoner release often emerges as a key element in peace talks. As one prominent member of the Palestinian negotiating team summed up with regard to their priorities for negotiations with the Israelis in the 1990s: 'first the land, then the prisoners' (cited in Gormally and McEvoy, 1995: 13). As discussed in Chapter 1, in most conflicts the prisoners have been fellow members of the armed groups, they have engaged in violent acts on behalf of those organisations, and they and their families may well have endured considerable hardship while in prison. Certainly in South Africa, Spain, Indonesia, Northern Ireland and elsewhere, negotiations on alternatives to armed struggle have all been preceded by discussions with prisoners belonging to the respective groupings. Indeed, in many instances, those who actually do the political negotiations are themselves former prisoners (Crawford, 1999; Buntman, 2003; Schulze, 2004; Woodworth, 2001, 2004). In short, other than through military defeat, it is difficult to conceive of a successful conflict transformation process which ignores the context of prisoners incarcerated as a result of the preceding conflict.

That said, there can be important distinctions in the ways in which the question of prisoners is addressed in political negotiations. In South Africa, for example, the release of certain key political prisoners including Nelson Mandela was a precondition on the part of the ANC before substantive political negotiations with the South African government could begin (Mandela, 1994). In the 'wars of the Yugoslav succession', the 1995 Dayton Agreement provided for a post-ceasefire immediate 'release and transfer without delay of all combatants and civilians held during the conflict' (Bell, 2001: 284). During the Irish peace process, the government in the Republic of Ireland began releasing prisoners soon after the declaration of the IRA ceasefires as a 'confidence building measure', long before direct negotiations on the issue ever took place (Gormally and McEvoy, 1995: 63). In Northern Ireland, Loyalists were focused upon the prisoner issue from the outset of their negotiations with the British government. Republicans on the other hand were reluctant to discuss the issue at all in the early stages of the process, apparently for fear that concessions on the prisoner issue might be offered up instead of substantive movement on other significant constitutional and political issues upon which they were focused (Bell, 2006). In different contexts, the sequencing, prominence and modalities concerning negotiation on the prisoner issue will inevitably vary.

The treatment of prisoners and particularly the question of their early release was directly linked to the political constitution of the conflict. In some instances, such as Israel (Bornstein, 2001), while the notion of 'terrorism' is deeply ingrained into the political lexicon, the parallel acceptance that such terrorism is politically motivated and that those imprisoned for such actions are also 'political' in that sense appears comparatively unproblematic (Teichman, 1996). In other places, however, such an acceptance creates significant difficulties. Some states, such as Spain over the last couple of decades, do invest considerable political, ideological and practical energies during a conflict into denying the political nature of the conflict and of those incarcerated as a result of violence. In such contexts, if releases are deemed necessary, they may be framed as technocratic or instrumental measures taken in response to a changed set of security circumstances.

Such was the case in Northern Ireland. In order to deal with Unionist misgivings on the prisoner releases section of the Agreement, the British government sought to downplay the significance of the move. Such efforts included a handwritten note to Unionist negotiators from the Prime Minister's Chief of Staff, dated the day of the Agreement, which pointed out the high numbers of prisoners who would have been released in any case under normal remission rules. Despite such exertions, the ideological significance of what was occurring was lost upon few of the actors.

As was noted previously, the issue of prisoner release spoke directly to the conflicting perceptions of the conflict between Nationalists and Unionists. For many Unionists, prisoners appeared to serve as useful focal points, the living embodiment of a perspective on the conflict where 'blame' for the conflict could be laid entirely at these incarcerated 'men of violence'. The symbolic and political impact upon the Unionist community was predictable. Given such important political ramifications, the two governments and the other negotiators to the Agreement had to be convinced that prisoner releases were not only politically necessary in terms of the broader process but that prisoners would not return to violence once released back into their communities. This relationship, between release of prisoners and levels of violence, is worth examining in a little more detail.

In other jurisdictions, prisoner releases have occurred whilst violence was ongoing. However, in some such contexts (for example, Italy and elsewhere in the 1980s), early releases were used at various junctures more or less as counter-insurgency strategies, designed to encourage individual prisoners or groups of prisoners to 'break away' from militant groups in return for early release (Moss, 1989). In Italy, while political violence continued until the mid-1980s, early prisoner releases began in 1979 with the Decree Law (which granted remission to *pentiti* or repentant 'terrorist' prisoners in return for information) and a more generous *Pentiti* Law in 1982 (expanded again in 1987), which granted remission in return for 'disassocia-tion' from violent groups (Tarrow, 1989; Meade, 1990; De la Porta, 2006). In Spain, following a general amnesty for political prisoners in 1977 two years after the death of Franco, phased releases were introduced for prisoners from a faction of ETA (ETA Politico Militar) in 1981 which had abandoned the armed struggle (Aguilar, 2001; Barros et al., 2006; Carlos and Gil-Alana, 2006). Since the 1980s, the Spanish government has continued a policy of offering early release and 'reinsertion' for prisoners who split from ETA which usually entails a degree of cooperation with the authorities as well as a public denunciation of the use of violence (Clarke, 1987; Woodworth, 2001). In Israel/Palestine, in the wake of the Gaza/Jericho Agreement of 1994, thousands of prisoner releases occurred while violence was ongoing. However, only prisoners belonging to the Fatah faction (loyal to Yasser Arafat) were released and the prisoners had to sign a controversial declaration supporting the peace process and agree to live in Gaza or Jericho, then the only sites under control of the Palestinian National Authority. Prisoners from other factions including Hamas and Islamic Jihad were not eligible for release and violence continued.

In the Northern Ireland context, a number of factors suggested that the confidence of the Agreement negotiators in devising a feasible scheme to effect prisoner release was well placed. First, while the conflict was ongoing, the recidivism rate for the most serious of prisoners was reassuringly low. Between 1985 and the first ceasefires of the mid-1990s, 374 indeterminate sentenced prisoners were released on licence, only eleven of whom had their licences revoked for unreasonable behaviour, while only one was reconvicted for a 'terrorist' offence (Gormally and McEvoy, 1995). Obviously, in the light of the ceasefires by the major paramilitary organisations, the risk of reoffending was correspondingly reduced. Second, the temporary-release 'home leave' schemes had previously shown that released prisoners were capable of neither reoffending while on release nor failing to return once their furlough was completed. Of course the behaviour of temporarily released prisoners had previously been, in effect, 'guaranteed' by the organisations to which they belonged. However, the entire peace process was arguably constructed on a similar belief. Whatever the occasionally very 'ragged edges' to the integrity of the ceasefires (see Chapter 7), if the leadership of the major groups were genuinely determined to steer their organisations out of violence, the vast majority of their members (including released prisoners) would follow suit. Finally, as is detailed below, the terms of release 'on licence' for the some of the most high-profile released prisoners were designed explicitly to engender public confidence that they could not reoffend with impunity but rather could be returned to prison with a lower evidential threshold than would be required to be convicted in a criminal court. With these factors well reviewed in the public domain at the time, and with an apparently shared view amongst the negotiators that the Agreement was simply not viable for the Republicans and Loyalists without early release of prisoners, a 'workable consensus' was reached concerning a practical mechanism to effect the releases.

OPERATIONALISING PRISONER RELEASE

The first formal acknowledgement of the British government's openness to movement on prisoner release came in a high-profile meeting between the then Secretary of State for Northern Ireland, Mo Mowlam, and senior Ulster Defence Association (UDA) prisoners in the Maze prison. In January 1998, UDA prisoners voted to withdraw their support for the peace process. This move, coming in the wake of a number of UDA killings over the Christmas 1997 period, was viewed as such a serious development that the Secretary of State took the politically risky decision to enter the prison and be filmed in discussions with some of Northern Ireland's most notorious prisoners. Dr Mowlam was successful in persuading the UDA prisoners to reinstate their support for the process (Mowlam, 2003). Key to that success was the presentation of a document to the prisoners which included provisions on the question of early release. As promised in the document to the prisoners, in February 1998 the British government submitted a paper regarding prisoners to the talks process. Having received position papers from some of the political parties (Ulster Democratic Party (UDP), Progressive Unionist Party (PUP), SDLP, Sinn Féin and the Irish government (the remaining parties did not address the issue)), the British government indicated a willingness to 'work out an account of what could happen in respect of prisoner releases in the context of a peaceful and lasting settlement being agreed'.[2]

For Sinn Féin and the Loyalist parties, there were two broad objectives on the question of prisoner release. The first was to ensure that prisoner release would be completed within a given time-frame. The second was to resist any direct linkage in the relevant enabling legislation between prisoner release and the decommissioning of paramilitary weapons, a move which was viewed as politically untenable at that juncture by both factions (McEvoy, 2001). Both of these objectives were ultimately achieved. For the British government, on the other hand, and, to a lesser extent, their colleagues in government in the Republic of Ireland, the challenge was to design a release method which would achieve the political objective of effecting prisoner release, avoid fatally undermining political confidence in the Agreement (particularly amongst a sceptical Unionist community) and be sufficiently robust to sustain any expected legal challenges. In designing such a system, they were faced with a number of options.

One obvious method of achieving prisoner releases was simply to introduce an Amnesty Act for all those convicted of politically motivated offences. Although there are now some strictures concerning the contents of any such amnesty law (Mallinder, 2007),[3] such a course of action would certainly have been legally viable for the government (Livingstone, 1995). However, an amnesty was never a likely course of action in the British context. Although an Amnesty Act was passed shortly after the outbreak of the First World War for suffragettes, no such act has been passed after a period of violence in Britain since 1798 (Mullan, 1995). Such a move would have been highly controversial and would almost certainly have lacked the subtlety required to persuade Unionist negotiators.

Less dramatically, perhaps, the government could have utilised the Royal Prerogative of Mercy to give effect to prisoner releases (Smith, 1983; Harris, 1991). This was the method used by the Unionist government at Stormont to release all prisoners within one year of the cessation of hostilities after the 1950s IRA border campaign. The fact, however, that the Royal Prerogative effectively precludes parliamentary scrutiny would again have rendered it politically difficult. The government could have established a complex legal process to assess what was, or was not, a 'political' offence and released prisoners accordingly. This has been done in other jurisdictions including South Africa and Namibia. In these contexts, using the definitions provided in humanitarian or extradition law, systems were established to make determinations on release based upon whether the object of an attack could have been described as a legitimate 'military' target. In both instances, however, the ensuing process has proved cumbersome and legalistic and actually obstructed the political objective (that is, prisoner release) for which it was established (Van Den Wyngaert, 1980; Keightley, 1993; Marks, 2000).

Instead the option ultimately developed in Northern Ireland was one which took advantage of the technocratic and instrumentalist definition of 'terrorism' contained in the Emergency legislation. In so doing, the government circumnavigated the difficulties which would have hampered any attempt to determine prisoner releases based upon the nature of the targets attacked. Under the Northern Ireland (Sentences) Act 1998, an independent commission was set up and tasked with overseeing the release of 'qualifying' paramilitary prisoners.[4] Qualifying prisoners are defined in the Act as prisoners who:

- were convicted of a 'scheduled' or 'terrorist' offence before 10 April 1998 when the Agreement was signed;
- were not a supporter of an organisation yet to declare a ceasefire;

- would not, if released, be likely to become a supporter of such an organisation; and
- would not be a danger to the public if released from serving life sentences.

All qualifying prisoners were released on licence. The terms of the licence stipulate that he/she does not support an organisation not on ceasefire; does not become concerned in the commission, preparation, or instigation of acts of terrorism; or, in the case of life-sentenced prisoners, that he/she does not become a danger to the public. This licence remains in force for fixed-term prisoners until the date that the prisoner would otherwise have been released (that is, 50 per cent of the sentence) and for the rest of his or her life for life-sentenced prisoners (see also Sentence Review Commission, 2004, 2006).

The legislation also provided flexibility for the Secretary of State to 'specify' organisations under Section 3 (8–10), thus giving such groups 'official' recognition that they were on ceasefire and rendering prisoners belonging to such groups eligible for early release. This power allowed for a monitoring function to make judgements as to whether organisations were maintaining their ceasefires. It also gave power to the Secretary of State to recognise officially 'new' ceasefires from organisations who had not yet declared a cessation at the time of the Agreement and for such prisoners to benefit also from early release provisions. This power proved a significant 'carrot' for smaller organisations such as the Loyalist Volunteer Force (LVF) and the Irish Nationalist Liberation Army (INLA) which subsequently declared ceasefires later in 1998 and whose prisoners subsequently became eligible for release (McEvoy, 2001).

Under the Act, prisoners were required to make an individual application to the Commission by a specified date. These applications were then passed to the NIPS to confirm details regarding the sentence, offences and whether or not prisoners were members of an eligible group. The applications were then returned to the Commission and prisoners were given a 'preliminary indication' as to whether or not they were to be freed early, which was then followed by a substantive determination.[5] Prisoners serving fixed-term sentences had their sentences reduced by two-thirds.[6] For life-sentenced prisoners, the Commission calculated how long they would have normally served and reduced it by one-third.[7] Any remaining qualifying prisoners were to be released by June 2000 (that is, within two years of the legislation being passed). The Secretary of State retained an overall power to suspend or later revive the scheme or prevent the release of a person adjudged to be failing to meet any of the criteria outlined above. Any prisoner whose licence was revoked by the Secretary of State could have their case reviewed by the Sentence Review Commission.[8]

Overall, the legislation to affect prisoner release as part of the Northern Ireland peace process was actually a well-designed vehicle of conflict transformation. As Dwyer (2007) has argued persuasively, while the legal and policy frameworks of the Sentence Review Commission were ostensibly permeated with the 'scientific' methods of 'risk assessment' more traditionally associated with releasing ordinary prisoners, in reality much of the practical work of the Commission appears to have been characterised by political pragmatism. Almost uniquely amongst the various institutions arising from the Agreement, it delivered 'on time'. All qualifying prisoners were released within the two years of their organisational ceasefires being recognised as stipulated under the Agreement (Sentence Review Commission, 2004). The British government withstood sustained pressure from the Unionists and the Conservative opposition to link the release process directly to decommissioning which might well have scuppered the whole process (McEvoy, 1999). Its operating practices proved robust enough to withstand a number of legal challenges, both from victims of violence and from prisoners who had their licences revoked.[9] Although there were suggestions in at least one case that a licence revocation was based on political rather than security grounds,[10] the licensing arrangements did arguably provide some public reassurance that prisoners could not simply reoffend with impunity.

Most significant, perhaps, is the fact that the prisoner release programme has demonstrably worked. As noted previously, since 1998, 449 prisoners have so far qualified for early release under the scheme. To date, only 16 prisoners have had their licences revoked of which 12 were life-sentence prisoners. Some 28 prisoners have been reconvicted of other offences, none of which were for murder.[11] Leaving aside the fact that there may have been some overlap between those who had their licence revoked and those who were reconvicted of another offence,[12] even an approximate figure of 40 prisoners (or less than 10 per cent) being involved in either ordinary or politically motivated offending almost a decade after the Agreement is quite striking.[13] By way of comparison, recidivism rates in Britain for 'ordinary' offenders released from prison reveal that 58 per cent are reconvicted of another offence within two years (Home Office, 2001). In Northern Ireland, the equivalent figure is 48 per cent (NIPS, 2003). These figures suggest that this controversial measure, which was widely adjudged by the negotiators of the Agreement as necessary, has not placed the community in Northern Ireland at significant risk. Certainly in criminological terms, the early release programme has been a striking success. The judgement on its effectiveness in terms of conflict transformation can only be made by a closer examination of the measures put in place to facilitate the reintegration of these prisoners.

EFFECTING PRISONER REINTEGRATION

In Chapter 8 we look in more detail at the broader implications and lessons to be learnt from the reintegration of former politically motivated prisoners in Northern Ireland. For current purposes, however, it is sufficient to offer a brief analysis of how the process was actually implemented. As noted above, once those prisoners who benefited from the early release provisions were released back into the community in Northern Ireland, they joined thousands of other former prisoners who had been released throughout the conflict after serving their proscribed terms of imprisonment. All were supposed to benefit from the provisions for the 'reintegration' of politically motivated prisoners contained in the Agreement. The Agreement stated:

The Governments continue to recognise the importance of measures to facilitate the reintegration of prisoners into the community by providing support both prior to and after release, including assistance directed towards availing of employment opportunities, re-training and/or re-skilling, and further education. [Agreement, 1998, Annex B, para. 5]

Despite this reference to its importance in the Agreement, the practice of prisoner reintegration in Northern Ireland remains controversial. As in other societies emerging from conflict, the source of that controversy has a number of aspects. As noted above, for some, the allocation of any financial resources towards people who have been involved in violence is controversial *per se*. Usually juxtaposed to the treatment of victims, such criticisms are normally framed as the 'men of violence' being 'rewarded' for the suffering and hurt they have inflicted (Gormally, 2001). In addition, many politically motivated former prisoners and former combatants would argue that the very term 'reintegration' denotes a misunderstanding of the relationship between them and the communities from which they come – implying that they are somehow 'other' in such communities, or required to change in order to 'fit back' into society. Certainly in other comparative jurisdictions as diverse as South Africa, Colombia, Indonesia, Sierra Leone, Italy, Spain and Palestine, former politically motivated prisoners and ex-combatants have expressed precisely this discomfiture at the term (McEvoy et al., 2008).

In the Northern Ireland context, the particularities of the prison experience also cause some former prisoners to bridle at the usage of the term 'reintegration'. In particular, many associate the expression with what they regard as 'residual criminalisation' (discussed further below). Former prisoners also contend that the term denotes a failure to acknowledge the broader causes of violence and the continued structural exclusion of former prisoners from the normal entitlements of citizenship (Coiste, 2003a, 2003b, 2003c, 2003d, 2003e, 2004). Finally, a number of commentators have argued that the actual delivery of reintegrative measures has also been contentious, denoting, for example, a lack of political will and inadequate resourcing on the part of government (for example, Rolston, 2007). As explored in more detail in Chapter 8, some of these broader political and ideological connotations associated with the term 'reintegration' and suggest a more appropriate framework for addressing the post-conflict needs of politically motivated prisoners. At this juncture it might be useful to offer some background to the ways in which the reintegration programmes were put into effect.

Between 1995 and 2003, £9.2 million in funding came from the Community Foundation for Northern Ireland (CFNI)[14] and the European Special Support Programme for Peace and Reconciliation (Peace I and II) and was directed towards prisoner and former prisoner issues. Following the personal commitment of outgoing European Commission President Jacques Delors, the EU sought to underpin the peace process by giving practical support to a range of 'bottom-up' funding initiatives of local community programmes which included former prisoners and victims in one of their measures designed to 'target vulnerable groups'. From 1995 to 2000, Peace I accounted for some £500 million while the second programme, Peace II (2000–06) provided a further £450 million for peace-related projects. Between 1995 and 2003, 61 former prisoner groups and a further 29 affiliated projects received £9.2 million from these funds, less than 1 per cent of the overall budget (CFNI, 2003: 47, 50; Shirlow et al., 2005: 5).

The chosen mechanism for delivery of the EU monies was interesting. Rather than funding coming directly from government, a local grant-giving organisation, the Northern Ireland Voluntary Trust (NIVT) – later renamed the Community Foundation – was tasked with distributing the monies to both former prisoners and victims.[15] The British government also pledged to provide 20 per cent of matching monies from the appropriate local government departments, a relationship which led to some unusual encounters in the early days of the peace process.[16]

In order to achieve a level of transparency in its disbursement of monies to the former prisoner projects, NIVT established an advisory group consisting of the main Republican and Loyalist former prisoner groupings as well as other organisations with a history of working with prisoners; these included the Quakers, NIACRO and the Irish Commission for Prisoners Overseas (Gormally, 2001). The Community Foundation saw themselves explicitly as engaged in 'taking risks for peace' in funding the former prisoner reintegration projects (CFNI, 2003). Certainly the funding of prisoner reintegration work and the organisation in general was the object of a constant barrage of criticism from Unionist politicians and prominent critics in the media.[17] Despite some perhaps predictable mishaps (including the discovery of an arms cache at one UDA-linked former prisoner project which led to a suspension of the group's funding),[18] CFNI in general and its charismatic director Avila Kilmurray in particular have received considerable local and international plaudits for the ways in which such monies were distributed and in particular for the willingness to engage in 'risky' funding strategies.[19]

The reintegrative model developed was essentially a self-help model wherein former prisoners managed and staffed their own reintegration programmes. The actual work of the projects is discussed elsewhere in this book. The projects were organised on a factional basis, broadly mirroring the various paramilitary organisations to which the participants had previously belonged. Thus Coiste na n-Iarchimí became the umbrella organisation for former IRA prisoners, EPIC serviced former UVF and RHC prisoners, Prisoners Aid acted for UDA/UFF, Teach na Failte for former INLA prisoners, and a range of programmes catered for different smaller and non-aligned groups. Undoubtedly, this model resulted in some duplication of effort. However, no other method would have been feasible in the early days of the transition. Over the years, as evidence by the research upon which this book is based, there has been increased collaboration and joint lobbying initiatives by former adversaries on issues of mutual concern. Such developments emerged organically and could not have been imposed by government or other funding bodies.

CONCLUSION

This chapter has explored the context and practice of the early release and reintegration programme established under the Agreement. As was noted above, the prisoners who qualified for such releases joined thousands of others who had been previously released throughout the conflict. The difference for these prisoners was of course that, at least for most of the mainstream paramilitary organisations, the Agreement-linked releases signified the formal ending of generations of political imprisonment. In the post-ceasefire era, the changed political and security circumstances transformed the nature of former prisoner groups which had existed for much of the conflict. There was no longer a need to provide direct financial and practical assistance to prisoners and their families. While new organisations emerged during the transition, in part as a result of the funding available for reintegrative work, it is important to understand the historical context and impact of former prisoners groups which had operated for much of the previous conflict. Such groups are the subjects of Chapter 3.

3

The History and Evolution
of Former Prisoner Groups

Politically motivated former prisoner groups are a relatively recent phenomenon in Northern Ireland, the first two examples being established as recently as 1995. The impetus for such groups arose for at least two reasons. First, given the long-standing resistance of politically motivated former prisoners to the tag of either criminals or offenders, accessing existing services provided by statutory agencies would have constituted an admission of criminality. Second, they generally embraced the concept of self-help, seeing themselves as possessing the necessary expertise to assist others in similar circumstances, while believing that the existing service providers lacked the experience or empathy to deal with former prisoners (NIVT, 2001).

This chapter examines both Republican and Loyalist groups with particular regard to the role of prisoner issues in the broader shifts within their respective movements towards transitional politics both before and after the ceasefires of 1994. Following a brief discussion of funding, we then examine the groundbreaking talks initiated by the Quakers in 1990 which led to a joint approach on the issues of reintegration and funding for self-help groups, the difficulties encountered by those involved in this joint approach, and the reasons for its eventual failure. The chapter further considers the aims, objectives and funding of past and present Republican and Loyalist former prisoner groups, before concluding with an assessment of their future role, both in terms of funding and also their overall contribution to former prisoner reintegration and conflict transformation.

PRISON REGIMES AND THE 'DOWNTOWN CENTRE'

Differences between Loyalists and Republicans were obvious from the very beginnings of the process of creating former prisoner organisations. As is discussed elsewhere, as pro-state paramilitaries, Loyalists had something of an ambivalent relationship with a polity to which they owed loyalty but which, none the less, imprisoned them for actions carried out in 'defence' of that state (Bruce, 1992). Again for Loyalists, prison struggle had never been a particularly prominent feature of their history or cultural psyche (Crawford, 1999). As one Loyalist former prisoner stated: 'In the 1930s Dawson Bates [the then Minister of Home Affairs in the Stormont Government] would have been paying us to do what they began imprisoning us for in the 1970s' (Loyalist: workshop).

While Loyalists believed that their actions were politically motivated, they were less inclined to join what many regarded as 'Republican-type' prison protests. On certain occasions in the late 1970s and 1980s when loyalists did engage in protests demanding segregation, such actions were represented by Unionists as giving succour to Republicanism and other anti-state discourses. This animosity toward political struggle prevented a sustained, systematic and 'resistant' focused approach toward prison-based regimes. The inability, for example, of the 'Loyalist blanketmen' to maintain a prolonged political campaign was recognised by Loyalists linked to the UVF/RHC as being due to a lack of collaboration from other Loyalist groups and a wider Unionist community who 'offered little support for the protestors': 'Republicans were able to draw on a whole reservoir of tradition within prisons, but there was nothing for us. What we had to do to a large degree was to start and lay the rules and traditions which could be followed by others. It was very difficult because we had an antagonistic regime' (Loyalist: workshop).

Unlike Loyalism, Republicanism has a history of imprisonment stretching back many decades and is associated with political conflict in Ireland in both the north and south (see, for example, Coogan, 1987). During the various IRA campaigns, prisoner welfare groups emerged to organise the provision of parcels and to raise funds for prisoners and their families. When the current 'Troubles' began, a number of welfare groups materialised; these included: Green Cross, the Prisoners' Dependency Fund and the Central Citizens Defence Committee. Following the introduction of internment in 1971, more groups (most notably the Irish Republican Prisoners Welfare Association) were established as political campaigns focused on conditions both in Long Kesh/Maze and HMP Belfast (Crumlin Road, colloquially known as the 'Crum'). As one former prisoner put it:

Our whole system was based on the same welfare that had existed in campaigns as far back as the '40s with the PDF and Green Cross ... When I went into gaol in 1972, they provided the transport, they helped with parcels, that was their role outside, to raise funds. We were making things to send out to be sold and they were also taking part in the political campaigns. [Republican: workshop]

The groups involved in welfare and in the support of political campaigns were independent of each other and of the wider Republican movement, reflecting the many factions that then existed within Republicanism. These included the Official Irish Republican Army (OIRA), the Irish National Liberation Army (INLA) and the IRA. While there may have been little cooperation between these groups outside, cooperative relationships did develop inside prison, while the first intimations of a centre to deal with the resettlement of former prisoners also came from Loyalist-Republican interaction in Long Kesh.

This latter initiative evolved into the so-called 'downtown centre', the first serious attempt to address their welfare and resettlement needs by the prisoners themselves (Crawford, 1999). The Camp Council in Long Kesh, which represented the interests of all the paramilitary prisoners, conceived the idea in 1974. The 'Camp Council' was widely credited with contributing to a degree of 'tranquillity and understanding between bitter opponents', so much so that both its Republican and Loyalist representatives wanted to 'export' the cooperation outside gaol into the establishment of a 'downtown' office in Belfast (Garland, 2001: 194). Gusty Spence, Officer Commanding UVF prisoners, and David Morley, Officer Commanding IRA prisoners, both drew up documents on the proposal for consideration at Camp Council. The IRA document, 'Outline Scheme for Resettlement', argued for an effective after-care scheme including the establishment of a Belfast office, controlled by the Prison Welfare Service with a coordinating committee. This committee would comprise voluntary, probation and prison welfare groups and enable interaction between the welfare wings of the five main paramilitary organisations (White, 1998; Crawford, 1999).

The detailed problems faced by prisoners and their families during and after prolonged imprisonment were outlined in the Loyalist document, 'Proposals for a Resettlement Programme'. It suggested that a 'downtown' office could be used as a base 'where the representatives of the various Prisoners' Welfare bodies could meet, discuss and work for the common welfare of all prisoners' (Crawford, 1999: 45). The Camp Council agreed that a joint submission be put to the Northern Ireland Office (NIO) for consideration. The potential of the centre was not lost on those involved in discussions, as Gusty

Spence commented: 'Heaven only knows where such cooperation could have led Northern Ireland' (Garland, 2001: 194).

In the end, the British government's decision (discussed in Chapter 1) to end Special Category Status and to introduce 'criminalisation' in 1976 led to the abandonment of the 'downtown centre' idea.[1] Loyalists interpreted this as being due to 'hardliners' within the Republican movement not wanting 'any form of cooperation with the [NIO] or other British authorities' (Garland, 2001: 194). Republicans counter this, arguing that, at this time, they were 'up to their necks' in negotiations with the NIO. Because of their wider ideological concerns, they also contend that they were less motivated by the concept of the 'downtown centre' than their Loyalist counterparts. One Republican former prisoner stated:

You can chart the attempts made from 1975 to de-politicise the whole conflict ... it was aimed at Republicanism and it's something we knew from the very beginning, something we always resisted ... the downtown office ... Republicans almost got involved in it and then realised just exactly what was going on. The British government was removing themselves as a party to the conflict. They were handing it back and creating confusion ... to say that it was two tribes fighting. [Republican: workshop]

The idea of a 'downtown centre' conflicted, therefore, with Republican ideology and their determination to view the conflict as a war with the British state and not with Loyalism. Endorsing the concept of a centre would have meant lending credence to the British government's policy of criminalisation and its counter-claim that the conflict was essentially internal and between Loyalists and Republicans.

FORMER PRISONER GROUP DEVELOPMENT

Although the centralisation of the prisoner issue within Provisional Republicanism started around the time of the removal of Special Category Status, it gradually became a more important aim of the movement towards the end of the 1970s and early 1980s. In 1978, as the 'no-wash' phase of Republican protest began inside and outside the H-Blocks, Relatives' Action Committees (RACs) were formed in many areas throughout Northern Ireland. These committees comprised mainly friends and families of prisoners and, over the next three years, they campaigned to highlight the ongoing protests inside the Maze (Campbell et al., 1994). As public support grew in Nationalist areas, efforts to coordinate publicity and protests resulted in the formation of the National H-Block/Armagh Committee. Sinn Féin, long the junior partner within militant dominated Republicanism, became increasingly significant in the mobilisation concerning these protesting prisoners (Collins, 1986; Von Tangen Page, 1998). In demonstrating that the prisoner issue had significant levels of support from the wider Nationalist community, politically inclined Republicans were able to gain increased support within the movement for a dual so-called 'Armalite and Ballot Box' strategy, which combined an IRA armed campaign with the political contestation of elections.[2] They also learned the valuable lesson that building broad coalitions around a particular issue and beyond their own immediate constituency could add legitimacy to their various campaigns (McEvoy, 2001). For some, the change in prison regime was the catalyst for a rethinking of the issues affecting prisoners. Whereas Long Kesh had been a more open system allowing for some, albeit restricted, interaction between the differing political persuasions, the new cell system in operation in the Maze severely limited any contact between Loyalists and Republicans.

By the mid-1980s, Sinn Féin's POW Department had been established to coordinate the many campaigns being fought around prison-related issues, including strip-searching, repatriation and extradition. In February 1988, the Campaign for Lifers began to protest against a review system put in place by NIPS in March 1983. As one Republican 'ex-lifer' noted:

After all the ups and downs, hunger strikes, escapes etc., for the first time you had POWs taking a long hard look at people who at that stage had been in twelve years or longer, mostly in the category of lifers ... the POWs themselves [decided] that a campaign to deal with life sentences and SOSPs needed to be embarked upon. [Republican: workshop]

As pressure grew from Unionist and Nationalist politicians criticising the lack of transparency in the decision-making processes of the Life Sentence Review Board, the NIO eventually detailed the operation of the system in 1985. The process was heavily criticised by political parties affiliated to paramilitary prisoners as the criteria for release included consideration of the actions of the paramilitary group outside (Sinn Féin Prisoner of War Department, 1986).

The Campaign for Lifers 'concentrated its efforts to bring about change in the NIO criteria for the release of life and SOSP prisoners' (The Captive Voice/An Glor Gafa, 1989: 1). Although the same criteria remained in place for some time, as was discussed above, the authorities did introduce numerous initiatives to aid the release of prisoners such as the 'home leave' and 'working out' schemes (McEvoy, 2001). Thus the problems associated with release after prolonged periods of imprisonment became the topic for discussion not only among the released but also those still in prison:

the campaign to deal with life sentence and SOSPs ... was a forerunner, although nobody seen it at the time, to asking the question about people getting out of gaol, 'what are they going to do once they are out?' You are going to get this influx of people released and nothing there for them ... I left gaol in 1990 and was asked to take on the responsibility of the POW Department, and to carry forward the ideas that had been put together in the gaol in terms of an ex-POW centre. [Republican: workshop]

Those ideas were further developed when Loyalists and Republicans next came together through a Quaker initiative that became known as PROPP (Progressive Release of Political Prisoners).

The lack of a tradition of imprisonment in the Loyalist community was readily apparent when its first high-profile representative, Gusty Spence, was sentenced in 1966. He did have support among the Shankill Road working class but as Spence himself has repeatedly acknowledged, elsewhere within Unionism there was significant disapproval. For example, as Spence was a member of the local Orange Order, his lodge continued to recognise him by stopping outside Crumlin Road gaol during the 12th July parades. However, the governing body, the Grand Orange Lodge of Ireland, ordered Spence's expulsion and, when it refused, his lodge (Prince Albert Temperance) was threatened with the removal of its warrant (Garland, 2001). Again, there was no loose network of welfare groups – prisoners depended on friends and family for sustenance. As the 'Troubles' intensified, however, and additional UVF members were convicted and sentenced, welfare groups associated with the organisation were fashioned.

The first such group was the 'Orange Cross', replicating the Republican Green Cross. This group performed a similar function for UVF prisoners by organising collections and 'supplementing parcels destined for the prisoners with basic necessities like soap, a comb, hair cream, face flannel and shaving soap' (Garland, 2001: 129–30). A Loyalist former prisoner sums it up:

We had no culture or history of prisoners, we started from scratch trying to work out systems ... When Gusty Spence went to prison, that was the first time that Loyalists went outside the law. In that era that was the first time a welfare system the 'Orange Cross' was formed. Among working-class areas we were the same as IRA prisoners but once you went outside of those areas you'd no support ... within the general Unionist population we were outcasts. [Loyalist: workshop]

There was a difference, too, for those from a rural background:

Maybe in places like the Shankill, where there's a high concentration of Loyalist prisoners, the working-class people supported former prisoners, but you go to a place, portrayed as the 'bastion of Unionism'... Portadown, within the Loyalist and Unionist community there, is outright hostility to our very existence. Unionism in Portadown has manifested itself in many extreme forms politically, but they still do not have much time for people who do not have the cloak of legitimacy around them ... that in many ways has curtailed the development of Loyalist former prisoner groups. [Loyalist: workshop]

As the number of Loyalists imprisoned began to increase in the early 1970s, particularly with the introduction of internment, the UVF established the Loyalist Prisoners' Welfare Association (LPWA). This was 'a loose group whose main focus was transport, family welfare, prisoners' rights, street protests, hoax bombs, blocking roads ... replicating the Black Taxis [old London cabs brought in to act as 'public transport' in North and West Belfast] to generate funds for families' (Loyalist: workshop).

The Orange Cross was subsumed by the LPWA, which was the only welfare group in existence for UVF prisoners and former prisoners until as late as 1995. The LPWA functioned as part of a movement. It had close ties to the UVF outside and to its prisoners inside who appointed a welfare officer to liaise with the LPWA. This close connection allowed the mobilisation of support for protests and provided extra help when needed: 'It was a movement. People underestimated the size of the operation that organised parcels at Christmas, transport and things like that' (Loyalist: focus group).

The LPWA also organised protests outside prison to highlight the conditions of those incarcerated. One of the first was when Republican and Loyalist prisoners in Long Kesh stopped taking visits for 14 weeks in protest at restrictions put in place after a IRA prisoner escaped during a visit. The LPWA was also instrumental in the discussions around the idea of a 'downtown centre', as one former prisoner recalls: 'The concept of the "downtown centre" came from inside. Gusty [Spence] was involved and the NIO bought into it ... Trying to bring all the paramilitary groups in from the cold ... the LPWA did the negotiating ... the Republicans blocked it' (Loyalist: focus group).

Loyalists were involved in protests throughout the late 1970s and early 1980s, particularly in relation to the campaign for Special Category Status in the Maze and the campaign for segregation in Crumlin Road (McEvoy, 2001). As was the case for Republicans, the next main issue for the movement centred on the Life Sentence Review Board introduced in 1983. Members of the LPWA and parents of SOSPs and life-sentence prisoners formed the 'Justice for Lifers' campaign in 1985 (Justice for Lifers, 1985; Loyalist: focus group). Eddie Kinner, a former UVF SOSP, explains:

The first campaign was aimed at SOSPs. All the parents got together to push the issue. That started in and around 1983–84. The first indeterminate sentence prisoners to be released were Gusty [Spence] and two Republicans. The pressure then grew about SOSPs. What kicked off the genuine acknowledgement of having to release prisoners was the attempted escape of Benny Redfern and Ned Pollock. Benny Redfern got crushed to death in a bin lorry. The desperation of that – there was a recognition that at some stage they [the prison authorities] were going to have to do something especially if people were going to go to that extent to try and escape. [interview, 8 December 2004]

The idea that indeterminate-sentenced prisoners had to take part in interviews and answer particular questions in order to be considered for release was seen by some as reinforcing the government's policy of criminalisation. It caused a split within the UVF compound in Long Kesh, with around 15 indeterminate-sentenced prisoners (out of around 90) refusing to take part in the process. Eddie Kinner was one of the 15:

As far as I was concerned it was a charade. No one had been released and I couldn't justify taking part. There was ground still to be won. There was still scope to negotiate what kind of release procedure you would be going through. Once people began to take part then they accepted the terms and conditions. Once people started moving out through the 'working out scheme', the thing was in place and you were only cutting off your nose to spite your face. I had a decision to make – get another three-year knock-back or bite the bullet and go through the process. I was harming no one but myself. [interview, 8 December 2004]

Kinner, like many others eventually went through the process. The first two Loyalist SOSPs were released in 1988 along with the first Christmas parole for indeterminate-sentenced prisoners. This marked the beginning of releases of those serving prolonged sentences, many Loyalists believing that this was the catalyst for the development of former prisoner support groups during the 1990s: 'As the first life sentence prisoners began to be released around '88–'89, it was then that it dawned on people the problems that were there' (Loyalist: focus group).

PROGRESSIVE RELEASE OF POLITICAL PRISONERS (PROPP)

The first real initiative in this regard came from the creation of the organisation, PROPP.[3] In 1990, Martie Rafferty, a Quaker and social worker who worked in the Quaker Family Centre at the Maze, approached some Loyalist and Republican former prisoners to ask them if they had encountered any difficulties since their release. During separate discussions, Rafferty recognised that each side had similar concerns about the needs presented by release after prolonged imprisonment and the lack of resources to address them. The Quaker movement in Northern Ireland had recognised that politically motivated former prisoners would have difficulties working with state agencies. Rafferty suggested that Republican and Loyalist former prisoners should cooperate in providing a forum to articulate the problems and complications faced by former prisoners returning to their families and communities.

The initial meeting of PROPP took place in Quaker House, Belfast in 1991. It was attended by nine Republican and three Loyalist former prisoners, together with Rafferty and three 'human rights activists'. As more meetings were organised, the numbers eventually levelled off to a nucleus of two or three from each side. The idea was that PROPP would grow and develop into a recognised body that would articulate the reintegration issues affecting politically motivated former prisoners, the case strengthened by its joint Republican and Loyalist members, who had the approval of their respective organisations to form the group (Green, 1998; Crothers, 1998; EPIC, 2004). Martin Snodden regarded PROPP as: 'the transition from issues concerned with "inside" to issues "outside" while the LPWA continued in their role of looking after prisoner welfare' (interview, 14 December 2004). The meetings took place against the backdrop of continuing violence, and the risks involved for the participants were twofold:

being targeted not only by the 'other' side but also by our 'own' side ... you have to remember there were no ceasefires in place ... over the course of the next few

years, we were 'observed' by the Republican war machine – there were people
sent from that particular constituency to check us out and see what we were
at ... we had an unwritten contract with regard to security and confidentiality.
[Martin Snodden (EPIC): interview, 14 December 2004]

There were times when events caused particular tensions within the
group. Former Republican prisoner Tony Catney recalls one such
episode:

There was an explosion, September '92, A Wing in the Crumlin Road and two
Loyalist prisoners were killed. At our meeting the next Monday night, I was the
only Republican. They started into me asking me to condemn the bombing,
nearly asking me to apologise for it. I said no it wasn't the right way to go about
it, if I did that then we would start every meeting condemning the latest incident
and it would get us nowhere. The tensions we had between us were massive.
It was a toss up whether I jumped out of the window or [they] threw me out.
[interview, 14 December 2004]

A number of issues were crucial to the concept of PROPP. These
centred on the belief that the government had a responsibility to fund
the cost of reintegrating political prisoners back into the community
and that this would enable the establishment of two separate self-help
centres to replace the unacceptable services provided by NIACRO
and the Probation Board for Northern Ireland (PBNI). Tony Catney
explains how PROPP viewed the role of government: 'Government
had a responsibility to fund – that's it, that's all. They had the resources
to make things happen. We had the know-how and the experience
to make things happen' (interview, 14 December 2004).

Unlike the earlier idea of a 'downtown centre' catering for the needs
of all political former prisoners, PROPP never envisaged anything
other than separate self-help centres. As Martin Snodden recalls:

It was always the case of separate centres. We had to look at reality. It was
unthinkable at that particular time, no ceasefires; in fact things had got worse.
It simply wasn't an option to have a joined-up centre. We had an unwritten
agreement regarding the exchange of information but it was never envisaged
as one structure to house all factions. [interview, 14 December 2004]

Due to the Hurd Principles (a highly controversial measure named
after former Northern Ireland Secretary of State Douglas Hurd which
was designed to ensure that public funding could not be allocated to
any community organisation with an alleged paramilitary affiliation),
PROPP could not approach government directly; instead, people

lobbied on PROPP's behalf as well as meeting with NIACRO, PBNI and other potential funders. Members believe that this 'chipping away' had a slow but positive effect, strengthened by the fact that Loyalists and Republicans were 'making the pitch' together. The Quakers secured the first funding:

against the backdrop of violent conflict and probably 'subversive' stamped all over your record. The first funding is always the hardest to secure. To be fair it never covered anything other than meeting as PROPP but it was about staking the first claim. Then the statutory bodies started to take notice for fear of being left behind. [Tony Catney: interview, 14 December 2004]

Ironically, according to Martin Snodden, difficulties arose within the group when a large amount of funding was offered from backers in the United States who insisted that PROPP become legally constituted and encouraged it in seeking additional funding to match that already on offer. Discussions continued for many months on the issue of a legal constitution and approaches were made to the NIO regarding statutory funding, using the offer from abroad as leverage. Then, a few months after the ceasefires were called in 1994, new Republican representatives replaced Tony Catney and his colleague. This changed the dynamic of the group. Eddie Kinner felt the move was deliberate:

The other Reps [Representatives] were perceived as being too familiar with the Prods – so they were pulled out and two others put in ... they would have nothing to do with meeting NIO ministers because the NIO at that stage were refusing to meet with Sinn Féin ... they couldn't be seen to be used to undermine that connection so they scuppered any early chance of funding. [interview, 8 December 2004]

Snodden attributes these changes to a combination of Republican ideology and the Republican movement's desire for control over the issue of prisoners. From a Republican perspective, PROPP was always a tactical rather than a strategic initiative. While welcome as a forum for exchanging views, the prospect of a joint project was always problematic to them. The issue that undermined the development of PROPP, according to Republicans, was the lack of a shared political analysis between them and Loyalists. Republicans argue that they were focused on the conflictual axis between themselves and the British state, whilst Loyalists appeared to invest more importance in an analysis of the Loyalist/Republican axis of conflict.

In any event, the Republican former prisoners' group Tar Anall was already established (though not yet funded) and the issue of attracting funding could not, from the Republican perspective, rest upon the parallel establishment of Loyalist services. Additionally, PROPP appeared to be predicated upon 'matching funding for matching development' in Loyalist and Republican structures. Republicans argue that, had this approach taken root, the significant development of Republican groupings that subsequently took place would not have been possible, given the 'relative lack of capacity and interest amongst loyalist former prisoners' (Republican: interview, 22 August 2005). According to a Republican source:

Moreover, those initially involved in PROPP from the Republican side failed to give necessary feedback to other stakeholders within the Republican family. When what Loyalists interpret as an exertion of control took place, this was really an organisational view that individuals claiming to represent Republicans really needed to adopt a more collegial approach. [Republican: interview, 22 August 2005]

In the event, from a republican Perspective, PROPP lost its relevance. The development of services for Republican former prisoners took priority as against a forum which was likely to impede the attraction of the required resources. Once the EU Peace Programme came on stream, the need for a parallel funding approach that tied Republicans into what Loyalists had the capacity for would have been counterproductive (Republican: interview, 22 August 2005).

Again, there is a suggestion of different capacities between Republican and Loyalist former prisoner groups to deliver results in their respective communities:

EPIC [the UVF/RHC prisoners' resettlement organisation] were trying their best to do a good job but it was a lot harder for them than it was for us, because we had a great springboard in our community, they hadn't. That was one of the reasons for the demise of PROPP. It was the development. We got our own funding, did our own work, we had our own centres. So there was really no need for PROPP after that other than as somewhere to meet and talk and to keep up ... they met at the very, very difficult times of the struggle. They met when Loyalist assassinations were going on. They met throughout times like the Shankill bombing. It was very difficult risky work. And I think it was very important work. [Republican: interview, 12 December 2004]

The difficulties experienced by the group meant that other avenues had to be explored. One such avenue was offered by NIVT which, following a series of meetings, agreed to fund two six-month contracts, one each for a Loyalist and Republican development worker, in the hope that more funding would be secured down the line. This led to the setting up of EPIC on the Shankill Road and Tar Anall on the Falls Road. This initiative coincided with the inauguration of the first round of European Peace and Reconciliation funding which, ironically (and something of an indictment of 'single-identity' work), eventually led to the demise of PROPP. As one disillusioned Republican noted who had been involved in PROPP since its inception: 'Peace I brought in the concept of separate access ... the Republican community could have total control over the former prisoners issue and there would be no need to work with Loyalists' (Republican interview, 14 December 2004). 'When Peace I money was secured, the groups started to develop separately. The joint approach was no longer needed to secure funding and Republicans would no longer approach the state' (Eddie Kinner: interview, 8 December 2004). 'There was a very clear divide in regards to the focus of PROPP and the separation of PROPP, that is, when the Peace money came on stream and both groups were then able to access it independently of the other. There was then a growing separation and PROPP eventually dissolved' (Martin Snodden: interview, 14 December 2004).

The interviewees believe that PROPP never managed to fulfil its objective, the issue of statutory funding still remaining very high on the agendas of former prisoner groups today. Although the dialogue that took place helped to develop relationships, some of which still endure, the unrealised potential of the group in terms of conflict transformation was noted by Eddie Kinner: 'If the government had have funded that and taken on its responsibilities, it could have developed something which could have been more powerful and more influential in terms of strengthening and cementing the peace process' (interview, 14 December 2004).

CONTEMPORARY FORMER PRISONER GROUPS AND ISSUES

Since EPIC and Tar Anall were founded in 1995, as noted above, many other former prisoner self-help groups have been established right across Northern Ireland, supported, primarily, by European Union funding. Most groups have similar aims and objectives, namely to support the reintegration of politically motivated former prisoners into their families and communities. While these aims remain a 'live' issue for the groups, the decreasing number of individuals seeking practical assistance has drawn a question mark over the sustainability and future of the groups. In particular, it begs the question as to the contribution they can offer in building peace.

As we have seen, EPIC was established in 1995 as a self-help centre to address the problems surrounding the resettlement of politically motivated prisoners, in particular those from a UVF or RHC background. It opened a drop-in centre to deal with the many practical issues facing former prisoners on release, including housing, benefits and employment prospects, as well as offering emotional support and counselling to former prisoners and their families. The specific objectives of EPIC are:

- identify the needs of prisoners and prisoners' families during the post-release period;
- provide resources and facilities which will help former prisoners and their families in the process of reintegration into the family and community;
- provide a reference point for prisoners during the pre-release period and after release;
- link former prisoners and their families with other existing agencies, where appropriate, and support them in making use of their services; and
- provide opportunities, both formal and informal, to share experiences and encourage the development of mutual support services (Crothers, 1998).

In the run-up to the 1998 Agreement, EPIC developed regional centres in various parts of Belfast, Derry/Londonderry and Armagh to cater for the many politically motivated prisoners to be released under the terms of the Agreement. It also conducted a number of studies into the experiences of Loyalists inside prison and the problems associated with reintegration, this latter work being aimed at refining and developing the services specifically targeted to meet the needs identified in the research (Crothers, 1998; Green, 1998). Over the years, EPIC has developed and diversified its services; in the organisation's own words: 'while successful reintegration of ex-combatants in itself makes a significant contribution to peace-building, EPIC have, through a wide range of activities, made a much wider contribution to peace building in Northern Ireland' (EPIC, 2004: n.p.). Its activities now include:

- creating opportunities for ex-combatants and others to engage in dialogue;
- using the experience of former prisoners to influence and persuade young people of the value of non-violent methods of conflict resolution;
- empowering and training former paramilitary activists with the skills to pursue their objectives in a non-violent way while contributing positively to the community; and
- sharing experiences of conflict with others in conflict zones around the world to identify common themes and construct models of best practice in peace-building.

EPIC also continues to work on addressing the issues that prevent the full reintegration of politically motivated former prisoners into society.

Tar Isteach, which is both a charity and a company limited by guarantee, was launched in 1999 and provides counselling and welfare rights services for Republican former prisoners and their families in the North Belfast area. It is a community-based organisation providing support services to 'a highly marginalised group in one of the most deprived areas of Northern Ireland' and ensuring that the barriers which 'persistently prevent political former prisoners, and by association their families, from achieving full and equal citizenship' are overcome (Tar Isteach, 2004: 3). As well as these counselling and welfare services, Tar Isteach is involved in:

- youth projects;
- a not-for-profit social economy construction firm providing employment and training;
- development of other former prisoner projects throughout North Belfast such as Amach agus Isteach in Ardoyne; and
- cross-community projects promoting dialogue and peace building among all sections of the community.

Although Tar Isteach's main aim is to act as a support mechanism for former prisoners and their families, the organisation's welfare rights services are available to the wider community. A priority for the group is to work 'for the overall social, economic and physical improvement of the entire community' (Tar Isteach, 2004: 3). As observed above, Tar Isteach is part of a larger network of Republican former prisoner groups integrated into Coiste na n-Iarchimí. Coiste's aims are to:

- secure the full integration of the Republican former prisoner community through recognition of the contribution they have made to the community in the past and can make in the future;
- facilitate Republican former prisoners in deepening and developing their contribution to justice and peace in Ireland; and
- deepen the mutually beneficial links with community organisations, employers and other groups.

At its peak Coiste included some 24 groups and employed 95 staff throughout the island of Ireland (Gormally, 2001). Coiste and their affiliated groups' work has included: counselling and advice services; job and training-related activity; a not-for-profit construction company; a political tours business (which links up with a Loyalist former prisoner project and includes a 'hand-over' between the two groups); considerable work within Republicanism and beyond on truth recovery and dealing with the past; as well as lobbying and advocacy on behalf of the Republican former prisoner constituency in relation to continuing discrimination. Coiste's 'nation-building' programme has included a concerted work programme to 'outreach' to various constituencies including Loyalist groups, former British Army and Royal Ulster Constabulary (RUC) personnel, the Orange Order, Unionist politicians and a range of other historically estranged constituencies north and south of the Irish border (Gormally et al., 2007).

As observed above, most funding for politically motivated former prisoner groups has come from EU schemes. Since its inception, EPIC has mainly been funded by the Peace and Reconciliation I and II programmes. Tar Isteach and Coiste have also received support under Peace I and II. This funding is awarded in grant form by Intermediary Funding Bodies (IFBs) who are contracted to administer funds in relation to certain 'measures' or criteria. As the core funding body for former prisoner groups, CFNI sets out clear criteria for funding, priority being given to projects which:

- support the healing process and help those who are victims of the conflict to come to terms with their losses;
- support community involvement, retraining and the development of skills among people who have been marginalised by society; and

- encourage self-help and user involvement in the provision of quality services for marginalised groups and people (NIVT, 2001: 2–3).

Independent evaluations carried out on the projects have concluded that they 'have more than met the objectives of the EU Peace Programme' (NIVT, 2001: 8). As well as meeting the aims set out above, the evaluation stated that:

- There now exists a comprehensive support structure for former prisoners and their families; that structure is led by former prisoners and so is a clear model of self-help in practice.
- Linkages have been initiated and developed across the divides.
- Some innovative approaches by former prisoners and the awareness of their potential contribution for good in society have been significantly highlighted.
- Networks and alliances with some statutory bodies have been formed (NIVT, 2001).

One of the most significant comments in the evaluation concerns the impact of the funding programme and it is worth quoting in full:

The Programme has had impacts which are both quantifiable and intangible. The most important single benefit of the programme has been the impact it has had on peace building. Peace building has involved building confidence within communities as well as developing contacts between what had been warring combatants, fostering those contacts so that collaborative working can be initiated, and identifying ways in which the issues facing former prisoners and their families can be addressed. All of this has led to many former prisoners and their families feeling much less alienated and seeing that they have a place in this society. [NIVT, 2001: 6]

As noted above, the media portrayal of peace funding has at times been less than complimentary. Rather than highlighting its potential benefits, some journalists have reported on the Peace Programme in a negative and sensationalist way, focusing, for example, on funding for former prisoner groups in comparison to that for victims' groups.[4] Former prisoner groups are concerned that the positive role that they have undertaken is often obscured by such media coverage, which appears bent upon stereotypical interpretations and demonisation of former paramilitaries.[5] As a member of Tar Isteach observed:

We received funding from Comic Relief and we used those funds to do crucial work with young people. It was all based on conflict resolution and peace and reconciliation work. When sections of the press found out they ran a piece on how former bombers were getting money from a well-known charity.

The day that press stuff came out was the same day that we were arranging taking a group of teenagers up, from New Lodge, to meet the Apprentice Boys of Derry. There was nothing written about that, about us doing something that challenged stereotypes. We were stereotyped and attacked without any consideration or even mention of what the funds were used for. [Republican: interview, 25 August 2005]

The issue of additional funding is at the core of the future sustainability of the groups. Given the dependence on Peace Programme money and the absence of statutory funding, former prisoner groups are constantly seeking alternative ways of funding projects. Coiste has started a 'political tourism' business, showing groups of tourists and other interested parties around various parts of West Belfast, including both Loyalist and Republican areas. A leaflet promoting the tour has been produced in a number of different languages, together with a promotional DVD (Coiste, 2004). Tar Isteach has created a new social economy enterprise called AAI Construction. This 'not-for-profit' firm provides training and employment for former prisoners (although not exclusively so) and offers affordable building services to people in North Belfast (Tar Isteach, 2004). EPIC continues to lobby government and statutory agencies. There are, however, significant constraints: 'What they [the government] have tended to do is channel funds to "safe hands" – sanitised people – and with all the will in the world they can't make a button of difference. Once government get their head round that it may lead to a place for us' (Loyalist: focus group).

Moreover, it can be argued that:

Money won't sustain conflict transformation – it has to be the skills and the ideology that you leave the young people ... financial sustainability is a myth – you are not charging for the services you provide in conflict transformation. The money you get from funders [for conflict transformation work] has to be transformed into social profit. [Loyalist: focus group]

In that regard, it was argued in the Loyalist focus group that funders 'are forcing groups together without thought [as to] the consequences and are setting criteria that are absolutely meaningless ... [the] terminology ... is mad ... "holistic approaches" ... "capacity building"

... what do they mean?' Instead, it was contended, 'we need funders who are prepared to take risks': 'Conflict transformation training – we don't need to go and buy that from Palestine, Peru or South America ... let's look at our model of practice or the creation of our own models' (Loyalist: focus group).[6]

THE FUTURE OF FORMER PRISONER GROUPS

As to the future of politically motivated former prisoner groups, for some time evaluators have been suggesting that while some of the groups had been actively considering their future but that 'too many are focused on the availability of grant aid and see their survival and growth as fully dependent on continuing grant aid' (NIVT, 2001: 37). That is clearly not the case with all the groups as outlined above. Liz McShane argued in her 1998 Interim Report that mainstream funding would enable groups to continue and develop their work instead of devoting considerable time to raising funds.

The groups themselves believe that regardless of the source of their funding that their work in resettling former prisoners is far from complete, According to Tommy Quigley, Project Coordinator of Tar Isteach:

Notwithstanding the positive contribution [to peace-building], we are still waiting for full citizenship in legal terms. The effect of the 'criminal' record in a wide variety of life from employment through to adoption needs to be addressed. There is a responsibility on both governments across Ireland to fulfil the Agreement commitment in this regard. But this doesn't stop former prisoners from being involved in promoting justice, peace and community empowerment ... former prisoners refuse to be passive. They are agents of change not objects of transition. [Tar Isteach, 2004: 5]

Again, for Tom Roberts, Director of EPIC:

We have a pretty good handle on all the practical issues that ex-prisoners face. Unfortunately we haven't made much impact on the legislation that impacts upon former prisoners and that will continue for quite a while. Our role has become much wider now than former prisoners. It leads into the next phase; our future is in providing assistance and support to our respective paramilitary organisations, the UVF and RHC, in their own transformation process. [interview, September 1995]

Evidently, politically motivated former prisoner groups see their purpose as being unfulfilled and, while they can be innovative in terms of their future *raison d'être*, it is difficult to envisage what the future holds in the absence of secure or mainstream funding. If, as Tom Roberts suggests, former prisoner groups move into a new phase that assists and supports paramilitary organisations to transform themselves into something other than that associated with violence, then mainstream funding would be a timely initiative.

It is this dichotomy between the personal and communal goals of former prisoner groups that shapes the next three chapters which deal with the research results from the perspectives, successively, of

- the ways in which imprisonment and release impacted on family life, self-esteem and other social relationships but are also implicated in processes of resistance and transition;
- residual criminalisation and the ways in which this can act as an impediment in the contribution of former prisoners to their respective communities; and
- the contribution of former prisoners to conflict resolution, management and transformation in their respective communities.

The focus in Chapter 4 is within the communities, Chapter 5 deals with impediments both within and between such communities, while Chapter 6 focuses primarily on the role of former prisoners seeking to work within and outside their own communities.

4

Imprisonment and the Post-Imprisonment Experience

As mentioned in the introduction to this book, most of the survey and qualitative work conducted with or about former prisoners is done by former prisoner groups themselves. This research is the first to examine the post-prison experiences of both Loyalist and Republican former prisoners in a manner which situates those experiences in familial, community and broader social contexts as well as within the broader academic and policy literature. One of the benefits of this approach is that it acknowledges both community cohesion and heterogeneity within those communities. In so doing, the findings undermine the stereotypical construction of armed groups as unqualifiedly tribal and 'controlled/controlling'. While members of paramilitary organisations possess an obvious group loyalty, this by no means removes their agency or capacity to criticise leadership decisions. Similarly, the nature of relationships within paramilitary organisations is more fluid and reciprocal than is often acknowledged in the literature.

In seeking to explore the effects and impact of imprisonment and of the state policy of 'criminalisation' of political violence, we are also concerned to investigate post-prison trajectories by examining involvement in community and political organisations and attitudes towards conflict transformation. The issue of victimhood is also addressed in order to determine attitudes within and between the politically motivated former prisoners and their families.

THE CHARACTERISTICS OF SURVEY RESPONDENTS

Over half of all former prisoner respondents in the questionnaire survey conducted for this book were aged between 36 and 55 (see Table 4.1), a finding that reflected the high level of imprisonment among young persons in the 1970s and 1980s. The sample included interviewees who had been released from as early as 1967 through to 2000 and, as such, covered all of the various prison regimes during the contemporary conflict. To reiterate, these latter included: internment, criminalisation after 1976, the hunger strikes of the early 1980s, and the more managed prison regimes of the late 1980s and 1990s. Unsurprisingly, relatives covered a wider range of age groups ranging from parents to children.

Table 4.1 Age of respondents (percentage Republican and Loyalist respondents)

| Age | Republican | | Loyalist | |
	Former prisoners	Relatives	Former prisoners	Relatives
18–25	0.0	9.6	5.3	14.7
26–35	18.7	26.0	18.7	16.0
36–45	26.7	26.0	29.3	40.0
46–55	49.3	28.8	32.0	14.7
56–65	4.0	1.4	12.0	4.0
66 plus	1.3	8.2	2.7	10.6
Total	100.0	100.0	100.0	100.0

The gender of former prisoners was heavily biased, being predominantly male (see Table 4.2). Only 5 per cent of Loyalist former prisoners were female, compared to 20 per cent of Republicans. Loyalists were generally less supportive of women being included in direct action although both groups recognised that women played other key roles in culture and welfare within their communities when the men were in prison.

Table 4.2 Gender of respondents (percentage Republican and Loyalist respondents)

| Gender | Republican | | Loyalist | |
	Former prisoners	Relatives	Former prisoners	Relatives
Male	80.0	27.0	95.0	29.3
Female	20.0	73.0	5.0	70.7
Total	100.0	100.0	100.0	100.0

Women have always played a more defined role within the history of Republicanism and thus there was a precedent for the direct role of women in the newly emerging Republican movement after 1969. Initially, women tended to be allocated subsidiary roles in that movement, although this began to change, particularly from the mid-1970s onwards (Corcoran, 2006). Nevertheless, the number of Republican female activists imprisoned (in Armagh Gaol) was always much lower than their male counterparts (in Long Kesh). The masculine preponderance within the prison population was paralleled by a family-based support network within which females were predominant and, as noted in both Loyalist and Republican focus group meetings, there has been a strong demand by many female partners that their role be adequately recognised. Thus, for example, in being figured as a site of resistance, Long Kesh undoubtedly became part of the 'façade of [Republican] hypermasculinity'. But, paradoxically, this also allowed the prison to be linked to the mythology of the Republican homeplace where women, left to support and take care of 'thousands of families' (Dowler, 2001: 62), also endured, in the words of Gerry Adams (2000) the 'terrible burden' of the 'weekly trek to Long Kesh'. While marital and other relationships in the 'ordinary' population could break down, it was important that those within prisoner families were maintained. Such sentiments acknowledge something of the complexities of imprisonment and hint at the problems attending the reintegration of partners back into family life within a post-imprisonment environment. This process could often be problematic in that it disrupted family relationships built up when the combatants were imprisoned.

The deprivations which conflict brought continue while many lives remain unpredictable and emotionally difficult (Shirlow and Murtagh, 2006). So much about conflict is obvious, but the disposition of gendered relationships and the impact of conflict upon them have generally been invisible, especially with regard to understanding the post-imprisonment condition (Dowler, 2001). This is peculiar given that conflict shaped many women's lives as they endured violence, parented while their partner was imprisoned and had their homes subjected to violence or security force raids. What is also evident from this and other research is that during the incarceration of their husbands and partners women often assumed increased responsibilities as the *de facto* head of the household. In some instances, they also came into contact with new ideas through support groups and other networks, some of which were and remain heavily influenced by a feminist discourse. Cumulatively over the course of incarceration, such processes occasionally directly altered power relations between such women and their imprisoned partners, children, or parents (see McEvoy et al., 1999).

There is a compelling need to understand the intent and impact of violence and how conflict entered what would be deemed as the female territory of the home via searches, attacks and other related violence, in addition to the potential onset of stress-related disorders. Other studies of women in Northern Ireland include not only examinations of the disruption of normative notions of femininity as combatants and agitators, but also as the underpinning of gendered roles given that women sometimes fed and sheltered male combatants. However, for the most part, examinations of women in this conflict have focused on their supportive roles, at the expense of examining how some women transgressed these supposed roles by testing masculine-centred renditions from within their ethno-nationalist constituency. The relatively invisibility of women in the narrative of conflict and sacrifice is ultimately tied to a process of relative gender blindness.

DURATION OF IMPRISONMENT

Virtually half of all the former prisoners spent five years or less in jail. More Republicans (38.7 per cent) than Loyalists (24 per cent) served five to ten years in jail, whereas a similar proportion of Loyalists (25 per cent) and Republicans (21 per cent) were incarcerated for more than ten years. One in eight Republicans, compared to around 7 per cent of Loyalists, served more than 15 years in jail. Most respondents had been sentenced to fixed terms, while 14.7 per cent of Loyalists and 17 per cent of Republicans had been sentenced to life. One in five Republicans had been interned without trial, compared to one in ten Loyalists. As noted above, this differential impact of internment echoed the British state's primary desire to tackle Republicanism, with internment only being used against Loyalists over a year after it had begun in 1971. As one Loyalist stated in relation to internment: 'Republicans were interned in the first phase of internment because internment was brought in to protect the state and it was they who were threatening it' (Loyalist: workshop).

Nearly 70 per cent of Republicans interviewed were first imprisoned between the age of 16 and 20, a finding which, again, reflects the differential impact of internment upon Republican and Loyalist communities. Conversely, only 30 per cent of Loyalists initially experienced imprisonment when aged between 16 and 20. It was suggested during the relevant focus group meeting that Loyalist former prisoners tended to be slightly older and that this was due to individuals joining paramilitary organisations during the peak of violence in the early-to-mid 1970s. The Republican focus group argued that their prisoners were likely to be younger than Loyalists due to the more general community reaction to increasing militarisation in the early 1970s and beyond. It was also maintained that many of the early members of Loyalist groups would have been older than Republicans as they had joined paramilitary organisations after spending time in the British Army. According to evidence from the Republican focus group, a wide range of age groups had been introduced to active Republicanism for the first time when the conflict started in late 1960s. In later years, as the conflict progressed, it would have been unusual for people to wait until they were in their late twenties or early thirties before becoming involved. Indeed, persons in their late twenties and early thirties seeking to join the Provisional IRA would have been viewed with suspicion and concerns that late-comers may have been informants or lacked the type of motivation required while younger.

Former prisoners were also asked to provide their age at last release from prison. Around 20 per cent of respondents had served more than one period of incarceration, including being on remand; being on remand and never sentenced; and being sentenced. About 20 per cent of both groups were released between the ages of 16 and 23, while 40 per cent of Republicans and 25 per cent of Loyalists were aged between 23 and 29. A fifth of both groups were aged between 29 and 35, while more Loyalists (28.3 per cent) than Republicans (17.4 per cent) were aged over 35. In sum, the majority of respondents had been incarcerated during their late youth and early to mid-twenties.

THE IMPACT OF IMPRISONMENT

Imprisonment had a series of effects on both the prisoners and their families which, however, did not necessarily disappear with the end of incarceration. For many respondents, the effects of imprisonment upon post-release outcomes were not directly linked to the period of time spent in jail or the nature of the imprisonment regime when incarcerated. The effects of imprisonment detailed by the former prisoners in this sample resonated with many of the consequences long identified in the generic prison literature; these include difficulties with physical and psychological health, relationship problems, complications in obtaining and maintaining long-term employment, and concerns centred around coping with life on the outside (see, for example, Goffman, 1961; Bukstel and Kilman, 1980; Zamble and Porporino, 1988; Gibbs, 1991; Sappington, 1996; Liebling and Maruna, 2005).

While most of these studies on 'coping' with the impacts of imprisonment involved non-political rather than political prisoners, there are, none the less, obvious similarities in experience. Political prisoners are not inured to the normal 'pains of imprisonment' by virtue of their political motivation (McKeown, 2001; McEvoy, 2001). Nevertheless, political prisoners arguably have a number of advantages compared to non-political inmates. They may, for example, be sustained by their political motivations and ideology, a greater emphasis upon imprisonment as a collective rather than an individual process, and a lack of social stigma and resultant higher levels of support from family, friends and community than their non-political counterparts.

The reality that many Republican prisoners, in particular, viewed imprisonment as another 'site of struggle' may in itself have been a 'coping' mechanism (McKeown, 2001). However, the ability to cope with social and psychological deprivations of imprisonment and forced confinement is not the same as coping with and maintaining 'normal' social and family relationships. In their study of the partners of 200 Republican and Loyalist former prisoners, McEvoy et al. (1999) found that political motivation did not prevent prisoners and their families from experiencing emotional stress. Grounds and Jamieson (2003) and McEvoy et al. (2004) detail similar findings in their respective research on politically motivated former prisoners and their families. A new set of challenges faced prisoners on release as in many instances they entered an environment that was alien to them. Evidence from the focus groups suggested that long periods of incarceration, in particular, had removed prisoners from wider societal and technical changes. For example, 'When I got out I went for a job and had to draw a plan in metres and centimetres. I simply didn't know what these things meant. When I went inside everything was pounds, shillings and inches. I just couldn't do what was a very simple test' (Republican: focus group).

Other comments pointed to difficulties in coping with new technologies, the impact of urban redevelopment and a subsequent failure to recognise places that were once familiar to prisoners. In addition, children had grown up and this in many cases reaffirmed a sense of loss. For others, there was a strong sense that only those who had been incarcerated operated at the same emotional level. The initial sense of joy that accompanied the return to family life was sometimes short-lived and replaced by children questioning the authority of a parent who was relatively unfamiliar to them, or probing their involvement in violence. In some cases, prisoners, their partners, or other family members had deliberately masked the fact of imprisonment from their children.

Among former prisoners interviewed, slightly more Republicans (61 per cent) than Loyalists (56 per cent) were married or in a long-term relationship. A quarter of Republicans and 18.7 per cent of Loyalists were divorced or separated while twice as many Loyalists were single (24 per cent and 12 per cent respectively). Former prisoners and relatives were asked to comment as to whether incarceration had led to a positive or negative impact on various relationships. In the main, most of these relationships were seen to have been adversely affected. Among those who were married when incarcerated, around two-thirds stated that their imprisonment had a negative affect upon their relationships with partners and child/children.

There was more variation in responses concerning parents and extended family members; 53.3 per cent of Loyalist former prisoners, compared to only 18.7 per cent of Republicans, stated that imprisonment had a negative impact in their relationships with parents. Unsurprisingly, few former prisoners held that imprisonment had a positive impact upon relationships with their extended families but even then, Republicans (20 per cent) outnumbered Loyalists (10 per cent). Again this demonstrates the more positive attitudes toward imprisonment within the Republican former prisoner group and the stronger sense of support from relatives and the community compared to Loyalists with their far more ambiguous intra-community relationships. In the words of one Loyalist former prisoner: 'Unionists seem obsessed with this notion of respectability. If my brother [a B Special] had his state uniform on and slaughtered all round him it would have been quite acceptable. He had the legitimacy of the state around him' (Loyalist: focus group).

Similar numbers of Republican (21.3 per cent), and Loyalist (24 per cent) respondents stated that imprisonment had had a negative impact on relationships with their children although, again, a higher percentage of Republicans (12.0 per cent) compared to Loyalists (2.7 per cent) argued that imprisonment had created more positive relationships with their children. Former prisoners who pointed to a negative impact upon family life generally argued that imprisonment led to them 'missing out on their children growing up', or even to complete estrangement. Children themselves, now adults, talked of never having experienced a complete parent-child relationship.

In general, with regard to parent-child relationships, incarceration equated with notions of loss and hurt, as well as a strong sense of alienation and suffering.

Relatives were also asked to comment on the effects of imprisonment on personal relationships. More Republican (38.7 per cent) than Loyalist (28 per cent) relatives felt that imprisonment had had a negative impact on their relationship with the prisoners. This reverses the trend noted above in that Loyalist former prisoners were generally more likely to acknowledge a negative relationship than their Republican counterparts. No convincing explanation of these findings emerged from the focus groups.

Small majorities of both Republican (54.1 per cent) and Loyalist (54.7 per cent) former prisoners stated that they had found it easier to cope on a day-to-day basis while in prison. This reflected a lack of worries over personal finances, and a strong and durable sense of the defined comradeship developed during imprisonment. Equally, 37.3 per cent of Republican and 38.7 per cent of Loyalist former prisoners found it difficult to adapt to a post-imprisonment environment. The vast majority of both Republicans (93 per cent) and Loyalists (84 per cent) had experienced financial problems when first released and nearly two-thirds of Republicans and just under a half of Loyalists (48 per cent) were currently experiencing financial difficulties. Sizeable majorities of Loyalist and Republican former prisoners (over 80 per cent in both cases) stated that they found it easier to talk about their prison experiences with other former prisoners than to discuss such issues with non-prisoners. Only 34.7 per cent of Republicans and 22.7 per cent of Loyalists found it easy to relate to people from within their own age group who had not been incarcerated. A similar share of Republican (42.7 per cent) and Loyalist (43.8 per cent) relatives stated that former prisoners found it difficult to talk to them about their prison experience.

The experience of imprisonment was more commonplace among Republican former prisoners and their relatives than was the case within the Loyalist group. Around two-thirds of Republican former prisoners and relatives had other family members or relatives who were imprisoned, compared to just under 50 per cent of the Loyalist sample. Again, 80 per cent of Republican former prisoners had friends who were imprisoned, compared to 62.7 per cent of Loyalists, and a similar trend was characteristic of relatives. Nevertheless, despite the dissimilarities between the groups, it is evident that both sets of respondents held a highly significant knowledge of imprisonment compared to the norm, especially when it is recognised that, overall, those imprisoned during the Troubles for 'political' reasons constituted no more than between 2 and 3.5 per cent of the total adult population.

Within the Republican community, imprisonment clearly impacted on a more significant share of the population and was recognised by some as a community phenomenon. Conversely, in Loyalist areas, fewer individuals were affected by imprisonment and this is reflected in the lower rate of direct experience regarding prisoner issues. In addition, the dissimilar experience of imprisonment between Loyalist and Republican communities was matched by differing political organisations, strategies and tactics and the uneven ability of Loyalists to politicise the prisoner issue. In direct contrast, Sinn Féin and other Republican groups have mobilised around prisoner-related questions and, in so doing, have developed wider strategies of political resistance and related community concerns.

The different representation of prisoner issues within each community may partly explain the finding that around 70 per cent of Republican former prisoners, compared to half of the Loyalist respondents, found it 'easy to fit in with' their community after release. Similarly, 85.3 per cent of Republican former prisoners, compared to half as many Loyalists, claimed that they had received support from their community whilst they were imprisoned. This contrasting sense of support was acknowledged by the Loyalist focus group which noted that Loyalist former prisoners were still treated by many members of their residential community with senses of loathing and mistrust, even after a long period of release. During the focus group session with Loyalists, there was significant reference to those who had returned to their communities several years before and who had since then been in full-time employment. Such persons were, it was contended, not likely to spend considerable amounts on items such as cars, home improvements and holidays, given the fear that to do so would lead to them being labelled as a 'drug dealers'/criminals who had access to significant amounts of disposable income. Hence, Loyalist former prisoners, even those released decades ago, were often depicted by members of their own community as being directly involved in criminality such as drug dealing and other illegitimate sources of income generation without any specific information which could have justified such labelling.

THE IMPACT OF CONFLICT

Former prisoners and their families experienced extremely high levels of personal loss during the conflict. As shown in Table 4.3, a third of Loyalist and Republican former prisoners lost a family member as a result of political violence. Furthermore, a third of Republican relatives had members of their families killed, compared to 17.8 per cent of Loyalist relatives. More than half of the Republican former prisoners (54.7 per cent) and 48 per cent of their relatives had lost a relative, compared to 42.7 per cent of Loyalist former prisoners and their relatives. A highly significant 94.7 per cent of Republican former prisoners and 78.7 per cent of Loyalist former prisoners had lost a friend, as had 58.7 per cent of Republican relatives and 45.9 per cent of Loyalist relatives. The lower figures for relatives may relate to former prisoners knowing other members of their organisation who had been killed.

Table 4.3   Death caused by the conflict (percentage Republican and Loyalist respondents)

	Republican		Loyalist	
	Former prisoners	Relatives	Former prisoners	Relatives
A family member	32.0	36.0	34.7	17.8
A relative	54.7	48.0	42.7	42.7
A friend	94.7	58.7	78.7	45.9

Given that deaths in the Troubles equated to 0.25 per cent of the population of Northern Ireland, it is evident that the former prisoner community experienced a far greater intensity of direct violence and experience of loss. Moreover, violence was at its most intense in specific areas, including the Greater Shankill and North Belfast, which accentuates the knowledge of loss and inevitably intensifies subsequent community focus upon the need to commemorate and acknowledge such hurt. Both Republican and Loyalist focus groups agreed that critics of non-state combatants sought to undermine the status of victimhood within Republican and Loyalist communities and, in so doing, aimed at de-legitimising the meaning and impact of their losses. Such attitudes simplify the conflict into uni-dimensional notions of perpetrators and victims, with little room for acknowledgement that many individuals in conflict-affected communities may at times have direct experiences of both.

Again, there were some marked differences between Republican and Loyalist experiences of conflict-related death and injury. Republican former prisoners and their families were more likely to have suffered serious personal injury in comparison to Loyalists and their families. Over a quarter of Republican former prisoners (26.7 per cent) and 14.7 per cent of relatives had suffered serious injury as a result of the conflict, compared to 9.3 per cent of Loyalist former prisoners and 1.3 per cent of their relatives. Republican explanations for these differentials pointed to the uneven impact of mistreatment within the prison system, the nature of policing within their community, more numerous house searches and the higher level of rioting within Republican areas in the early 1970s and during the period of the hunger strikes in 1980–81 (see Table 4.4).

Table 4.4   Serious physical injury (percentage Republican and Loyalist respondents)

| | Republican | | Loyalist | |
	Former prisoners	Relatives	Former prisoners	Relatives
Self	26.7	14.7	9.3	1.3
Family members	37.3	38.7	32.0	17.3
Relative	34.7	30.7	37.0	24.0
Friend	57.3	36.0	49.3	20.3

As noted above, politically motivated prisoners in Northern Ireland endured many of the familiar pains of imprisonment. They have had to cope with the intrinsic personal and familial problems familiar to any long-term prisoners, such as the fear of mental deterioration, familial strains and fears of harassment by the security/state forces after release. Analyses have shown that the consequences of imprisonment and related stresses upon former prisoners and their families were somewhat masked during the conflict (see McEvoy et al., 1999). However, the period since the ceasefires has seen a greater willingness to acknowledge such human costs more openly. Thus the study also sought to explore the psychological impact of imprisonment and related conflict experiences.

The rates of reporting of serious psychological trauma affecting themselves, or people close to them, was particularly high among Republican former prisoners and their relatives. A quarter of Republican former prisoners (24 per cent) and 27 per cent of their relatives stated that they themselves had experienced serious psychological trauma as a result of the conflict. These figures rose significantly with regard to reporting the experience of family members, relatives and friends. Nearly half (48 per cent), for example, of Republican former prisoners reported serious psychological trauma among family members and friends. The figures for relatives were 40 per cent and 29.3 per cent respectively. In general, Loyalist former prisoners and their relatives tended to report fewer experiences of conflict-related trauma. Nevertheless, 17.4 per cent of former prisoners stated that they had experienced trauma compared to more than a quarter of family members and 38.4 per cent of relatives (see Table 4.5).

Table 4.5   Psychological trauma due to the conflict (percentage Republican and Loyalist respondents)

| | Republican | | Loyalist | |
	Former prisoners	Relatives	Former prisoners	Relatives
Self	24.0	28.0	17.3	8.1
Family member	48.0	40.0	26.7	28.4
Relative	33.3	36.0	18.7	32.0
Friend	48.0	29.3	38.7	21.6

Given that the respondents lived in North and West Belfast, which were among the most politically violent areas, it is not surprising that many had experience of being intimidated from their homes. Nearly 40 per cent of Republican former prisoners (38.7 per cent) and 25.3 per cent of their relatives had been so intimidated. According to Republican former prisoners, Loyalists were the principal intimidators (58.6 per cent of cases). Two respondents identified their intimidators as 'state forces' and one the 'Official IRA'. All other Republican former prisoners (38 per cent) blamed a combination of Loyalists and state forces, reflecting the common supposition that security/state forces conspired with Loyalists to perpetuate such intimidation.

Within the Loyalist sample, 32.9 per cent of former prisoners and 20.3 per cent of relatives had been intimidated from their homes. These figures rose dramatically when respondents were asked if they knew of friends (58.9 per cent) and relatives (36.5 per cent) who had suffered this experience. The majority of respondents identified other members of the Loyalist community as the intimidators, a reflection of more recent feuds within Loyalism: two-thirds of relatives (67.3 per cent) and 44.2 per cent of former prisoners blamed other Loyalists.[1] A quarter of former prisoners (26.9 per cent) and 21.2 per cent of relatives blamed Republicans for this particular form of intimidation (see Table 4.6).

Table 4.6   Intimidated out of home (percentage Republican and Loyalist respondents)

| | Republican | | Loyalist | |
	Former prisoners	Relatives	Former prisoners	Relatives
Self	38.7	25.3	32.9	20.3
Family member	33.3	41.3	35.6	40.0
Relative	38.7	28.0	32.9	27.0
Friend	49.3	33.3	58.9	36.5

EMPLOYMENT STATUS

While accurate official figures on rates of unemployment among politically motivated former prisoners have not been collated, it is possible to gain some insight into the extent of the problem by crosschecking research carried out by academics, community groups and former prisoner groups themselves (see Table 4.7). In one study, for example, conducted by the Republican former prisoner group, Tar Anall, it was found that only 27 per cent of Republican former prisoners released before 1990 were in employment at the time the study was completed in 2003. Some estimates suggest that up to one in four of those unemployed and living in West Belfast were former prisoners.

Table 4.7   Employment status (percentage Republican and Loyalist respondents)

| | Republican | | Loyalist | |
	Former prisoners	Relatives	Former prisoners	Relatives
Employed	41.3	40.0	53.3	61.3
Self-employed	8.0	8.0	2.7	27.0
Unemployed	40.0	28.0	29.3	16.0
Sickness/incapacity	18.7	14.7	14.7	8.0
Pensioner	1.3	10.7	2.7	12.0
Student	2.7	5.3	0.0	2.7
Training scheme	2.7	0.0	0.0	0.0

Thus, despite the lack of precise figures, the claim that long-term unemployment is a widespread problem for politically motivated former prisoners is not really contested by any of the relevant statutory bodies. Such high levels of long-term unemployment are due to a range of factors, including a lack of skills, or the possession of skills or qualifications that were no longer valid following long periods of incarceration. Other factors that lead to high levels of unemployment include an inability to work in areas dominated by the 'other' community, as well as issues concerned with illness and trauma-related conditions. But above all, perhaps, are issues related to continued structural exclusion due to the past involvement in violence and experience of imprisonment:

When you listened to the stories of people trying to get access to work, it was clear that they fell into a number of categories: there were those who were able, not necessarily easy but able, to get access to jobs in their own community because they knew people or whatever; there were those who were able to go a bit beyond that, but who conceal their past, which meant they were always vulnerable, and meant that if the past came out then there was a high chance that they would lose the job or chances of promotion or whatever it might be … There are undoubtedly obstacles, if people don't declare they are vulnerable, and clearly they should declare, if they do declare then there is a high possibility in many cases that they will be ruled out of consideration. [interview: member of civic society, 8 February 2005]

In the research for this book, the unemployment rate among Republican former prisoners was found to be 40 per cent, a higher rate than that of their Loyalist counterparts (29.3 per cent). Relatives also showed higher than average rates of unemployment at 28 per cent for Republican relatives and 16 per cent for Loyalists. Given that the average rate of unemployment within the study area was around 14 per cent, it is obvious that rates of unemployment are well above community norms. After excluding those in employment and pensioners, the observed levels of economic inactivity were 58.2 per cent and 44 per cent respectively for Republican and Loyalist former prisoners (see Table 4.7).

In part, the differential unemployment rate between former prisoners and relatives may be explained by the different age profile, especially regarding younger persons who are less likely to have experienced long-term unemployment. Furthermore, relatives who have not been imprisoned are obviously less likely to be directly affected by the effect of a criminal record in their search for work (see Chapter 5). Among those in employment, it was suggested that former prisoners tended to find jobs such as taxi drivers, doormen and labourers, usually for relatively low pay and within their own communities. However, relatives were also likely to have limited employment opportunities. Many were employed in the service industry as shop assistants or waiters/waitresses. Since the advent of Peace I and II funds, many relatives and former prisoners have found employment within the community sector. The fragile nature of employment and self-employment was also clearly noted by a Republican respondent:

It is obvious that it is hard to get well-paid and long-term work at that. Some of us get into the community sector, which is fine, but there is always the problem with long-term finance and job sustainability. You can get a bit of door work, but then again it's late nights and it's more 'brawn than brain'. You can set up on your own but then you have to have a few pounds behind you which most of us don't have.

For me it's like always being a teenager. No money. No regular money and still waiting to start a career. A teenager without the kicks. [Republican: interview, 15 December 2004]

Although the economic situation of Loyalist former prisoners and their relatives was relatively better than that of Republicans, it was still, however, significantly worse than the average for both Northern Ireland in general and their local areas in particular. Interestingly, there appear to be major differences in the economic experiences of Loyalist former prisoners and their relatives, which are not as apparent within the Republican community. Relatives of Loyalists seem to fare significantly better in the labour market in terms of the employment/ unemployment differential than each of the groups studied. They also tend to be less dependent upon incapacity benefits. The differences in economic experience between the Republican and Loyalist former prisoners also appears to be borne out by the finding that nearly two-thirds of Republicans (64 per cent) were currently experiencing financial problems, compared to 48 per cent of Loyalists.

Both groups of former prisoners stated that they had encountered difficulties gaining employment. One key factor, shared by 91.4 per cent and 82.4 per cent of Republicans and Loyalists respectively, was a refusal to work in places dominated by the 'other' community. Virtually all Republican former prisoners and their relatives felt confined to their own areas when seeking work, a situation linked to chill factors (that is, fear of entering a place dominated by the other community) and other issues concerning immobility (Bairner and Shirlow, 2002; Shirlow and Murtagh, 2006). Similar shares of respondents from both groups suggested that their prison records constituted a barrier to gaining work for which they were qualified. Moreover, 15 per cent of Republican and 9.6 per cent of Loyalist relatives stated that their association with a former prisoner had also caused them difficulties gaining work for 'which they were qualified'.

A majority of Republicans (60 per cent) stated that they would not include the possession of a prison record when completing job application forms. This reflects the pragmatic experience that such disclosure could lead to the cessation of an interview or, indeed, a failure even to be shortlisted for one. Most argued that their refusal to list criminal records on such forms was explained by a desire not to criminalise their own actions. However, the opposite was the case among Loyalist former prisoners, 67.7 per cent of whom stated that they would declare a prison record if asked to. This reflected, essentially, a 'damned if you do and damned if you don't' perspective. The majority of both Republican (86.7 per cent) and Loyalist (89.3 per cent) former prisoners said that the attitudes of employers were a barrier to them finding work.

Table 4.8   Receipt of benefits (percentage Republican and Loyalist respondents)

	Republican		Loyalist	
	Former prisoners	*Relatives*	*Former prisoners*	*Relatives*
Benefits	77.3	78.7	64.0	53.3
Job Seeker's Allowance (income-based*)	14.7	4.0	17.3	1.3
Job Seeker's Allowance (contributions-based)	2.7	0.0	0.0	0.0
Income Support*	24.0	28.0	13.3	9.3
Housing Benefit*	16.0	26.7	4.0	9.3
Incapacity Benefit	9.3	8.0	5.3	8.0
Disability Living Allowance	16.0	16.0	9.3	5.3
Tax Credits*	8.0	13.3	0.0	5.3
Child Benefit	26.7	42.7	1.3	8.0
Pension	0.0	0.0	2.7	6.7

(* indicates means-tested benefits)

The lack of job opportunities available to former prisoners and the low level of income within their communities were reflected further in the numbers dependent upon welfare benefits (see Table 4.8). More than three-quarters of Republican and almost two-thirds of Loyalist former prisoners were in receipt of at least one form of benefit, as were many of their relatives. In addition, 64 per cent of Loyalist former prisoners and 53 per cent of their relatives were also in receipt of benefits. Some benefits are universal such as pensions and child benefit whilst others are linked to disability. Republican former prisoners were more likely than Loyalists to be recipients of employment/unemployment linked benefits and also much more likely to be in receipt of Disability Living Allowance, Child Benefit and Tax Credits, suggesting, obviously, that they were more likely to have disabilities, children, and low income levels. Loyalist former prisoners were more likely to be in receipt of Job Seeker's Allowance. Notwithstanding the differentials between groups, it is clear that both Loyalist and Republican former prisoners and their relatives are heavily dependent on a range of state benefits, the reliance on means-tested benefits in particular reflecting their low economic status.

CONCLUSION

From this account of the personal characteristics of Republican and Loyalist former prisoners and their relatives, it is apparent that both sets of respondents have been disadvantaged in various ways by imprisonment, although there are variations between the two groups. As a generalisation, the key point seems to be that in addressing their personal difficulties, Republican former prisoners have a higher degree of community and personal support than their Loyalist counterparts. This implies that they may therefore be more influential in promoting transition within their own communities but also possibly more widely effective in the former prisoner role. Moreover, despite their shared personal difficulties, they can more effectively rationalise their status through constructs of continuing resistance than can their Loyalist counterparts.

Regardless of the reality of those consequences of imprisonment and conflict for many individual former prisoners, it would be wrong to give the impression that they view themselves as passive victims of circumstance. Indeed, quite the opposite is the case. Many Republican former prisoners have been explicit that while the focus of their 'resistance' many have changed, they remain committed political activists within the broader Republican 'struggle'. Similarly, Loyalist former prisoners, particularly (although not exclusively) those from a UVF/RHC background, have also sought to channel their experience, leadership and energy into activities to benefit both the former prisoners themselves and the Loyalist community in general. As we have seen in Chapter 3, analysis of the conflict and views of peace-building may differ between Republican and Loyalist former prisoners, many similarities exist in the form of organisation and the type of projects developed by both groups.

Nevertheless, while the personal circumstances of former prisoners can be overcome in engaging in committed work within their communities and families, it is evident that additional impediments, especially criminalisation and victimhood, remain and these require approaches that stretch beyond a singular community approach. These obstacles are the focus of Chapter 5.

5
Residual Criminalisation and its Effects

In the past, both during the recent and previous phases of conflict in Northern Ireland, former prisoners had to make a number of choices on release – whether to continue with their political activism, whether to curtail or alter it, or whether to give it up completely. It was important for both Republicanism and Loyalism to harness support for their positions among activists past and present. For both groupings, the support of former prisoners also provided a vital legitimacy to their respective political leaderships in attempting to promote the move away from violence to their respective support bases. At a practical level, they also needed to ensure that former prisoners remained 'on board', not least to deny them lending their potential experience, skills and resources to emergent dissident groupings opposed to the wider leadership strategies.

As noted above, despite the release and reintegration provisions to the Agreement, neither British or the Irish governments have yet been prepared to remove all the barriers to full citizenship and social inclusion faced by former prisoners (Gormally et al., 2007). In particular, what many former prisoners refer to as 'residual criminalisation' has remained as a key obstacle to former prisoners in the transition from conflict. Following some discussion on the contextual of residual criminalisation, this chapter provides some concrete examples of the ways in which such obstacles constrain former prisoners and indeed contribute to some of the negative stereotyping and stigmatisation which appeared as a perennial source of frustration to many of the former prisoners interviewed for this research.

RESIDUAL CRIMINALISATION

'Residual criminalisation' is used as a catch-all phrase by many former prisoners to describe the range of legislative, attitudinal and practical obstacles which speak to the failure to acknowledge their status as former political rather than criminal prisoners. The term appeared several times in the fieldwork for this book from both Republican and Loyalist former prisoners. Although some prisoners tend to deploy the expression in a instrumental fashion which suggests a co-ordinated over-arching strategy (reminiscent of the criminalisation era discussed in Chapter 1), it is probably more useful to conceptualise residual criminalisation as a series of hegemonic discourses which persist in pockets of the state system, political unionism and elements of civil society where the logic of the peace process has yet to be fully internalised.

As noted above, on the legislative front, politically motivated former prisoners receive little protection from unfair discrimination in terms of employment or access to goods and services. Anti-discriminatory employment legislation, established through the 1976 and more robust 1989 Fair Employment Acts, are now firmly embedded within recruitment and employment practices in Northern Ireland (CAJ, 2006). However, since its inception (the current iteration is Section 2(4) of the Fair Employment and Treatment (Northern Ireland) Order 1998), this legislation has explicitly permitted discrimination, which would otherwise be unlawful, against those whose political opinions 'approve or accept the use of violence for political ends, connected with the affairs of Northern Ireland, including the use of violence for the purpose of putting the public or any section of the public in fear'.

In addition, the legislation states that discrimination against those who are 'proven' to be a threat to national security, public safety and public order is not unlawful. In simple terms, the possession of a conviction which upholds membership of a proscribed organisation permits the denial of an interview and any legal redress to job applicants who are politically motivated former prisoners. Indeed, in a recent employment tribunal case in Northern Ireland, the validity of that exception was upheld. The Fair Employment Tribunal found that two former IRA prisoners (John McConkey and Jervis Marks) had been 'unlawfully' discriminated against by the SIMON homeless charity because of their 'political opinions'. The Tribunal accepted that both men no longer support the use of violence and dismissed their cases 'not without some reluctance'. But the Tribunal also held that the 'clear wording' of Section 2(4) of the Order *required* them to find against the two former prisoners. One source of comfort to former prisoners was that the Tribunal did call for the law to be amended because of the 'changed environment in Northern Ireland' – noting that 'there may be good reasons to consider appropriate amendments to the said article, or even its repeal, to reflect those changed circumstances'. The case is currently being petitioned to the Northern Ireland Court of Appeal.[1]

Moreover, in recent years, it has become common practice for employers to require applicants to declare their previous 'criminal' convictions (NIACRO, 2006). This practice too is viewed by former prisoner groups as a form of criminalisation since many refuse to accept that their convictions are for 'criminal' offences (Gormally et al., 2007). Often employers may dismiss an applicant who has failed to declare a conviction if they subsequently discover the omission. Since former prisoners are aware that the 'political opinion' exception appears to rule them out of protection under the Fair Employment Act, they simply don't appeal such decisions. As noted by Mike Ritchie, Director of Coiste;

We usually are asked to look into the issue of declaring convictions about 20–30 times a year. However, in most cases it is obvious that former prisoners simply don't bother either applying for jobs or taking up cases when it is clear that they have been rejected because they have 'convictions'. The legislation's main impact is that it creates a sense of fatalism and rejection. [interview: 15 December 2004]

Former prisoner groups thus constantly campaign to ensure that issues of criminalisation remain within the respective human rights and equality arenas. Concerted attempts have been made to ensure that the Northern Ireland Human Rights Commission (established under the Agreement) includes former prisoners within the Draft Bill of Rights for Northern Ireland. After considerable lobbying, the Draft Bill of Rights now contains a non-discrimination clause, which stipulates that: 'Everyone has the right to be protected against any direct or indirect discrimination whatsoever on any ground (or combination of grounds) such as race or ethnic origin, nationality, colour, gender, marital or family status, residence, language, religion or belief, political or other opinion, possession of a criminal conviction' (Northern Ireland Human Rights Commission, 2002; Article 4). The Draft Bill of Rights also contains a clause which stipulates that 'The State shall take effective measures to ensure that favourable conditions are created for the reintegration of former prisoners into society' (ibid.: Article 15).

However, the same Draft Bill does not distinguish between politically motivated and non-politically motivated convictions as it includes the exception that discrimination on the grounds of a criminal conviction may be adjudged legitimate if the character-istics used to discriminate constitute 'a genuine and determining requirement'. As such, politically motivated former prisoner groups have been unsuccessful in lobbying to have the Draft Bill of Rights distinguish between 'politicals' and other offenders on the grounds of motivation.

For a number of years, civil servants have been involved in a process designed to bring together under one legislative Act the various equality provisions designed to outlaw discrimination on a number of grounds including the basis of religion, gender, ethnicity, sexuality, or disability. That process has also seen intensive lobbying from disparate organisations trying to get their 'sector' included as a protected group under such legislation. Former politically motivated prisoners have also been busy in that regard. After significant pressure from former prisoners, in 2002 the Equality Commission for Northern Ireland suggested that legislation could be introduced 'to outlaw discrimination against those who have past convictions, with proper safeguards in place through necessary exemptions from dangerous individuals' (Equality Commission for Northern Ireland, 2002: para. 4.1).

The Equality Commission also deliberated whether separate consideration needs to be given to those who considered their offences to have been based on political grounds and that the legislation should consider a formulation wherein discrimination could not occur on the basis of 'irrelevant criminal convictions' (Equality Commission for Northern Ireland, 2002: paras 3.8.8.1 and 3.8.7). At time time of writing, the Single Equality Act process has yet to be completed although there is little reason for optimism that it will include politically motivated former prisoners as a designated protected grouping.

While no formal legislative proposals designed to tackle discrimination against former prisoners have as yet been tabled, in 2007 a British government-led task force which had been meeting sporadically since 2005 produced a voluntary code for employers and others to assist in dealing with people who have convictions related to the conflict (OFM/DFM, 2007).[2] That document advises that:

conflict-related convictions of 'politically motivated' former prisoners, or their membership of any organisation, should not generally be taken into account [in accessing employment, facilities, goods, or services] provided that the act to which the conviction relates, or the membership, predates the Agreement. Only if the conviction, or membership, is materially relevant to the employment, facility, goods or service applied for, should this general rule not apply. [OFM/DFM, 2007: 4]

The report goes on to indicate that conflict-related convictions should not be a bar unless the conviction was 'manifestly incompatible' with the job, facility, goods, or service in question. The onus of demonstrating incompatibility would rest with the person making the allegation and the offence would not, *per se*, constitute adequate grounds. Any applicant affected by a negative decision should have a right of appeal and 'it is expected that only in very exceptional circumstances that such grounds could be successfully invoked' (OFM/DFM 2007: 5). As well as practical advice to employers on making decisions regarding conflict-related convictions, the document also provides for an appellate structure (made up of the Northern Ireland Office, the Confederation of British Industry and the Irish Congress of Trade Unions) known as a Tripartite Review Panel. That Panel, which will have a part-time secretariat, will be able to receive complaints from individuals and is required to produce an annual report to the Secretary of State. The operation of the voluntary code will be reviewed in 18 months. The document concludes: 'if there is evidence that the voluntary arrangement is demonstrably not working it is the view of the Government that the voluntary arrangement should be put on a statutory basis' (OFM/DFM, 2007: 13).

Despite this voluntary code, the significant achievements of politically motivated prisoners in resisting criminalisation during their incarceration (McEvoy, 2001), and the explicit recognition of the political nature of their offences as evidenced by the accelerated release provisions, it is evident that politically motivated former prisoners remain confronted by an active series of policies and processes which reproduce criminalisation. As a result of this, at the time of writing, they remain legally or indirectly barred from a significant number of political, social and economic positions.

The questionnaire survey addressed these issues through a succession of questions aimed at assessing the awareness of residual criminalisation. These were concerned with examples of such constraints and also problems encountered in dealing with statutory agencies, employers and training providers. In addition, questions were asked concerning stereotyping by state forces and the media.

EXAMPLES OF THE EFFECTS OF RESIDUAL CRIMINALISATION

In an attempt to measure something of the practical effects of residual criminalisation, the survey included questions related to such issues as obtaining: Public Service Vehicle (PSV)/Heavy Goods Vehicle

(HGV) licences, compensation for criminal injuries or damage to property, pensions, visas, and loans/mortgages. Republicans tended to be more aware than Loyalists of the constraints placed upon former prisoners through criminalisation, although this did not apply to pensions or loans/mortgages (see Table 5.1). One important caveat to the points raised below is that we have no means of ascertaining how widespread these difficulties are in the wider non-prisoner community while, again, as multiple criteria are involved in, for example, loan applications, it is sometimes difficult to isolate the precise effects of residual criminalisation.

Anyone wishing to drive a public service or heavy goods vehicle requires a PSV or HGV licence. Nearly three-quarters of Republican (74.7 per cent) and just over half of Loyalist former prisoners (53 per cent) were aware of difficulties in obtaining these licences and it is instructive to pursue this example in some detail, as it does demonstrate the practical difficulties of residual criminalisation. Taxi driving is important in terms of employment within socially deprived communities in Belfast where many public taxis operate on a community-bus service level. The occupation does not require significant skills and can also be undertaken on a part-time basis, which provides the opportunity to raise income levels. These licences are issued through the Department of the Environment. Routinely, a politically motivated former prisoner is informed that he is 'not a fit person' for employment as a taxi driver. Such decisions are usually appealed in the magistrate's court where the refusal is normally confirmed. An appeal is then made in the County Court where, eventually, some licences are granted. As one Loyalist remarked: 'It's all right to be an ex-prisoner in charge of our children's education in the form of Martin McGuinness[3] but it's not all right for an ex-prisoner to drive a taxi' (Loyalist: focus group).

The central problem for politically motivated former prisoners lies in the arbitrary nature of such processes. The judgement as to a person's suitability is not made on the basis of ability but rather on the presumed 'morality' of the applicant. One prominent case was that of Damian McComb, a former Republican prisoner who had been released under the early release provisions of the Agreement. He challenged a ruling by the Recorder in Belfast which upheld a Department of Environment determination that he was 'not a fit and proper person to hold a taxi driving licence in all of the circumstances'. McComb's lawyers successfully relied upon the commitment to reintegration in the Agreement and the determination that a person released under the Northern Ireland Sentences Act was, by definition, deemed no longer to represent a danger to the public. Mr Justice Kerr, now Lord Chief Justice of Northern Ireland, held that:

The Agreement contemplated that mechanisms would be put into place for the accelerated release of prisoners and that those prisoners who benefited from that programme would be reintegrated into society. It appears to me therefore that particular attention should be paid to the fact that a prisoner released under the terms of the Northern Ireland (Sentences) Act has been adjudged not to be a danger to the public.[4]

However, while the McComb judgement is of particular utility to prisoners who benefited under the early release provisions of the Agreement, it is of limited use to the thousands of Republican and Loyalist prisoners who served their sentences and were released prior to the Agreement.

Table 5.1   Awareness of issues and experiences arising from residual criminalisation (percentage republican and loyalist respondents)

| | Republican | | Loyalist | |
	Former prisoners	Relatives	Former prisoners	Relatives
Awareness – PSV/HGV licence	74.7	48.0	53.0	22.7
Personal experience – PSV/HGV	13.3	34.7	17.3	18.7
Family experience – PSV/HGV	2.7	5.3	0.0	6.7
Awareness- compensation	81.3	82.7	62.7	45.3
Personal experience – compensation	26.7	62.7	25.3	34.7
Family experience – compensation	4.0	20.0	8.0	12.0
Awareness – visa	86.7	88.0	70.7	42.7
Personal experience – visa	49.3	68.0	33.3	36.0
Family experience – visa	24.0	25.3	1.3	9.3
Awareness – pension	30.7	13.3	44.0	10.7
Personal experience – pension	8.0	8.0	6.7	10.7
Family experience – pension	4.0	4.0	1.3	1.3
Awareness – loans/mortgage	37.3	24.0	37.3	21.3
Personal experience – loans/mortgage	10.7	13.3	24.0	13.3
Family experience – loans/mortgage	2.7	5.3	2.7	2.7

Again, there was a higher awareness of problems in criminal injuries compensation among Republican former prisoners and their relatives than was true of Loyalists. Nevertheless, the relatively high numbers of Loyalist former prisoners (62.7 per cent) and their relatives (47.2 per cent) aware of such problems could be related to events in the aftermath of the Loyalist feud in 2000. Both EPIC and a number of families affected by this were refused compensation by the Northern Ireland Compensation Agency because former prisoners were either family members or, in the case of EPIC, part of the management committee; EPIC has since won its appeal through the courts.

There was relatively little difference in the awareness of problems in this regard except for the comparatively low percentage of Loyalist relatives (42.7 per cent). Republican former prisoners had more experience of actual problems – 49.3 per cent compared to 33 per cent of Loyalists – in obtaining a visa (usually for travel to the United States or Canada), although the reasons for this difference are not transparent.

Whilst it is difficult to say conclusively why Republicans tended to be less aware than Loyalists of problems arising from pensions and other financial factors, part of the answer might lie in the historic economic and employment experiences of Republican communities. For example, people will only be aware of pensions if there is a community tradition of receiving them while those who tend to spend most of their lives unemployed or in low-income employment tend to depend on means-tested benefits at retirement age. The slightly younger age profile of the Republican former prisoner sample compared to its Loyalist counterpart sample may also have been a factor.

Equal numbers (37.3 per cent) of Republicans and Loyalists were aware of difficulties in obtaining loans/mortgages/insurance although compared to Republicans (10.7 per cent), twice as many Loyalists (24 per cent) had personally experienced difficulties. These issues also had the lowest awareness for all categories of respondents.

DEALING WITH STATUTORY AGENCIES

The interaction between former prisoners and their relatives and the statutory agencies of the state seems to provide another important dimension to residual criminalisation (see Table 5.2). Nearly half of Republican (46.7 per cent) and just over a third (34.7 per cent) of Loyalist former prisoners were aware of difficulties in dealing with statutory agencies, and 25.3 per cent compared to 20 per cent had personal experience of such difficulties. Both groups tended to cite what is now the Department of Health, Social Services and Public Safety (DHSSPS) (formerly the Department of Health and Social Security – DHSS) as the agency with which problems were most frequent, followed by the Northern Ireland Housing Executive (NIHE). Interestingly, this was one of the few areas in the survey in which the difficulties experienced by Loyalist relatives scored higher percentages than their Republican counterparts. Over a fifth (21.3 per cent) of Loyalist relatives compared to 8 per cent of Republican relatives cited difficulties with NIHE; additionally 18 per cent compared to 5.3 per cent had experienced problems with social services/social workers. Again, the Shankill feud of 2000 may offer one explanation for this trend (see Chapter 7).

Table 5.2   Difficulties in dealing with statutory agencies (percentage Republican and Loyalist respondents)

| | Republican | | Loyalist | |
	Former prisoners	Relatives	Former prisoners	Relatives
Awareness of difficulties	46.7	37.3	34.7	9.7
Personal experience	25.3	25.3	20.0	5.6
Family experience	10.7	13.3	4.0	2.8
Housing Executive	26.7	8.0	20.0	21.3
Social Security	42.7	14.7	28.0	20.0
Social Services/workers	17.3	5.3	13.3	18.0

Table 5.3   Difficulties in dealing with employers and training providers (percentage Republican and Loyalist respondents)

| | Republican | | Loyalist | |
	Former prisoners	Relatives	Former prisoners	Relatives
Awareness – public-sector employment	70.7	53.0	52.0	21.3
Personal experience	20.0	32.0	13.3	9.3
Family experience	14.7	22.7	10.7	6.7
Awareness – private employment	54.7	28.0	36.0	10.7
Personal experience	22.7	16.0	20.0	5.3
Family experience	2.7	8.0	1.3	2.7
Awareness – training	32.0	12.0	22.7	4.0
Personal experience	8.0	8.0	5.3	1.3
Family experience	0.0	2.7	0.0	1.3

DEALING WITH EMPLOYERS AND TRAINING PROVIDERS

In relation to employment and training, 70.7 per cent of Republican and 52 per cent of Loyalist former prisoners were aware of problems in obtaining public-sector employment, while 20 per cent and 13.3

per cent had direct experience of such issues. Republican former prisoners were also more aware of difficulties with regard to private employment and training. The rates of awareness were considerably higher among Republican prisoners than their Loyalist counterparts, but the personal experience of employment and training difficulties was less uneven. The awareness and experience rates among Loyalist relatives were significantly lower when compared to the other categories, Republican relatives having similar awareness levels to Loyalist former prisoners. The politicisation of the Republican movement could explain these variations in levels of awareness, especially with regard to relatives. But the relatively similar levels of experience among prisoners would suggest that imprisonment, irrespective of group membership, influences both the awareness and occurrence of such difficulties (see Table 5.3).

STEREOTYPING

At least a third of Republican former prisoners (33.3 per cent) and over a quarter of Loyalist former prisoners (26.7 per cent) stated that they had experienced unfair treatment by state/security forces – that is, Royal Ulster Constabulary (RUC)/ Police Service of Northern Ireland (PSNI)/British Army – since their release (see Table 5.4). Fewer Loyalists had experienced personal harassment (16.0 per cent of former prisoners and 22.7 per cent of relatives) compared to Republicans (24.0 per cent former prisoners and 13.3 per cent relatives). Perhaps unsurprisingly, the majority of all respondents concluded that such treatment undermined the peace process.

Table 5.4   Treatment by state forces (percentage Republican and Loyalist respondents)

	Republican		Loyalist	
	Former prisoners	*Relatives*	*Former prisoners*	*Relatives*
Personal harassment	24.0	13.3	16.0	22.7
Personal unfair treatment	33.3	13.3	26.7	24.0
Generally undermines peace process	93.3	92.0	76.0	68.0

The representation of former prisoners in the media was also an issue of concern. Nearly a quarter of Republican former prisoners said they had experienced harassment at the hands of the media and a third said they had been treated unfairly. Smaller but still significant numbers of Loyalist former prisoners and Republican relatives had similar experiences of such harassment. Interestingly, this was one of the few areas in the survey where Loyalist relatives scored more highly than Republicans. Nearly a quarter of Loyalist relatives had personally experienced harassment from the media (22.7 per cent) compared to 13.3 per cent of Republican relatives. A majority of both Republican former prisoners (93.3 per cent) and relatives (92 per cent) believed that the media's representation of former prisoners undermined the peace process. Three-quarters of Loyalist former prisoners and two-thirds of Loyalist relatives concurred. Coiste regards this issue as one of importance:

we ... challenge media reports. For example, last week Jim Allister [Member of the European Parliament] put out a very negative press statement opposing us getting EU funding. We challenged that – though it was not carried by the media. But at least the media hears a different voice even if they decide not to let anyone else hear it. [Mike Ritchie: interview, 15 December 2004]

The majority of all respondent groups also interpreted the first report in April 2004 of the Independent Monitoring Commission (IMC), the body established to monitor paramilitary activities and the pace of security normalisation, as undermining the potential for peace-building.[5] Both Sinn Féin and the PUP were fined as a result of the suppositions made within this report. One aspect, which particularly angered former prisoners, was the supposition that community groups should vet members to ensure that they had no linkages with paramilitary groups. Such declarations were held to be reminiscent of political vetting programmes that were commonplace in the 1980s. Respondents also noted that such vetting practices ignored the efforts of many former prisoners who were engaged in the promotion of social, welfare and conflict transformation projects.

The comments of Loyalists were particularly scathing. It was claimed that the IMC report 'reintroduces the justification for violence', as it is perceived as being centred upon the 'scapegoating of former prisoners'. Furthermore, the establishment of the IMC was heralded as creating 'another stick to beat the bad boys'. For Loyalists, in particular, the report ignored 'all the good work being done'. According to the PUP, the IMC had focused on 'the further marginalisation of those working hardest ... It narrows the ground of those actively involved in building peace and gives the "wreckers" a leg up' (Progressive Unionist Party, 2004: n.p.).

CONCLUSION

No substantive legislative protection yet exists to deal with the residual criminalisation experienced by politically motivated former prisoners. That said, it was lobbying by former prisoner groupings which led to the creation of the British government-led task force which produced the recent voluntary code for employers and others involved in the provision of goods and services to former prisoners. Of course, Republicans demand that such policy initiatives should be replicated on both sides of the border (Gormally et al., 2007). Broadly, Republican former prisoners are more likely than their Loyalist counterparts to be aware of the tangible and potential problems caused by residual criminalisation, although actual personal experience does not vary significantly between the two groups. Republican relatives have far greater awareness of these issues than Loyalist relatives. Both sets of relatives tend to be most – or least – aware of the same issues as do the respective sets of former prisoners. For example, Republican relatives, like Republican former prisoners were least aware of issues concerning pensions and loans/mortgages, whereas both Loyalist former prisoners and their relatives were more conscious of these concerns. The number of Loyalist relatives who were aware of a particular issue was also usually very close to the number that had actually experienced difficulty. It thus seems to be the case that Loyalist relatives were usually only aware of those residual criminalisation issues that had affected them personally. It may also be the case that all difficulties experienced by former prisoners in the areas assessed above will be attributed to residual criminalisation, although other factors are involved, while the survey lacked a 'control sample' of non-prisoners.

Nevertheless, the trends discussed here do seem to confirm the findings of Chapter 4 and point to Republican former prisoners and their relatives as having a higher awareness of residual criminalisation than their Loyalist counterparts. At a general level, criminalisation has become part of Republicanism's oppositional politics. Financial issues apart, Loyalist former prisoners are less aware of the impact of criminalisation and this may point to the differences in the ways in which the prisoner issue has been politicised in the two communities, former prisoners being far more visible within – and central to – the politics of Republicanism than is the case within Loyalism (see Chapter 7). The much higher awareness levels among Republican relatives also supported this conclusion. Conversely, while Loyalist former prisoners have been informed of difficulties through the network of former prisoner and other groups, their relatives have encountered the effects of residual criminalisation only when they had directly experienced them. We return to these issues in Chapters 6 and 7 because, together with the personal difficulties of former prisoners, they constitute significant obstacles to the ability of former prisoners to work both within and between their respective communities. Above all, residual criminalisation leads to the stigmatisation of former prisoners, most especially for Loyalists, who have a much more ambiguous relationship to their own community.

6

Community and Conflict

In the next two chapters, the emphasis of this book shifts to consider the ways in which the groups have become involved in conflict transformation work despite the impediments discussed in Chapters 4 and 5. Following on from our previous concerns with resistance and criminalisation, the focus here is very much on former prisoners and community, both within their own communities and between historically estranged communities. We then focus on attitudes to victimhood amongst the former prisoners because these are fundamental to evaluating former prisoners' capacity in conflict transformation work.

By way of background, it is also important to reiterate the division between Loyalists and Republicans regarding the nature and meaning of the conflict. For Republicans, their relationship to the British and Irish states remains primary whereas for Loyalists, the conflict with Republicans is acknowledged as being of greater significance than their relationship to the state. Notwithstanding this ideological division, it is obvious that working between culturally and politically polarised communities is important for both Loyalist and Republican former prisoner groups. It is also apparent that there has been a significant rise in initiatives and interventions by these organisations during the years of the peace process. This has involved engagement, in various forms, with academics, members of civil society, political opponents, statutory agencies, and peace and reconciliation groups. The desire to engage with critics and those with alternative perspectives is also a sign of openness and a shift away from an inward-looking preoccupation among former prisoners which arguably characterised the early days of the transition. Indeed, permitting access to the authors of this book is part of that wider process of critical engagement and openness with regard to alternative perspectives and opinions.

WORKING WITHIN AND BETWEEN COMMUNITIES

Our research points to a marked contrast between Loyalist and Republican former prisoners concerning their involvement in community-based activities. A large majority of Republican respondents to the questionnaire survey (81.3 per cent) stated that they had been involved in community work since their release compared to just under half (46.7 per cent) of Loyalist former prisoners. The most significant form of community-based activity related to interface work and the attempts made to dilute the rationale and impact of violence within highly segregated areas. Two-thirds of Republicans compared to 33.3 per cent of Loyalist former prisoners had been involved in such efforts. There was also extensive involvement in youth and community safety/restorative justice schemes that aimed to lower incidents of anti-social behaviour. Other activities of former prisoners are shown in Table 6.1.

In each of the specific areas of community work, Republicans were more likely to be involved than Loyalists, a further reflection of different linkages between community-based politics and ideology which, within Republicanism, accords a higher status to former prisoners. The lower level of involvement among Loyalists was viewed as being a feature of that community's more conservative attitude towards the British state and social change more generally, but also to the lesser status of former prisoners. One Loyalist commented that many of his compatriots ceased their role as activists upon release: 'Most UVF men saw themselves as irregulars. When the war ended that was it. They went back to being plumbers, welders, or whatever their trade was. It was over. Militant Republicanism had ceased and that was it' (Loyalist: focus group).

Table 6.1   Involvement of former prisoners/relatives in community work since their release (percentage Republican and Loyalist respondents)

	Republican		Loyalist	
	Former prisoners	*Relatives*	*Former prisoners*	*Relatives*
Interfaces	63.3	70.6	33.3	34.7
Youth work	53.3	54.9	26.7	30.7
Community safety	51.7	45.1	24.0	22.7
Elderly	25.0	17.6	12.0	5.3
Women's groups	30.0	23.5	6.7	1.3
Environment	36.7	33.3	12.0	5.3
Restorative justice	33.3	33.3	25.3	29.3
Economic regeneration	46.7	43.1	9.3	8.0
Other	16.9	8.0	6.7	8.0

The Republican focus group concluded that the higher share of Republicans involved in community work reflected the interconnection of politics and community representation in which Republican former prisoners were viewed as part of a defined community of shared aspirations and allegiances. The political commitment of Republicans was seen as having close links to the overall tradition of Republican 'volunteerism'. Moreover, involvement in community work was also seen to reflect the regard and support for Republican former prisoners within their own community, as well as the importance that they and their community attach to community-based work. Involvement took many diverse firms including a plethora of party political and community organisations as well as former prisoner groups.

Table 6.2 Reasons for contact with former prisoner groups (percentage Republican and Loyalist respondents)

| | Republican | | Loyalist | |
	Former prisoners	*Relatives*	*Former prisoners*	*Relatives*
Housing	46.8	24.0	56.0	37.3
Benefits	77.4	32.0	58.7	44.0
Relationship problems	14.5	13.3	10.7	16.0
Illness/alcohol/drug issues	4.8	5.3	5.3	4.0
Work-related issues	43.5	14.7	46.7	29.3
Training/education	62.9	28.0	40.0	21.3
Legal impediments	35.5	10.7	12.0	20.0
Counselling	12.9	8.0	14.7	21.3
Friendship	74.2	29.3	52.0	44.0

A substantial majority of both Republicans (81.3 per cent) and Loyalists (73.3 per cent) interviewed for the questionnaire survey had availed of the services offered by former prisoner groups (see Table 6.2). Of these, 95 per cent considered the services offered to have been valuable. More Loyalist (62.7 per cent) than Republican (45.3 per cent) relatives had used a former prisoner group while their family member was in prison and this trend continued after release. The reasons offered for the lower use rate among Republican relatives included the lack of specific former prisoner groups and the availability of support services provided by other community organisations.

The main areas of support offered by former prisoner groups to Republicans were linked to benefits (77.4 per cent), friendship

(74.2 per cent), training/education (62.9 per cent), and housing and work-related issues. More Republican former prisoners than Loyalists have used the groups for help with benefits, possibly because of their higher rate of unemployment. Republican former prisoners were also nearly three times more likely than Loyalists to seek help with legal issues, a further reflection of the link between political discourse, resistance and legal redress (McEvoy, 2000). The principal reasons for Loyalist usage centred on housing (56 per cent), benefits (58.7 per cent) and work-related issues. Among the four categories of respondents, counselling was most used by Loyalist relatives (21.3 per cent) but friendship was considerably more important for all groups. A central explanation for the high usage of former prisoner groups was that of trust.

Among former prisoners who had not used such groups (18.7 per cent of Republicans and 26.7 per cent of Loyalists), the main reasons given were the lack of need, a desire to 'move on' and a lack of knowledge as to the services offered by such groups. More than one-third of Republican and 10.7 per cent of Loyalist relatives stated that they had not used former prisoner groups because they 'did not need them'.

ISSUES AFFECTING COMMUNITIES

Respondents were asked to rank the five most important issues affecting their communities (see Table 6.3). Among Republican former prisoners (46 per cent) and their relatives (50.7 per cent), it was clear that anti-social behaviour was a major issue of concern. Within the Loyalist sample, 41.3 per cent of prisoners and 56 per cent of relatives shared the same anxieties.

Over 60 per cent of both Loyalist prisoners and relatives, compared to only half as many Republican respondents, selected 'drugs' as the leading issue of community concern. For Loyalist former prisoners, crime and drugs were identified as the new enemy within their communities: 'they are destroying our communities, this is the new war for our communities' (Loyalist: focus group). Loyalists also challenged the sanguine attitudes of Republicans in relation to the drugs issue. In their view, Republicans were complacent concerning drug usage within their own communities. In response to this, Republicans regarded drug usage as a much lower priority within their community, due to the methods employed to deal with such issues, and claimed that people from working-class Protestant

Table 6.3 Main issues affecting local community (ranked 1–5 in order of importance) (percentage Republican and Loyalist respondents)

| | Republican | | Loyalist | |
	Former prisoners	Relatives	Former prisoners	Relatives
Anti-social behaviour	46.0	50.7	41.3	56.0
Policing	37.3	30.7	29.3	34.7
Crime	30.7	29.3	50.7	56.0
Drugs	29.3	34.7	61.3	65.3
Lack of jobs	28.0	26.7	34.7	36.0
Lack of youth facilities	28.0	24.0	14.7	36.0
Youth anti-social behaviour	22.7	21.3	41.3	50.7
Human rights/equality	22.7	16.0	13.3	0.0
Peace process	21.3	12.0	30.7	29.3
Lack of housing	17.3	29.3	10.7	9.3
Relationships within the community	10.7	6.7	17.3	13.3
Relationships with other communities	5.3	4.0	17.3	18.7
Language issues	1.3	0.0	4.0	4.0

communities were responsible for supplying most of the existing drugs to Republican communities. There would appear to be little objective data to support this conclusion. Similar numbers chose policing as a key concern, although the concerns over policing may have been driven by alternative viewpoints. Republicans are more concerned with legitimacy while Loyalists complain about the inactivity of the PSNI regarding the growth in criminal activity and those Loyalist elements that have been opposed to peace-building.

CONTACTS BETWEEN FORMER PRISONERS AND POLITICAL GROUPS

Former prisoners involved in community work were asked if, as a result of that work, they had had contact with people with different political perspectives (see Table 6.4). More Republican (56 per cent) compared to Loyalist former prisoners (44 per cent) stated that such work had led to contact with people with other political allegiances. This probably reflected the greater numbers of Republicans who were involved in community work. While the highest percentages of contacts were with other political perspectives within the broad Republican and Loyalist ideologies, there were also relatively small but still significant contacts across the divide, indicating, perhaps, the role that former prisoners can play in conflict transformation.

Nearly one-third of Loyalists and Republicans had made contact with Sinn Féin. There was more contact between Loyalists and Sinn Féin than with the SDLP. Twenty-eight per cent of Republican prisoners had been in contact with the PUP. Interestingly, excepting only the PUP, more Loyalists had contact with Sinn Féin than with any of the Unionist parties within their own area. This may reflect the marginalisation Loyalists feel with respect to the other Unionist organisations (see Chapter 7), but also some openness to the possibilities for conflict transformation.

Table 6.4   Contact between former prisoners and people of different political perspectives* (percentage Republican and Loyalist respondents)

	Republican		Loyalist	
	Former prisoners	*Relatives*	*Former prisoners*	*Relatives*
Yes	56.0	30.7	44.0	41.3
No	24.0	34.7	17.3	18.7
Sinn Féin	30.7 (5.3)*	16.0	30.7 (26.7)	29.3
Irish Republican Socialist Party	36.0 (22.7)	12.0	21.3 (18.7)	2.7
Workers Party	14.7 (12.0)	5.3	20.0 (18.7)	12.0
Official Republican Movement	17.3 (13.3)	5.3	18.7 (16.0)	5.3
Republican Sinn Féin	14.7 (6.7)	5.3	8.0 (8.0)	0.0
32 Co. Solidarity Comm.	9.3 (8.0)	6.7	5.3 (5.3)	2.7
SDLP	32.0 (25.3)	17.3	14.7 (14.7)	16.0
UUP	20.0 (17.3)	8.0	24.0 (24.0)	28.0
DUP	13.3 (12.0)	4.0	20.0 (20.0)	20.0
PUP	28.0 (18.7)	13.3	40.0 (17.3)	33.3
Ulster Political Research Group	17.3 (13.3)	6.7	29.3 (13.3)	26.6
UK Unionist Party	4.0 (4.0)	1.3	8.0 (8.0)	10.7
Alliance Party	12.0 (10.7)	8.0	10.7 (10.7)	14.7
Parties in the South	30.7 (29.3)	12.0	17.3 (17.3)	21.3
Ethnic minorities	36.0 (29.3)	13.3	16.0 (14.7)	18.7

(* The percentages stating such contact occurred 'only when required' are in brackets.)

The reasons for such exchanges were extensive (see Table 6.5). Almost half of Republican respondents (46.7 per cent) and a third of Loyalists stated that contacts were linked to community work. Around a fifth of all activities involved prisoner projects, interface work, dealing with unrest between communities and political development work. Socialising proved a less common reason for inter-group cooperation.

Table 6.5   Reasons for contacts with people of different political perspectives
(percentage Republican and Loyalist respondents)

	Republican Former prisoners	Loyalist Former prisoners
Community work	46.7	32.0
Former prisoner project	18.7	22.7
Community initiative	29.3	21.3
Interface project	22.7	28.0
Unrest/tension	26.7	24.0
Political work	21.3	18.7
Socialising	10.7	4.0

AWARENESS OF AND ATTITUDES TO
CONTACTS BETWEEN FORMER PRISONERS

Loyalist former prisoners and their relatives were also questioned about their awareness of dialogue between former prisoners, political groups, state agencies and ethnic minorities (see Table 6.6). In addition, they were asked to consider how they interpreted such contacts. Over two-thirds of Republican prisoners and their relatives were aware of contact between Loyalists and Republicans, compared to only 42.7 per cent and 40 per cent of Loyalist prisoners and relatives respectively. Large majorities in all four groups supported these contacts, the only substantial resistance coming from the 10.7 per cent of Loyalist former prisoners who would not support such activities. A similar series of responses were found with relation to awareness of contact with state agencies, with over 80 per cent of all respondents supporting such contacts. Respondents, especially Loyalists, tended to be less aware of contact between their respective groups and ethnic minorities. However, between 75 and 80 per cent of respondents supported such exchanges.

When asked about the role of former prisoners in terms of peace-building, a significant percentage (over 80 per cent) of Loyalist and Republican former prisoners and relatives felt that the wider community did not understand the role being played by former prisoners in building peace initiatives within and between local communities. Many Loyalists were particularly annoyed at the 'holier than thou' attitudes of some of their detractors, who viewed them as 'scum'. One Loyalist noted: 'Quiet summers [that is, periods without rioting] do not happen by accident' (Loyalist: workshop), a statement that reflects the notion that groundwork undertaken by former prisoners has led to a reduction in interface violence.

Table 6.6　Awareness of and attitudes to contacts between former prisoners (percentage Republican and Loyalist respondents)

| | Republican | | Loyalist | |
	Former prisoners	Relatives	Former prisoners	Relatives
Aware of contact between Loyalists and Republicans	68.0	69.3	42.7	40.0
Would support contact	82.7	86.5	69.3	72.0
Not interested	0.0	8.1	5.3	8.0
Too soon	2.7	2.7	4.0	6.7
Would not support contact	1.3	0.0	10.7	2.7
Aware of contact between Republicans/Loyalists and state agencies	69.3	57.3	46.7	46.7
Would support contact	80.0	69.3	81.3	82.7
Not interested	0.0	10.7	5.3	9.3
Too soon	2.7	2.7	2.7	0.0
Would not support contact	1.3	2.7	2.7	1.3
Aware of contact between Republicans/Loyalists and ethnic minorities	60.0	44.0	28.0	24.0
Would support contact	84.0	76.0	74.7	80.0
Not interested	0.0	6.7	8.0	9.3
Too soon	1.3	0.0	1.3	1.3
Would not support contact	0.0	0.0	5.3	1.3

WHO ARE THE VICTIMS?

The issue of victimhood constitutes another important actual or potential constraint on the capabilities of former prisoner groups to work effectively within and between their communities. As a range of commentators have argued, the status of 'who is a victim', hierarchies of victimhood, 'deserving' and 'undeserving' victims – these and other heavily loaded debates have been a feature of the Northern Ireland transition (for example, Fay et al., 1999; McKittrick et al., 2004). So too is the status of those who were involved in armed actions with many eschewing the more loaded 'perpetrator' for terminology such as 'protagonist' or 'combatant'. The former prisoners in the Republican focus group argued strongly that 'victim' is a highly contested term which does not belong to any particular section of society and also one that cannot be used 'on every occasion'. Within Republicanism, it is evident that they conceive the Nationalist community as having been victims of British and Unionist oppression, of having been denied basic human and civil rights and, of course, having been subject to violence from state forces and Loyalists.

The question of victimhood and the attitudes to it lie at the core of the issues surrounding the stigmatisation and demonisation of politically motivated former prisoners. While impacting on the acceptability of those groups as agents of conflict transformation, attitudes to victimhood also help shape the ideologies of the groups. The question of victimhood has thus to be addressed at some length, the issue of civilian deaths being especially problematic as is demonstrated in the following exchange from the workshop which, although lengthy, we considered worth reproducing in full:

Republican: 'I for one was never led to believe or never led to see the Protestant community as collateral that was expendable in terms of the war.'

Loyalist: 'The statistics show that they were. If you take a head count of the number of civilians killed and the number of British soldiers killed then Prods were expendable.'

Republican: 'I've never heard anytime them going, "go and blow up the Co-op and if there's fifty Prods in it sure it doesn't matter".'

Loyalist: 'Try telling that to the victims. Try telling that to the communities.'

Republican: 'I'm not saying that's how it's perceived but it's important for you to be able to turn round and say that that wasn't part of the mentality ... .'

Loyalist: 'Well then what was the political ideology behind that? If we take La Mon and places like that there, to us it was just the same as Begin and the King David Hotel.'

Republican: 'During coffee break we were just having a conversation in terms of whole thing about collateral damage and stuff like that and I for one would accept, ya know it doesn't matter whether it was meant or it wasn't meant especially if your relatives are burnt or blew up or killed, it probably has the same impact. But again, just from a personal point of view, I think that it's important that these things are said because we talked about our humanity and stuff like that, but I do remember, the time of the Bloody Friday bombs, for example, I was actually going to work that morning.[1] I was in Oxford Street bus station ... we were working in Helen's Bay at the time and coming back and the place in chaos, and going into the house and my mother saying, "this is a fucking disgrace, look what's happening" and the images on the TV, and La Mon, Republicans being absolutely gutted by that. That might sound like some crocodile tears or somebody being disingenuous but genuinely saying, "what the fuck's this, where's this leading to, what's this gonna actually achieve?" Enniskillen was probably, I think, a landmark, in terms of Republicans questioning the rationale behind what they were doing.[2] I'm not saying questioning whether they were right or not but the efficacy, if you want, of the methodology and all the rest of it that was being used. And it's just a point, when you were saying, there was that level of callousness, I can't speak for everybody – there probably was, war is a brutalising thing. People do become brutalised, people do become vengeful and callousness creeps into it. But I would concur with what R's saying, is Republicans, I can never remember people saying "fuck them Prods" or "go out and kill them fucking Prods". There was a certain level of what you were saying, maybe that, there was that disregard in terms of the British state, when we deal with them, then we will deal with the Unionists in whatever way. And we always thought Unionists will see sense and stuff like that. And I know history shows us, history's taught us and that's why we're in the situation we are in today. That it's far more complex than that, it's not as simple as that. I think it is important just to make those general points that everybody's experience is sorta different in collateral damage sort of, I can understand where you're coming from but I don't think people ever viewed it in that context.'

Republican: 'It did occur, we went in and blew up the shop and it doesn't matter why people were killed or not.[3] There were people from the Protestant community who were put out of work there after being injured, and I was talking to —, his wife was killed up in the Shankill bomb and we became very close, we went to Scotland together and made dialogue and I said "I apologise for your wife", I was sitting in H4 [in Long Kesh] when the news came across. We thought it was Johnny Adair and that's when we were all sitting with our heads down, nobody gloated over it. And I sat and we talked about his wife and his child … and he says: "the point is, my wife was killed – no matter why you were going for Johnny Adair or not, it doesn't mean anything when my wife is up in that grave and I have to bring that child up". I agree with R – there was never any intention within the Republican movement to inflict any damage, but it did happen.'

Republican: 'See if people didn't mind, I rather they would stop using collateral damage as a term. People's deaths or civilian deaths and stuff, it's been awful, and you mentioned La Mon. You can take my word or not for it, La Mon certainly wasn't meant as it happened, there was phones out of action and stuff. But civilian deaths, I think as human beings here, we just have to say, yeah absolutely awful, combatants' deaths, it's not nice but sort of, if you buy into it, you buy into it. And from a Republican perspective, people who bought into situations, people say about the RUC deaths and British Army deaths, UDR [Ulster Defence Regiment] deaths and stuff, to a degree they bought into. I mean you don't join an army without knowing the outcome potentially of it. So from a Republican perspective it really isn't callous, but it's what you bought into and you were getting pretty well paid for it and if you get the outcome of whatever soldiers normally do expect in a war situation, then that's sort of tough, but the civilians, I wouldn't use innocent civilians, but the civilians – they weren't legitimate targets and when they were killed – it's bad. I can't apologise on behalf of the Republican movement but I didn't like it, right.'

In the vernacular, the key distinction in this exchange centres on attempts to differentiate between 'deserving victims' and 'those who deserved it'. Thus: 'We contend that there is a fundamental distinction between those who have suffered at the hands of terrorist groups and former terrorists who contributed to the terror campaign and wrought untold suffering through the period of the Troubles' (DUP, 2003: 4).

This distinction points to the recurring theme of a hierarchy of victimhood. Events in the area of truth recovery and acknowledgement in the Northern Ireland transition have well underlined such tensions. In 1998, the report, *We Will Remember Them*, was published by the former head of the Northern Ireland civil service Sir Kenneth Bloomfield, the then Northern Ireland Victims Commissioner. The report was widely criticised by Republicans and Nationalists for promulgating the idea that the 'undeserving' victims were inevitably Nationalists and Republicans killed by the British security forces and their agents and that the most 'deserving' victims were members of the security forces (see Healing Through Remembering, 2006). In partial response to that perception, one local Republican community established their own 'bottom-up' truth recovery process in Ardoyne, North Belfast. The resultant report (Ardoyne Commemoration Project, 2002) was itself criticised by Unionists for choosing victims based essentially on geography, that is, individuals who were 'from' the area. As two of the report's authors candidly acknowledge (Lundy and McGovern, 2005), while this criteria included some individuals deemed 'less deserving' by the local community (such as those who had been killed as informers), it excluded members of the security forces who were killed while on active service in the area or indeed other combatants and civilians killed elsewhere *by* people from Ardoyne.

This contested, hierarchical nature of victimhood is quite explicit in the data collected in this present research. A large majority of respondents in the questionnaire survey agreed that civilians were victims as were their own communities (see Table 6.7). With the exception of Loyalist former prisoners, over 80 per cent of respondents stated that their families had been victims. Eighty per cent of Republican former prisoners and 77.3 per cent of Republican relatives agreed that Republicans were victims compared to 48 per cent of Loyalist former prisoners and 66.7 per cent of Loyalist relatives. Nearly as many Republican (66.7 per cent) as Loyalist former prisoners (70.6 per cent) held that Loyalists were victims. There were relatively similar responses with regard to prisoners, although more Republican (74.7 per cent) than Loyalist former prisoners (58.6 per cent) self-identified themselves as victims.

Table 6.7   Attitudes to victimhood (percentage Republican and Loyalist respondents)

	Republican				Loyalist			
	Former prisoners		Relatives		Former prisoners		Relatives	
	Agree/ Strongly Agree	Disagree/ Strongly Disagree	Agree/ Strongly Agree	Disagree/ Strongly Disagree	Agree/ Strongly Agree	Disagree/ Strongly Disagree	Agree/ Strongly Agree	Disagree/ Strongly Disagree
Civilians	88.0	0.0	82.6	1.3	83.3	1.3	93.4	0.0
Your community	93.3	0.0	92.0	0.0	81.4	0.0	93.3	0.0
Your family	85.3	0.0	84.0	4.0	69.3	1.3	81.3	0.0
Republicans	80.0	1.3	77.3	4.0	48.0	10.6	66.7	2.7
Former prisoners	77.3	4.0	81.4	1.3	69.4	1.3	78.7	0.0
Yourself	74.7	0.0	65.4	5.3	58.6	1.3	72.0	0.0
Loyalists	66.7	5.3	53.3	14.5	70.6	0.0	86.7	0.0
RUC/PSNI	40.0	30.6	20.0	52.0	49.3	8.0	73.3	0.0
British Army	37.3	33.4	18.7	57.4	58.7	6.6	76.0	0.0
Prison officers	36.0	30.6	22.7	49.3	42.7	10.6	58.8	0.0
Judiciary	30.6	36.0	13.4	52.0	38.6	13.3	56.0	0.0

Turning to attitudes towards representatives of the state, two crucial points emerge. First, Loyalist former prisoners were much less inclined than their relatives to classify representatives of the security forces as victims. Second, and conversely, Republican relatives had a far more exclusive view of victimhood than did Republican former prisoners. Thus, comparable shares of Republican (40 per cent) and Loyalist former prisoners (49.3 per cent) stated that police officers were victims, although 30.6 per cent of the Republican former prisoner group disagreed with this proposition, compared to only 8 per cent of Loyalists. The difference was much more marked in the responses from relatives, three-quarters of Loyalist relatives believing that RUC members had been victims, compared to only one-fifth of Republican relatives. Interestingly, more Republican relatives (52 per cent) than former prisoners argued against police officers being classified as victims. Unsurprisingly, Loyalists were more likely than Republicans to regard the British Army as victims, although the percentage (58.7 per cent) is perhaps less clear-cut than might be anticipated; however, only 6.6 per cent of Loyalist former prisoners disagreed with this proposition compared to 33.4 per cent of Republicans. As one Loyalist explained: 'A lot of Loyalists who became involved in the conflict did so because they had an empathy with security forces and that is reflected in the figures. When Republicans killed security forces they were attacking us – they still can't get their heads round that' (Loyalist: focus group).

That said, however, there seem to be differences among some Loyalist former prisoners in their attitudes towards the different types of security forces. While a majority (58.7 per cent) viewed the British Army as victims, fewer were prepared to make the same assessment about local RUC/PSNI personnel (49.3 per cent).

Only 36 per cent of Republican former prisoners regarded prison officers as victims, although this was greater than the 30.6 per cent who disagreed. Republicans said that there was still a great deal of hostility towards prison officers over their treatment of Republican prisoners during 'the blanket' and other protests; one Republican stated that he was less inclined to view them as victims because they had received large salaries and had thus benefited more from the conflict than most. It is notable, too, that Loyalist former prisoners are less inclined to view prison officers as victims (42.7 per cent) than members of the security forces. Of all the categories, members of the judiciary were the least likely to be described as victims, a trend common across the four groups of respondents.

The dual trends – that Loyalist former prisoners were less inclined than their relatives to acknowledge victimhood while, conversely, Republican former prisoners were more inclusive than their relatives – together constitute what is, perhaps, the single most important result to emerge from the questionnaire survey. This is supported by the Republican focus group in which 'victim' was defined as: 'anyone who had been psychologically or physically hurt by the Troubles'. The difference within the Republican respondents was particularly pronounced when it came to describing opponents who were directly involved in the conflict. Whereas a majority of Republican relatives (53.3 per cent) did regard Loyalists as 'victims', this was considerably less than the corresponding figure (66.7 per cent) for former prisoners. Furthermore, while 14.5 per cent of Republican relatives disagreed/

strongly disagreed that Loyalists were 'victims', only 5.3 per cent of former prisoners concurred. Republican relatives were also less likely than former prisoners to regard the British Army and the RUC/PSNI as 'victims'. One possible reason for the differences within the two sets of respondents is that it may reflect the ongoing involvement of former prisoners in both political and conflict transformation work, but also an empathy between the two groups of former prisoners which could act as a significant resource in such work.

Finally, respondents were asked to consider the impact of harm with regard to conflict-related issues (see Table 6.8). 'Harm' was defined as 'inflicting physical, psychological or emotional trauma'. Unsurprisingly, given the findings regarding victimhood, the majority of respondents agreed that harm was caused to all sides in the conflict. No Republicans disagreed with the statement that 'harm caused includes inequality and/or discrimination', compared to only 10.6 per cent and 6.7 per cent of Loyalist former prisoners and relatives respectively. There were also significantly positive responses to the propositions: 'harm caused to my community and to others should be commemorated'; and that 'understanding the causes of "harm" can contribute to building a new society'. Over three-quarters of all respondents noted that 'harm caused remains an impediment to building a new society', with at least 60 per cent of Republican and Loyalist prisoners agreed that 'issues of harm caused may not have been resolved but wider peace-building initiatives should continue'. Just over half of Loyalist relatives agreed within this latter proposition.

CONCLUSION

Although there are significant differences between Republican and Loyalist former prisoners and their relatives in their responses to the questionnaire, there still does appear to be implications of a common ground and that the experience of imprisonment and release can be used positively in terms of conflict transformation. Many former prisoners felt that their experience of conflict and prison could be used to help others particularly as a 'deterrent to young people' and to 'show the motivations and help explain the cause' of conflict. The sentiment of numerous comments was that lessons should be learnt from those involved in the conflict so as not to repeat them. Clearly, however, the same experiences have produced impediments to the role of former prisoners in the transition from conflict to

Table 6.8 Attitudes to conflict (percentage Republican and Loyalist respondents)

| | Republican | | | | Loyalist | | | |
| | Former prisoners | | Relatives | | Former prisoners | | Relatives | |
	Agree/ Strongly Agree	Disagree/ Strongly Disagree	Agree/ Strongly Agree	Disagree/ Strongly Disagree	Agree/ Strongly Agree	Disagree/ Strongly Disagree	Agree/ Strongly Agree	Disagree/ Strongly Disagree
'"Harm" was caused to all sides in the conflict.'	89.4	4.0	94.7	4.0	90.7	9.3	88.0	8.0
'"Harm" caused includes inequality and/or discrimination.'	96.0	0.0	98.7	0.0	89.4	10.6	80.0	6.7
'"Harm" caused to my community and to others should be commemorated.'	92.0	1.3	92.0	1.3	94.7	2.7	82.6	2.6
'Understanding the causes of "harm" can contribute to building a new society.'	96.0	0.0	93.3	0.0	100	0.0	82.6	2.6
'"Harm" caused remains an impediment to building a new society.'	73.4	9.4	78.7	8.0	84.0	5.3	77.4	12.0
'Issue of "harm" caused may not have been resolved but wider peace-building initiatives should continue.'	68.0	0.0	68.0	0.0	61.3	1.3	52.0	1.3

conflict transformation. To summarise, these are the 'disabling' and alienation of former prisoners through their personal responses to imprisonment and release, residual criminalisation, the differing attitudes of their own communities which have the cumulative effect of making Republicans more effective in the former prisoner role, the legacy of the conflict, and the contested nature of victimhood. In Chapter 7, we move to examine the significance of these impediments through the idea of conflict transformation within and between the respective communities.

7

Former Prisoners and the Practicalities of Conflict Transformation

In this chapter we propose to look at some of the practicalities of the conflict transformation work of politically motivated former prisoners. Broadly, former prisoners have had three types of roles to play in conflict transformation within and between their respective communities. In the first instance, they are involved in practical community development work within these communities. Often such practical work requires communication and the development of relationships between historically estranged communities on matters of mutual interest. Second, they are involved in direct conflict-related work, such as projects designed to reduce sectarian violence at interface areas, during the marching season, or indeed find alternatives to paramilitary punishment violence through community-based restorative justice programmes. Finally, some former prisoners are more broadly involved in the creation of personal, communal and social narratives linked to the transition from conflict-exploring issues such as communal attitudes to truth recovery, commemoration and 'dealing with the past'. This dimension includes human stories of 'who we are and where we come from' and the history of the conflict and its transformation. The key factor linking all of these activities, however, is the focus on the local. While certainly almost all of those interviewed for this research continued to have a keen interest in the 'high politics' of Stormont, their daily attentions seemed more directed to 'sorting out' the real challenges facing them 'on the ground'.

The practicalities of conflict transformation explored in this chapter are examined under a number of headings. First, we examine the different styles of leadership which we believe are discernible amongst former prisoners in the Northern Ireland transition. These are characterised as political, military and moral forms of leadership. Second, we examine in more detail the practical efforts to reduce violence, particularly within Loyalism where the difficulties have been more obvious. Finally, we look at the related question of how the different relationships which Republican and Loyalist former prisoners have with their respective communities impact upon their conflict transformation capacities.

FORMER PRISONERS, LEADERSHIP AND CONFLICT TRANSFORMATION

Before discussing further the leadership claims of politically motivated former prisoners, it is important to enter two caveats. First, we are not suggesting that all former prisoners are necessarily 'leaders' in the traditional sense. As already noted, some Loyalist and Republican former prisoners have long since disengaged from their respective movements to re-establish a 'normal' life for themselves and their families. Even amongst those who, in different ways, have retained their allegiances, some might baulk at the description of themselves as even having been 'leaders' rather than 'foot soldiers'. However, the notion of leadership we are suggesting is more subtle than that of individuals who 'give orders' and who are, in turn, obeyed by others further down a hierarchical structure.[1] Rather what we discern amongst some former prisoners is a more organic style of leadership, wherein localised respect, legitimacy and authority is associated with them either as a result of their past action and 'sacrifices' (such as gaol time) on behalf of 'their' commmunity, or because of their evident skills and abilities, again which may have been developed during incarceration.

From this perspective, former prisoners involved, for example, in community work and community-based restorative justice programmes, or seeking to calm tensions at interface areas, or in reconciliation or 'nation-building' work, are all providing different forms of leadership in the transition from – and the prevention of – conflict.

Second, it is also important to stress again that we are not postulating some form of naïve eulogising of all of those who once took up arms. We have written elsewhere about the realities of Northern Ireland's transition from conflict as a bumpy and uneven process. While the recidivism rates discussed above in Chapter 1 are highly encouraging, of course, some former prisoners have become involved in acts of political or sectarian violence, or individual criminality. Certainly the high-profile activities of Johnny Adair (former UDA activist) did little to inspire public confidence in the trustworthiness of Loyalist prisoners in particular released under the Agreement. At an organisational level, as is discussed in the section below on reducing violence, all of the main paramilitary organisations have been involved in varying forms of political violence and criminality since the ceasefires. Those caveats aside, we would argue that, as former Secretary of State Mo Mowlam opined with regard to the integrity of the IRA ceasefire, judgements need to be made 'in the round' (Mowlam, 2003). The tendency to fixate almost exclusively upon individual acts of criminality and other violent acts in some parts of the local media in particular has in our view obscured a more sophisticated knowledge of former prisoners. It is now indisputable that, at leadership level, the IRA and the UVF/RHC have for some time been engaged in real efforts to transform their respective organisations and by extension, the communities from which they emanate. We believe that is possible to determine at least three overlapping styles of leadership demonstrated by former prisoners and ex-combatants in that process of conflict transformation – political leadership, military leadership and communal/moral leadership.

POLITICAL LEADERSHIP

There is a considerable literature on leadership in general and the notion of political leadership in particular (for example, Burns, 1978; Blondel, 1987; Gardner, 1995; Elcock, 2001). Of particular interest for this book is that work which focuses upon the ways that political leaders prepare, cajole and sometimes even bully their constituencies in national and international peacemaking processes (Sheffer, 1993; Westlake, 2000). Much of this also considers the intersection between agency and structure, the ways in which individual actors transform themselves from armed actors to negotiators, often as a result of changed political circumstances (McGarry, 1998).

As noted previously, at a general level, the political leadership provided by former prisoners in Northern Ireland has been obvious. Most of those who negotiated the Agreement from the Republican and Loyalist parties were former prisoners who had been convicted of politically motivated offences committed during the conflict (Mitchell, 2000). Indeed, many are quite candid that the negotiation skills employed were actually learned in their dealings with the prison regime when incarcerated (Sinnerton, 2003). In addition, both sets of protagonists have demonstrated finely honed antennae as to the potential for 'stretching' their political base and considerable dexterity at overcoming seemingly insurmountable political difficulties.

Such skills have also been evidenced at the micro-level through various community-based initiatives. In the working-class Republican and Loyalist communities in which such peacemaking activities take place, former prisoners are largely regarded as having 'done their bit' on behalf of their communities. While, as we discuss below, there are important differences between the attitudes of the two communities, the ex-combatants involved in community-based work do, on the whole, bring a considerable degree of credibility, respect and legitimacy to such programmes. As one former Republican prisoner commented:

Locally, ex-prisoners are involved in every aspect of their communities. Community restorative justice is an example where ex-prisoners are involved – trying to provide an alternative form of response to anti-social behaviour. Housing committees, community groups. I mean they are activists. They went to gaol for activism – a different type of activism but they are passionate about righting wrong, about bringing about change for people in these areas. And that type of culture is there still, despite people being released. They are giving leadership to people in their areas and they are leading by example, they are getting involved. [Republican: workshop]

The community-based restorative justice programmes in Republican and Loyalist areas are a useful illustration of the kind of leadership under discussion. Since their inception, the presence of former prisoners in these programmes as managers, staff and volunteers has been a defining feature (McEvoy and Mika, 2001, 2002). The programmes were established as direct alternatives to paramilitary punishment violence and involved extensive dialogue with the IRA and UVF/RHC. Almost since their inception they have received enormous national and international attention (Mika and McEvoy, 2001; Braithwaite, 2002; McEvoy, 2003; Sullivan and Tifft, 2006). They were the subject of a specific paper in the Northern Ireland peace negotiations, a substantial discussion in the review of the Northern Ireland criminal justice system, and a number of high-profile investigations by bodies such as the International Monitoring Commission and the Northern Ireland Select Committee. Despite intense 'party politicking' concerning these projects (particularly concerning the policing debate – see McEvoy and Eriksson, 2007), the quality of their work has increasingly garnered significant plaudits.

In his independent evaluations of the projects in Republican and Loyalist areas, Mika (2006) reports that in the eight sites which he evaluated between 1999 and 2005, the projects were involved in nearly five hundred documented cases which, without their intervention, would almost certainly have led to a paramilitary-led punishment attack. In 2004, the Justice Oversight Commissioner Lord Clyde suggested that the projects were 'engaged in valuable and effective work' and that 'they share a common intention and motivation to make a positive and peaceful contribution to the welfare of the communities in which they serve' (Justice Oversight Commissioner, 2004: 101). Similar views were recorded by the International Monitoring Commission in its third report in 2004. Finally, in April 2007, the independent Criminal Justice Inspectorate for Northern Ireland (CJINI) found that the project which works in Loyalist communities (Northern Ireland Alternatives) had demonstrated a 'high standard of professionalism and dedication' and they found no evidence of undue paramilitary influence on the programme or that it was a paramilitary front and '*every indication to the contrary*' (Criminal Justice Inspectorate, 2007: 4). The programmes in Republican areas – that is, Community Restorative Justice Ireland – have also recently been inspected by the CJINI but their report is not yet published at the time of writing.

These restorative justice programmes are a useful example of the leadership of former prisoners and ex-combatants at the grass-roots level. The task of persuading communities long used to relying on punishment violence to 'deal with' their policing problems, to adopt restorative justice and associated non-violent ways of dealing with crime and anti-social behaviour was formidable (McEvoy and Mika, 2002). The former prisoners and ex-combatants involved in this restorative justice work bring an enormous amount of credibility, respect and legitimacy to the programmes which might otherwise be dismissed as the work of 'do-gooders'. Individually, a number of the most prominent restorative justice activists are highly skilled and charismatic practitioners, but it is also clear that over the years there has been considerable 'routinisation of charismatic leadership' (Weber, 1958) institutionalised into the working practices of the organisations (McEvoy and Eriksson, 2006). As well as their previous organisational and prison experiences, many have also been involved in other long-term and dedicated forms of community work. By working with and proscribing in a very public fashion to values of non-violence, human rights, inclusiveness, and respect and tolerance for differences, such former prisoners have provided significant small 'p' political leadership in transforming community attitudes to violence. In addition, and in particular within Republican communities where it was considerably more politically sensitive, they also provided leadership towards the building of relations between the state agencies such as the police and other aspects of the criminal justice system from which communities have traditionally been estranged.

MILITARY LEADERSHIP

Within military studies generally, there is an increased recognition that the notion of leadership is much more complex than giving orders through rigid hierarchical structures and expecting them to be carried out (Matthews, 1999). Certainly the more sophisticated literature on the ways in which volunteer paramilitary organisations 'think' suggests that the exercise of leadership in a process of change is much more likely to be based on internal discourses, relationships, organisational cultures and mythologies than simply instructions being issued from the upper echelons and obeyed by the rank and file (Crenshaw, 1990; Irvin, 1999). Again, the notion of credibility is central to this behavioural response rather than an instrumental approach to military leadership. Put simply, unless those who bring the peacemaking message have credibility amongst current paramilitary activists and can frame it appropriately within the organisation's way of thinking, the message will not be heeded.

As one former Loyalist prisoner commented:

I think the analysis we give to the UVF has been good. It has been instrumental in a lot of interface issues and in that some responses have been measured. Since the ceasefires you can see the effect of good leadership. Other than interface stuff the organisations have been very disciplined. That has involved former prisoner analysis. If it wasn't for the rednecks things would be a lot better. [Loyalist: workshop]

Again the work of former prisoners and former combatants in the community-based restorative justice programmes is instructive. As well as working and volunteering in these programmes, former prisoners have been central to efforts at persuading paramilitary organisations to desist from punishment violence, to refer 'complainants' from the community to the programmes and to consider their own internal organisational attitudes towards violence. Such a process of persuasion or leadership in trying to move paramilitary organisations onwards is neither smooth nor easy. Nor is involvement in peacemaking work without its personal risks, particularly for former Loyalist prisoners. As one argued:

You could be shot dead – it's as simple as that! If you criticise about drug houses or individuals involved in drugs then those type of people want to do you as much damage as possible – they have the most to lose from the political and peace processes. It applies across the board. In terms of military leadership for example, if you try to clamp down on these people, the ones who are making a living from drugs or whatever, then you are making enemies. [Loyalist: workshop]

The biggest risk is going too far ahead of your constituency. And yet if we are CT [conflict transformation] practitioners then we have to go ahead of our constituency. [Loyalist: interview, 2 February 2005]

As was noted above, former prisoners have played a prominent role in other key aspects of the conflict transformation process. For example, they were at the forefront of the internal discussions within Loyalism and Republicanism which led to the production of two documents concerning the respective constituencies' attitudes towards truth recovery processes (Eolas, 2003; EPIC, 2004, 2005). Eolas ('information' in Irish) was established as a network of grass-roots individuals working in Republican communities who had experience in working with victims primarily of state and Loyalist violence, former prisoners and other community and human rights activists. Those involved were frustrated at the sporadic and uneven focus upon issues concerning 'victims and political prisoners' and related matters. Ultimately they produced a *Consultation Paper on Truth and Justice* (Eolas, 2003), which draws upon some of the relevant international experience of truth recovery, acknowledges the need for greater understanding of Unionist/Loyalist views and needs with regard to truth recovery, and sets out a mission and a series of principles and values which should guide any process of truth recovery. It also proposes three overlapping 'discussion models' of how truth recovery might be achieved, each of which had a strong investigative dimension (Eolas, 2003: 32).

A similar initiative was established within Loyalism by people largely focused upon the UVF/RHC section of that community. This initiative is the most significant to come from former Loyalist combatants concerning the debate on truth recovery. A discussion document emerged from two days of discussion amongst people from a Progressive Unionist Party, UVF/RHC background and a range of community organisations on the question of truth recovery. It is frank about its primary intent to focus the debate within Loyalism and the requirements of conflict transformation.[2] In a similar fashion to the Eolas process, it drew upon the international experiences of truth recovery in order to frame the broad range of concerns with regard to truth recovery. Although the document expresses considerable cynicism about the potential of truth recovery, and expresses a strong inclination towards 'drawing a line under the past', it does acknowledge the need to 'get the truth out as we see it' in order to counter the demonisation of Loyalists and prevent the future teaching of history as being too 'one-sided'. It concludes that, unless a clear answer can be provided to the question of 'what are the benefits for Loyalism', a truth recovery process has little chance of success (EPIC, 2004: 11).

Outside their own immediate base, both Loyalist and Republican former prisoners have played significant roles in other truth-focused civil society initiatives such as Healing Through Remembering (2006) and participation in events sponsored by the Glencree Centre for Peace and Reconciliation in Co. Wicklow. What is particularly interesting about all of these processes is the prominence of former prisoners and ex-combatants. Given the central role that individual members and paramilitary organisations would have to play in any successful process of truth recovery, it is precisely the leadership capacity of ex-combatants in terms of raising and engaging with a difficult debate such as this which is likely to shape the views of those constituencies.

Finally, as is discussed further in Chapter 8, the processes of internal debate within the IRA and more recently the UVF, which led to both organisations 'standing down' in favour of the political process, has of course been orchestrated by former Republican and Loyalist combatants, many of whom are also former prisoners. Managing a process which leads to the dissolution of a paramilitary organisation, and in the case of the IRA the decommissioning of its weaponry, is evident *par excellence* of military leadership in a transition from conflict.

MORAL LEADERSHIP AND COMMUNITY BUILDING

The third overlapping style of leadership provided by former combatants and former prisoners is the notion of transformative or moral leadership in the process of community building. As Burns has argued: 'transforming leadership ultimately becomes moral in that it raises the level of human conduct and ethical aspirations of both leader and led, and thus has a transforming effect on both' (1978: 20).

The issues of community building and the attention paid to the needs of former combatants are strongly connected (Auld et al., 1997; Babo-Soares, 2004; Verwimp and Verpoorten, 2004). Indeed, the process of being involved in community development work also guards against elitist tendencies which are sometimes identified with those who have been involved directly in armed struggle (for example, Irvin, 1999). None the less, involvement by ex-combatants in strong and independent community organisations – utilising their existing managerial and political skills as well as demonstrating a willingness to learn new ones – is an appropriately balanced organic relationship between such individuals and the communities from which they originate.

As has been discussed throughout this book, amongst both Republican and Loyalist former prisoners, the breadth of work has included campaigning on a vast range of issues on behalf of former prisoners and local communities. These include improved services, facilities and rights; establishing local employment and economic development schemes in local communities; welfare, education, counselling, advisory and advocacy roles; the establishment of advice centres, family projects, counselling services, children's activities, social activities, classes, campaigning for the rights of former prisoners and their families and organising meetings and tours for individual and groups; and working on interfaces to reduce tensions, especially at times of heightened risk (Shirlow, 2001a; Coiste, 2003a, 2004). As the Director of Coiste has argued: 'Our member groups at local level are actively pursuing dialogue and debate with people from perspectives traditionally hostile to Republicanism in order to increase understanding and build relationships' (interview, 20 December 2005).

In both communities, as with political and military leadership, the notion of credibility is the key attribute brought to the process of moral leadership. Challenging the tendency to resort to violence, either in response to local crime or anti-social activity, or in response to heightened sectarian tensions at interface areas or in the stewarding of contentious marches (Jarman, 2002, 2004), these are genuine, measured and practical efforts at transforming moral attitudes to violence in communities where it has long been a default option. As one former Loyalist prisoner suggested:

Because of the background that former prisoners have, they have been able to argue successfully for moderation in terms of dealing with conflict. It's difficult for people in the community to accuse them of unwillingness to engage in violence if it is necessary. If they advocate a non-violent response it tends to be respected more by the community. [Loyalist: workshop]

Community-building around issues such as the injustices of the past or exclusionary practices against anti-social offenders is key in the process of political transition. Former prisoners argue that as individuals who have been directly involved in committing acts of political violence, they are suitably placed to make the arguments to local communities about the difficulties that such practices can create. As the same Loyalist former prisoner cited above argued:

If it was an ordinary member of the community, they might be accused of cowardice for not engaging in conflict but they can't very well say that to a person who has lived that way before and came to the conclusion that there is better ways to do things. They also can provide leadership by encouraging people not to become involved in militarism and paramilitarism ... In the early days of the conflict those who became involved didn't have the benefit of people who had lived through a conflict to give them advice. Now younger people who may be tempted to go down that road, have the luxury of having someone who has lived the experience and drawn different conclusions. [Loyalist: workshop]

The notion of 'moral leadership' being provided by former paramilitaries may strike some as counterintuitive. To take such a view, however, is to conflate judgements concerning the morality (or indeed lack of moral justification) for engaging in extreme acts of political violence during a conflict with the potential for moral acts in subsequent processes of conflict transformation. Indeed, it is precisely because of their violent pasts that many former prisoners are ideally placed to provide leadership. For those who have both inflicted and been on the receiving end of extreme violence, often it holds little allure. Their rejection of the efficacy of violence as a strategy is itself a powerful exercise in both moral leadership and community capacity-building.

REMOVING VIOLENCE

In terms of the practicalities of all three forms of leadership in conflict transformation, the key benchmark is that of diminishing or removing violence. Since the paramilitary ceasefires of 1994, a clear disparity has emerged in the respective levels of community influence exerted by Republican and Loyalist organisations in which former prisoners are key operators. The IRA has successfully held together a broadly cohesive Republican position and for the most part avoided damaging factional splits, despite dissident campaigns by both the Real IRA and Continuity IRA (including the Real IRA bombing in Omagh in 1998, which caused the highest casualty rate of any single incident in the conflict, killing 29 people and an unborn child). However, the capacity of these groups to cause lasting damage to the peace process has been restricted by a number of factors. Dissident groups have been successfully infiltrated by the security forces on both sides of the border, and have been hampered by a lack of technical capacity, minimal community support, a lack of political prowess and have been subject to sustained pressure from within the broader Republican family (Tonge, 2004, 2005). Even on the issue of Republican acceptance of the PSNI – the most emotive issue of recent years, and one of the most powerful gestures of the entire process – Republican discipline and control has held firm. This political leadership has translated to community level, ensuring that the IRA has been able to deliver on their ceasefire promises and ensure the cessation of Republican political violence across Northern Ireland.

In contrast, Loyalism, always a more fragmented bloc (Bruce, 2004; Hall, 2005), became even more diffuse in the post-ceasefire period, with feuds and factional splits occurring at a number of critical moments and resulting in the emergence of a large regressive/criminal element. Discontented forces within Loyalism, such as the LVF, have openly tried to undermine transformative Loyalism through championing a discourse that depicts peaceful transition as duplicitous (Gallaher and Shirlow, 2006). However, reactionary Loyalist discourse has typically been disorganised and incoherent and has failed to mobilise a full-scale return to violence. Such violence as has occurred has typically been directed inwards, in internal Loyalist feuding and power-grabs, rather than towards the Republican or Catholic population.

Despite leadership support for peace-building from both the UVF and the UDA, rank-and-file members of both groups have openly flouted the ceasefire (Bruce, 2004). Support for the Agreement was always nominal within UDA ranks and this was further complicated by the lack of a coherent social or political wing to the UDA, as well as a distinctly horizontal leadership structure (Gallaher and Shirlow, 2006). By the mid-1990s, these divisions had crystallised into two broad pro-Agreement and anti-Agreement camps. The LVF, formed around Billy Wright and other disaffected members of the UVF, advocated unreconstructed Loyalist ideals of Protestant superiority, political and cultural allegiance to the Union, that were to be operationalised through ethno-sectarian territoriality.

In 2000, these intra-Loyalist tensions erupted in the Shankill area of West Belfast, in a feud which was dismissed by the then Secretary of State for Northern Ireland, Peter Mandelson, as nothing more or less than squalid murderous gang warfare (Henderson, 2000). The feud was considered as the outplaying of a criminal turf war rather than an ideological split. The journalist Jonathan Freedland argues that 'in true Monty Python style, no one can name a doctrinal difference that separates Adair's UFF from the Ulster Volunteer Force which it hates so bloodily' (Freedland, 2000). This anarchic disintegration of Loyalism has also been described as 'idiocy that comes with a fragmented culture that has lost both memory and meaning' (Howe, 2005), or as a movement which, self-defined as defensive and lacking a clear ideological 'vision', fundamentally lacks the capacity to transform itself (Alison, 2004: 453).

However, such conclusions have been superseded by announcements in May 2007 that the UVF was indeed going 'out of business'. Furthermore, the UVF understood the activities of 'C' Company as being directed against them and their pro-Agreement stance. This feud and that with the LVF was understood as being a conspiracy against the UVF by forces that aimed to destabilise the emergence of a transitional and conflict transformation-driven Loyalism. While neither of us would underestimate the UVF's desire to respond to a perceived threat to its prestige and authority (and indeed the safety of some of its members), many senior former UVF combatants have argued passionately to the authors that these were literally 'fights to secure the peace process'. The UVF has also expelled members involved in criminal activity and racist actions. Of course, this is not to deny, however, that this particular organisation contains significant regressive elements but it does indicate that there is a desire in key parts of the organisation to engage in genuine conflict transformation, a process which again should be judged 'in the round'.

By way of context, since 1994, Loyalists have been responsible for 89 deaths. More than half (53.9 per cent) of these killings were undertaken by, or against, the LVF, 'C' Company and the Red Hand Defenders (RHD). The 31 civilian Catholics murdered accounted for 34.8 per cent of all deaths. In the previous decade, around 80 per cent of all Loyalist victims were civilian Catholics. An indication of a significant decline in sectarian killings both by share and numerically. Fourteen of these deaths (45.1 per cent) were caused by the LVF, 'C' Company and the RHD (see Table 7.1). No organisation has claimed responsibility for the deaths of an additional seven Catholic civilians (22.5 per cent) while the UVF was responsible for four murders of Catholics (none of which were sanctioned at leadership level). Twenty civilian Protestants were murdered, half by the UVF. Many of these were punishment-based attacks while some were innocent bystanders or misidentified Loyalist paramilitaries. The statement by Police Ombudsman Nuala O'Loan in January 2007, that many of the murders attributed to the UVF were the responsibility of renegade UVF leaders in Mount Vernon, North Belfast, is instructive with regard to understanding the context of this particular violence.

Nearly 40 per cent of Loyalist victims were Loyalists killed by Loyalists. Of these, 35 individuals were killed in internal feuds and punishments and 15 were murdered in inter-group feuding. According to the PSNI, Loyalists were not been responsible for any killings between October 2005 and May 2007.

Table 7.1   Post-ceasefire Loyalist deaths

Victim	UVF	LVF*	'C' Company	UFF	Unknown	RHC	RHD	*Total*
			Group Responsible					
Catholic Civilian	4	8	2	5	7		5	**31**
Protestant Civilian	10	2	2	4	1		1	**20**
UVF	4	3	1	3			1	**12**
UDA/UFF	3		1	4			4	**12**
'C' Company				1				**1**
Police					1		1	**2**
IRA		1						**1**
RHC		1				1		**2**
LVF	4	1				1		**6**
RHD					1			**1**
PUP			1					**1**
Total	**25**	**16**	**7**	**17**	**10**	**2**	**12**	**89**

(*Source*: Shirlow and Monaghan, 2006: 6.)
(*Includes unsanctioned murder whilst LVF members were in the UVF.)

Police data record 489 'punishment' beatings in predominantly Protestant communities from the ceasefires of 1994 until the end of March 2006. More than half of these (51 per cent) have been attributed to the UDA and 42 per cent to the UVF. 'Punishment' shootings in the same period totalled 686, the UDA and UVF being responsible, respectively, for 48 per cent and 47 per cent of all such attacks. This particular type of violence, within Loyalist communities, declined by over 80 per cent between 2003 and 2007.

The use of violence by the UVF, in particular against other Loyalists, was based upon a need for internal control and a desire to immobilise groups that threatened both the organisation and the peace process. It was essential for the UVF to both retain its authority within Loyalism and to avoid driving members towards dissidents, as noted by a prominent member of the Red Hand Commandos:

In other words, if you were having to discipline someone within your own organisation, tactics became different because where you once would have expelled someone, you had to be conscious of what you were doing because then people would have run and jumped onto this other vehicle, so that vehicle had to be destroyed once and for all because the LVF, and there is proof beyond a shadow of a doubt, started five feuds and the last feud, people were adamant and determined, that this would be the feud to end all feuds. [quoted in Shirlow and Monaghan, 2006: 5]

These comments echo an earlier argument that the capacity to stop violence had become an internal problem for Loyalism. As Bruce (2004) illustrates, the IRA was the main impediment to 'thinking' Loyalism and the emergence of a political wing which could drive the transformation towards peace. Post-1994, however, the key obstructions were internal. The 'spoilers' came into opposition with 'old friends'. The reaction to them, although illegitimate, signified a desire to reduce the potential for future violence. UVF leaders are now 'confident' that the removal of such elements will provide a more stable arena within which to pursue conflict transformation.

As noted above, an important factor in the transformation of military organisations and promotion of non-violence is the extent to which military leadership is considered credible by the rank and file. Such credibility has been essential to dissuading a return to large-scale violence, as it provides direction to armed actors to pursue non-violent activities, as well as legitimising anti-violence discourse on a national scale. As former Assistant Chief Constable Sam Kincaid observes:

So I see for the first time, certainly in my experience in both sides [UVF/UFF] a real effort, probably the last time we had anything as determined as this in some sense would maybe go back to '94 to the Combined Loyalist Military Command but even then, I think that was more to do with PR statements, I think there is genuine effort being made by key people within organisations to say, 'Well, the point of all this has gone.' [quoted in Shirlow and Monaghan, 2006: 11]

Between 1994 and 2007, the IRA substantially reduced its armed operations and bombing campaign. It is estimated that the organisation was responsible for between 10 and 21 deaths since 1994, attributable to a variety of incidents, including the Canary Wharf bombing in 1996. IRA involvement in punishment violence, however, *rose* during this period (from 15 attacks in 1998, to 80 in 2001, falling back down again to 3 in 2005). As is discussed further below, between 2001 and 2005 the IRA also took action on decommissioning, a process which was verified by an IMC report which described the IRA as having put the totality of its arsenal 'beyond use' (for example, as reported by the BBC, 26 September 2005). Only the most superficial of gestures towards decommissioning occurred within Loyalism until the UVF announcement in May 2007 that it had put its own weapons conclusively 'beyond reach'.

Evidently, both the UVF and IRA have significantly reduced and even removed the capacity of their organisations to undertake organised armed action. In the explicit transition from 'armed struggle' to 'unarmed struggle', these groups have opened the door for the continued interpretation of identity through a variety of social, cultural and political approaches. To measure the peace process only in terms of political agreements and milestones ignores the day-to-day, incremental, essential work of community activists in preventing violence on the ground. Central to such work, are the efforts of former prisoners in mediating with their communities (particularly with the younger generation within these communities) regarding the undesirability of violence, especially sectarian violence, as a means for solving problems.

FORMER PRISONERS AND RELATIONS 'WITHIN' THEIR COMMUNITIES

In Chapter 5 we considered some of the structural obstacles associated with 'residual criminalisation' which prevent former prisoners of both communities from realising their full potential as conflict transformers. There are also, however, a couple of important distinctions in the relationship between Loyalists, Republicans and their respective communities which in particular impose practical limitations on the capacity of the former. Before detailing this, however, we should also recognise at the outset that not all prisoners became involved in conflict transformation work after prison. As discussed above, a small percentage became involved in criminality or returned to paramilitary activities. In addition, many Loyalists in particular appear to have 'disappeared' back into their own communities and jobs or other activities which do not afford them a significant profile. For those former prisoners who do engage in conflict transformation activities, the relationship with community is central.

Former Loyalist prisoners interviewed for this research suggested higher levels of isolation and social stigma than their Republican counterparts. Quite apart from the generic impact of residual criminalisation which affects both groups, they also report noteworthy levels of stigma even within working-class Loyalist communities. One former Loyalist prisoner articulated this sense of stigma in stark terms:

I would say that there is a greater understanding from Republican politicians that what there would be among Unionists in terms of the role that former prisoners can play ... one of the ironies is that among the Catholic/Nationalist community, I would find a better understanding of my position in life ... there is not the same prejudice. [Loyalist: focus group]

The Loyalist communities themselves have very different histories to their Republican counterparts. As was noted above, unlike Republicanism, Loyalism has no comparable history of political prisoners or the eulogising of the 'law-breaking'. Instead, Loyalists wore uniforms: 'We just put on a B-Specials uniform or police uniform and you could shoot as many people as you want' (Loyalist: workshop). Again, another Loyalist comments on his reasons for, and the consequences of, becoming a paramilitary: 'The UDR or the RUC ... were being totally ineffective at that time to try and combat an IRA campaign by civil means ... Because I stepped outside the law to do what I engaged in – that wasn't acceptable, even within my own family. I have problems with that. I became estranged from parts of my family' (Loyalist: workshop).

The attitudes of 'middle' or 'political Unionism', to which Loyalist former prisoners often refer (DUP and UUP) arguably contributes to this sense of community censure and alienation of these easily identifiable working-class 'law breakers'. Loyalist former prisoners involved in community work see themselves as working on behalf of:

a community within a community ... an underclass [marginalised] by middle Unionists, the media ... middle Unionism doesn't like [conflict transformation] because they don't want a working-class movement ... Educational disadvantage within working-class Protestant communities is abysmal. Those who are trying to take a lead are ex-POWs and there are very few of us. [Loyalist: workshop]

As was noted above, Loyalist former prisoners argue that they are all demonised by the prominent criminal activities of high-profile Loyalists who act with conspicuous impunity, in some instances because they are in fact paid agents of the security forces:[3]

What we're seeing is the criminalisation of whole communities within Loyalist areas ... by the selective handling and protection of key individuals involved in criminality. Drugs have been put into our community ... [creating] a criminal culture [organised] by the lowest element in Loyalist communities, that means the whole community is stigmatised by the media, politicians and in some cases by Nationalists. It's come to the stage now that many ex-POWs are afraid to build an extension, buy a new car or own their own house because they'll be stigmatised as drug dealers, criminals or gangsters. [Loyalist: workshop]

There is no evidence of a similar connotation of stigma towards Republican former prisoners in Republican communities. In fact, the converse is true. The status of former prisoner is more likely to be seen as a 'badge of honour', denoting an activist who was imprisoned by the British state for their part in the war and who now continues the 'struggle' by other means. Indeed, there are high levels of community expectation upon former Republican prisoners that they will take on leadership roles at all levels. As Mike Ritchie, director of Coiste, explains:

I've often described former prisoners as middle managers in the peace process. Because of their experience and aptitudes they naturally take leadership roles in local communities. When there are situations where most people would just head for home, potential riot situations, for example, former prisoners are likely to be the people who are trying to calm things down. That's happened again and again on interfaces. But also in terms of local community activity former prisoners have commitment and drive. What they would see is they were involved in armed struggle as a way of acting out their community's fears, concerns and aspirations. Now that there's a ceasefire they are still committed to their community's aspirations, fears and concerns so they'll be to the fore in articulating them. [interview: 15 December 2004]

FORMER PRISONERS AND RELATIONS 'OUTSIDE' THEIR COMMUNITIES

These very different ways in which Loyalist and Republican former prisoners are regarded within their own communities is replicated in their dealings outside – or without – those communities. Again this means, inevitably, that the effects of exclusions and impediments vary between the two groups. As discussed in Chapter 3, mutual prison experiences, originally built on simple everyday exchanges, paved the way for dialogue between some Loyalists and Republicans in the 1970s. However, on the whole, the normalisation of such dialogue between working-class Republican and Loyalist communities has been a painstakingly slow process developed since the ceasefires. Needless to say, it is often former prisoners who have been at the forefront of such dialogue.

It would be wrong, however, to underestimate the difficulties involved. Despite the small physical distances, there is often a sense of parallel worlds between such communities. Fundamental misunderstandings remain between Republican and Loyalist former prisoners, as do stereotypical depictions of the other. Republicans often appear to juxtapose insular Loyalism with their own 'non-parochial' Republicanism. As one former Republican prisoner acknowledged regarding his view of Loyalists: 'I found them quite insular in that they never really bothered looking at history, colonialism and I've always thought that if they did, the blinkers would fall off their eyes and they would see the reality here' (Republican: workshop).

Such patronising attitudes – either conscious or unconscious – clearly grate with Loyalists. Republican former prisoners are at times frustrated by what they perceive as a lack of strategic thinking amongst Loyalists and an ingrained reluctance to actively criticise and campaign against the state. As one individual put it, from his perspective the state 'is there to shit on you' (Republican: focus group). However, Republican efforts to make common cause with Loyalist former prisoner groupings on issues such as human rights for ex-prisoners or an amnesty for ex-combatants have had only very limited success. Loyalists on the other hand tend to depict their Republican counterparts as political automatons who largely 'tow the party line'. What Republicans self-identify as discipline, strategy and structure can be occasionally viewed by Loyalists as a lack of individuality (McEvoy, 2001). At best, it manifests as a grudging respect for their former adversaries' political success: 'The Republicans have been successful in changing their military clout into political clout which Loyalists haven't been able to do and are never likely to be able to do' (Loyalist: workshop).

Quite apart from their relations with each other, former prisoner groups have also been extensively involved in developing relations with other organisations including agencies of the state. As noted above, in Republican areas (where the issues are politically more sensitive), former prisoners have been at the forefront in developing relations with state agencies, including the police, which have customarily been alienated from such communities (McEvoy and Eriksson, 2007). Again, however, across the two communities, different patterns of relationships are apparent.

Loyalist former prisoners have a keen perception that their lack of political clout (in the guise of Sinn Féin) as well as the widely held perception in government circles of Loyalist criminality creates significant barriers in terms of their relationship with statutory bodies. Often such factors combine to mean that decisions are invariably referred upwards which causes significant frustration and delay: 'We have built up a working relationship with them [statutory agencies]. You have a good system of working with those on the ground but where we find great difficulty is when trying to get them to make decisions that have to get approval from above' (Loyalist: focus group).

Oddly, perhaps, Republican former prisoner groups seem to have an easier relationship with the state. In part, this is because funding is often channelled through EU programmes such as Peace and Reconciliation I and II which makes it easier for Republican groups to justify and rationalise these applications for grant aid. Republicans appear to have significant capacity in terms of grant writing and management experience. Again, the relationship with statutory agencies seems less fraught for Republicans, perhaps because of their sheer numbers and greater self-confidence in such dealings deriving from their more secure place within their own communities. In short, it is impossible for statutory agencies to operate in Republican communities without engaging with former prisoners.

CONCLUSION

Despite considerable challenges, both Loyalists and Republicans have made significant contributions to the process of conflict transformation both within and beyond their respective communities. They have played significant leadership roles in transforming cultures of violence in the communities in which they live and work. These have included political, military and moral styles of leadership in conflict transformation and their impact is discernible in the decreased levels of violence in such communities. Of course those contributions are shaped significantly by their relationship with their respective communities and indeed with 'other' communities with whom they have gradually begun to engage. In the final chapter below we attempt to draw out some of the broader lessons of the Northern Ireland experience concerning former prisoners and conflict transformation, at least some of which may be of more general applicability elsewhere.

8

Conclusion: Conflict Transformation and Reintegration Reconsidered?

In reflecting more broadly on the significance of this research, we wish to revisit three key themes that we believe are of particular importance. Cumulatively, we would argue that these three themes constitute the basis for a repositioning of the notion of reintegration with regard to former politically motivated prisoners. Such a repositioning, or reconsideration, is arguably of relevance not just in Northern Ireland but also in other jurisdictions that are emerging from conflict.

First, as we have argued throughout, attitudes to reintegration and the wider effects of the prison experience vary between Republican and Loyalist former prisoners. That variance speaks to the need for bespoke programmes which take into account such differences. The common experience of violence, imprisonment and the structural context of the Northern Ireland transition did not of itself shape the shared forms of reintegration which emerged. Rather, the particularities of reintegration experienced by Loyalist and Republican former prisoners were also fashioned by their differing operational capacities, distinct ideologies and particular relationships with their respective communities. That said, and despite these differences, a central point of this work is that the UVF/RHC and IRA former prisoners who were the objects of the study have managed to put into practice and sustain high-impact and sophisticated modes of conflict transformation within and beyond their communities.

Second, much of the international literature that focuses upon the role of ex-combatants in post-conflict contexts is dominated by the Disarmament, Demobilisation and Reintegration (DDR) framework. As is discussed below, a serious omission in this literature is the lack of attention regarding the specific needs and experiences of released political prisoners. DDR programmes must be shaped not only around the needs of combatants who primarily experienced conflict 'in the field', but also those who spent significant periods of time incarcerated. In addition, the reintegration element of any such programmes, and indeed reintegration programmes more generally (including programmes for both political and 'ordinary' prisoners), tend to focus largely on them as individuals rather than upon the social, economic and political context to which they return. Former prisoners in Northern Ireland have directly challenged the assumptions of passivity which often characterise such thinking. In so doing, they have underlined the significant agentic potential of such individuals and groups in the communities to which they return.

Finally, the style of conflict transformation advanced by former prisoners provides a practical and realistic corrective to the occasionally nihilistic responses to segregated communities and political discord in Northern Ireland. We argue that despite their ideological differences, the work of former prisoners here embodies a political generosity that is often absent from the self-proclaimed 'middle ground' in this and other conflict-affected societies. Former prisoners who have inflicted (and often endured) destructive violence, and who live and work in such highly segregated communities which have been most damaged by conflict, often have much to teach to those who would decry their own culpability in the production and reproduction of political violence.

THE DISTINCTIVE IDEOLOGIES AND CAPACITIES OF REPUBLICAN AND LOYALIST FORMER PRISONERS

As has been argued throughout this book, the nature and impact of the work undertaken by former prisoners has been configured by their distinct experiences and ideologies.

With regard to Republicans, they emerged into a society within which the electoral fortunes of Sinn Féin meshed with community support which broadly allocated them both status and influence (Morrison, 1999; Shirlow et al., 2005). The Republican emphasis upon collective debate and dialogue whilst imprisoned arguably influenced post-release outcomes and abilities in that it encouraged a sense of internal unity and purpose.

The transition in Republicanism from violence to non-violent strategies was influenced by a self-conscious reshaping of Republican ideology in the prisons from the 1970s onwards. What emerged was predominantly class-based in terms of the Republican electorate but the cohesion to this emergent consciousness was provided by Republican narratives of colonialism, Irish culture and music, the realities of oppression, and a promised ultimate delivery from British authority. The versions of Republicanism understood by young

IRA volunteers arrested in their teens and early twenties required considerable ideological honing to afford prisoners a cultural and political vocabulary to understand their own resistance to the prison authorities (Fields, 1973; Shirlow and McGovern, 1998; McKeown, 2001). As noted by a Republican former prisoner:

When I was in, in the 1970s, most of the lads knew as much about Coventry City football team than they did about Cu Chuhulain. These lads were into T-Rex and wearing their hair long. Then a few years after being in they were into all things Irish. See when they came in they met people who were steeped in Republicanism, so they had fellahs there who could teach them Irish history and that sort of thing. [interview: 20 June 2005]

Republican prisoners, more so than Loyalists, saw themselves as actors who were builders of history via collective action. Throughout the early days of the conflict, prison resistance was dedicated primarily to the needs of the military struggle. Gradually, however, and in parallel with the increased emphasis on 'political struggle' within Republicanism throughout the 1980s and 1990s, the vocabulary of collective action gradually shifted towards the language and privileging of conflict transformation (Bean, 2002; Tonge, 2005).

After the Agreement and the releases, Loyalists, conversely, remained somewhat isolated and condemned both by wider 'middle' Unionism and also by other Loyalists who wished to continue with armed conflict. In addition, many former Loyalist prisoners viewed themselves as 'irregular' adjuncts to the state security forces. Given this 'loyalty' to the state, the pervasive view that the conflict had 'ended' (as compared to Republicans' view of it having moved to a 'new' non-violent phase of struggle), and the fact that more were able to return to meaningful employment – the allure of community development was less compelling. In essence, conflict transformation within the Loyalist grouping studied for this book (the former UVF/RHC constituency) was leadership led and dependent upon a small cadre that worked internally to alter Loyalist thought.[1]

Loyalists emerged from prison without the same coherence and related electoral resources that Republicans had acquired. While a political direction for former Loyalist prisoners was assembled around the PUP and groups such as EPIC which are linked to the UVF/RHC and (for a period the UDP which was associated with the UDA/UFF), but the scale of such engagement is nothing like that associated with Sinn Féin.[2] The Loyalist political entities that have emerged sought to promote a leftist/populist notion of Loyalist working-class identity

(Bruce, 1992). Their *raison d'être* was to challenge a Unionism that dismissed them and/or had demonised Loyalist volunteers.

The Loyalist political parties had significant impact in terms of the pre-1998 peace talks and other related political developments but have never come close to matching the political successes of Sinn Féin. With regard to the PUP's elected representatives (two were elected to the original Northern Ireland Assembly and one seat was retained in the 2007 Assembly elections), it is apparent that they were among the most public and articulate challengers of the stereotypical depiction of Loyalism as merely dysfunctional sectarianism. What is quite remarkable is that a small cadre of Loyalist thinkers, many of whom are former prisoners, have been able to bring about Loyalist ceasefires and a recent near-cessation of Loyalist violence without the political clout and community coherence of Republicanism (Shirlow and Monaghan, 2006).

The PUP, with its close links to the UVF, has argued consistently that the sectarian nature of violence was futile and undermined potential dialogue and political stability (Sinnerton, 2003). It promotes an understanding of conflict transformation heavily influenced by a strand of radical democratic socialism that had come to influence certain UVF thinkers, especially from the Shankill Road area of West Belfast. The imprisonment of key UVF personnel from the Shankill in the late 1960s and early 1970s was crucial to a shift from a Protestant fundamentalist rhetoric, promoted by an earlier UVF leadership, to one that articulated pluralist ideals and inter-community aspirations (Garland, 2001; Gallaher and Shirlow, 2006). Whilst imprisoned, many of these influential UVF men engaged in discussions with the Marxist-inspired Official IRA (Gallaher and Shirlow, 2006), which further contributed to a belief that the conflict was engineered to divide the working class, and manifestly was not one over religion. These prisoners identified the perpetuation of sectarian violence within Loyalism as being counter-productive to working-class interests, while those elements that perpetuated sectarian violence were increasingly depicted as being unworthy Loyalists.

It was these same imprisoned UVF leaders who, on release, promoted and struggled to maintain the Loyalist ceasefires. It is also these same former prisoners who have been prominent in the difficult and at times dangerous conflict transformation in working-class Loyalist communities (McEvoy and Eriksson, 2006). On a material level, their contribution has been immense in the Northern Ireland context. More broadly, their experience speaks directly to the capacity of a relatively small number of individuals with patience, credibility and goodwill to tilt the conflict transformation axis, even amongst armed groups previously characterised by their lack of ideological coherency, military discipline, or political sophistication.

DISARMAMENT, DEMOBILISATION AND
REINTEGRATION (DDR) IN THE NORTHERN IRELAND TRANSITION

In the wider international context of political conflicts, DDR programmes are now a familiar element of the post-conflict recon- struction template (Gear, 2002; Kigma, 2001; Berdal, 2005). Often the rationale for DDR programmes, particularly from major donors, appears to be a fixation upon getting combatant groups disarmed, broken up and returned to civilian life as smoothly as possible, lest they prove a destabilising factor in efforts to move a society towards peace. As the World Bank detailed in its rationale for demobilisa- tion and reintegration in the Great Lakes region of Africa: 'The strategy's main premise is that the disarmament, demobilization and reintegration of ex-combatants is necessary to establishing peace and restoring security, which are in turn pre-conditions for sustainable growth and poverty reduction' (World Bank, 2002: iii).

One interesting feature for current purposes is the fact that so little emphasis in the DDR literature refers to the particular needs and experiences of released political prisoners. Rather the tendency is for DDR programmes to be shaped primarily around the needs of those combatants still 'in the field' (Marks, 2000). While perhaps understandable, given that these are the individuals and groups with the most obvious military capacity, it should be remembered that prisoners most often remain an important part of their broader social or political movement. As a prominent Republican former prisoner earmarked to the authors, 'the Maze for us was simply the IRA locked up, we were still an integral part of the Army's [IRA] structure' (interview: 6 June 2005).

The failure of DDR programmes to acknowledge formally the particular needs and, indeed, abilities of former prisoners (for example, as leaders in the transition to peace) is a serious flaw. Further, as Rolston (2007) has argued, the evidence would suggest that DDR works most effectively when it is a staged element of genuine efforts being made to develop a society socially, politically and economically (Baaré, 2001). Efforts to simply disarm ex-combatants, get them out of military structures and back into a civilian life where their social and political circumstances remain unchanged, is not generally a recipe for stability (Gear, 2002).

The version of DDR which has emerged in Northern Ireland has a number of distinctive features. Amongst the non-state armed groups, the IRA is the group that has moved most on demobilisation. In August 2005, former Republican prisoner Seana Walsh read out a statement on behalf of the IRA leadership which formally ordered the end of the armed campaign, and that volunteers should 'assist the development of purely political and democratic programmes through exclusively peaceful means' and that they should not 'engage in any other activities whatsoever'.[3] The International Monitoring Commission has repeatedly made reference to the 'disbandment of [IRA] paramilitary structures' (IMC, 2007a: 8).[4] There was a suggestion from some dissident DUP members (opposed to power-sharing with Sinn Féin) that the disbandment of the IRA ruling Army Council should also be a precondition before the re-establishment of the devolved administration in Northern Ireland in 2007.[5] However, the fact that this did not appear to undo the DUP/Sinn Féin negotiations on restoring devolution would suggest an implicit pragmatism that some form of leadership structure is required in order to oversee the transformation of such an organisation (IMC, 2007a: 26–7).

Amongst the Loyalist groupings there have been recent parallel developments. In May 2007, former UVF prison commander Gusty Spence announced that the UVF and the closely affiliated RHC would 'assume a non-military, civilianised role'. Spence also indicated the UVF/RHC would engage in a process of 'transformation from military to civilian organisation'.[6] Even the UDA, long considered the least disciplined of the Loyalist groupings and one of those most embroiled in criminality, has indicated a desire on the part, at least of some of its senior leadership, to engage in conflict transformation (Gribbin et al., 2005; IMC, 2007b). In effect, while elements of the paramilitary organisational structures have remained in place to date in the transition from conflict, all of the main groupings would now appear to be on some form of organisational transformation trajectory.

With regard to disarmament, the decommissioning of weapons has been partial. Only the mainstream IRA has apparently fully decommissioned and this process took almost nine years of parallel political developments, tortuous negotiations and complex oversight mechanisms (O'Kane, 2007). The 2007 UVF and RHC statement on their future also included a promise to put weapons 'beyond reach'. This has been translated as keeping them under the direct control of the respective leadership of these organisations. That said, the organisations have reappointed another prominent former UVF prisoner, Billy Hutchinson, as liaison with the International Decommissioning Body to explain in detail how they are controlling access to these weapons.[7] The LVF publicly decommissioned a token amount of small arms and munitions in December 1998 and the UDA have had meetings with the decommissioning body but have not, as yet, decommissioned any weapons. On the part of the state, while demilitarisation (termed 'security normalisation') was initially equally slow to respond the changed security circumstances (Rolston, 2007), this too has speeded up in recent years. For example, the number of army observation towers was reduced to just two sites by January 2007 and, overall, army bases have been reduced from almost a hundred at the height of the conflict to ten by August 2007. A permanent garrison is currently envisaged of not more than 5,000 troops, compared to over 10,000 at the time of the ceasefire declarations (IMC, 2007a, 2007b).

As for the reintegration aspect to the DDR axis in Northern Ireland, the reality of the Republican and Loyalist campaigns was that combatants were not, by and large, separated from their families and communities. True, small numbers were 'on the run' or active in Britain or elsewhere. However, unlike many ex-combatants elsewhere, the vast majority of combatants in Northern Ireland were not living 'in the bush' but rather combined their normal family and community life with their 'operating' lives as paramilitary activists (Sluka, 1995; Feldman, 1991). As members of clandestine organisations, membership of which remains illegal to this day, few combatants or ex-combatants publicly self-identify as 'members' of the IRA or UVF other than in their own communities where their identities are already well known.

Of course, as was noted above, the linkage between 'reintegration' and political imprisonment in Northern Ireland has brought its own problems. In particular, the presumed association with 'ordinary' criminal offending raised hackles immediately amongst former prisoners whose incarceration had been dominated by the struggles (detailed in Chapter 1) against criminalisation. Such controversy is not, however, a uniquely Northern Ireland phenomenon.

Even within the specialist criminological literature which relates to ordinary imprisonment, reintegration is a term replete with definitional wranglings and occasional heated scholarly and policy debates (Braithwaite, 1989; Maruna and Immarigeon, 2004). In particular, the assumption that much reintegration research focuses predominantly on the attitudes and behaviour of the released prisoner, rather than the society to which he or she is returning, is a source of particular ire for many criminologists working in this field (Maruna and Le Bel, 2003). Perhaps most useful for current purposes is a genre of reintegration literature which is referred to as the 'strengths-based' style of reintegrative work. This is an approach which focuses upon the particular strengths or skills that former prisoners may have in terms of a potential contribution to their families or community and seeks to build upon these as a way of helping them desist from future crime (Ward and Gannon, 2006; Ward and Maruna, 2007). Utilising the strengths-based approach, policy-makers and practitioners are encouraged to deal with prisoners and former prisoners as 'subjects rather than objects' and to 'treat them with respect and demand reciprocity' (Duguid, 2000: 18). In particular, the importance of mutual support from other former prisoners who have been through a similar experience is often viewed as crucial in developing 'a sense of belonging' amongst former prisoners and an indication that some sovereignty is being returned to their lives after the regimented life of incarceration (Burnett and Maruna, 2006).

This strengths-based variant of reintegrative literature resonates strongly with the reintegration experiences of politically motivated prisoners in Northern Ireland. It speaks directly to the 'self-help' approach of former prisoners taking ownership over their own projects rather than assuming passive roles of accepting individualistic forms of 'treatment' or 'aid' (Gormally et al., 2007). The fact that it was former prisoners themselves who have largely managed and implemented their own reintegration in Northern Ireland (and indeed the Irish Republic)[8] rather than 'professional' agencies, has, in turn, encouraged a greater willingness amongst such individuals to acknowledge the personal and familial costs of the years of imprisonment (Hamber, 2005). The personal consequences of imprisonment explored in Chapter 4 have been much more honestly admitted and discussed (Shirlow, 2001a; Grounds and Jamieson, 2003; McEvoy et al., 2004). Finally of course, one of the strengths of the continued collective approach to the post-imprisonment experience has been that such organisations have provided the basis for continued resistant efforts against structural exclusion (Coiste, 2003b: 3).

As well as EPIC and Tar Isteach, the two groups primarily involved in this study, other former prisoner groups in Northern Ireland and the Republic could detail similar programmes of work since the signing of the Agreement. In the near future, there is likely to be a significant diminution in the number of groups receiving bespoke reintegration funding from the EU under Peace III which will cover the period 2007–13. As noted above, and bearing in mind that it is now almost a decade since the signing of the Agreement, there is a lively debate as to whether these groups should now morph into generic community development organisations or whether they should continue to play a distinctive role as former prisoner groupings (Gormally et al., 2007).

Such discussions apart, we would reiterate our view that the contribution of former prisoners and the groupings to which they belong has been highly significant to date. Despite significant obstacles, including their own misgivings about the term (either as an element of the Northern Ireland version of DDR or the criminological concept associated with 'ordinary' prisoners), and an arguably lacklustre government follow-through upon the commitments in the Agreement, former prisoners have well used the resources afforded them. Through the reintegration framework, they have become key agents of embedding the process of conflict transformation in Northern Ireland in communities most affected by violence and from which violence would emerge first if the process were to fail.

EMBEDDING RECONCILIATION: TOWARDS A 'REAL' SHARED FUTURE

Finally, we return here to the vexed question of reconciliation and in particular its current guise under the 'Shared Future' framework. As we have noted above, many Republican and Loyalist former prisoners are now involved in difficult areas of grass-roots community-based reconciliation but they express serious reservations about the utility of this term (McEvoy et al., 2006). As has been evident from the discussion in the introduction to this book, we share many of their misgivings.

We have argued that the work undertaken by former prisoners and prisoners' groups represent conspicuous examples of real leadership in attempting to transform and remove cultures of violence in Northern Ireland. Some of these men and women have been at the forefront of taking forward the most difficult issues of the peace process; these include working on interface violence at flashpoint areas, negotiations concerning contentious parades, the decommissioning of paramilitary weapons, engagement with the victims of political violence and other former combatants, and promoting and encouraging the emerging debate on truth recovery.

It is precisely because of their violent past as having fought 'on behalf of' those communities that they have the credibility to engage in such *real* reconciliation work in the working-class areas in which it is most needed. It is also they who have arguably taken the greatest risks in the peacemaking process on the basis that they do not want future generations to share their experiences of violence, exclusion and demonisation.

The reality is that for the many people who live in conflict-affected communities a 'middle ground' free of sectarianism or intolerance is not a present reality. However, the capacity to create such a reality is more likely given the substantive reconciliation work carried out by former prisoners. Such work has been characterised by a number of key features.

First, Republican and Loyalist former prisoners are very conscious of the role and responsibilities of the state as a protagonist to the conflict and of the need for effective mechanisms to ensure *state accountability*. Although former Loyalist prisoners may not pursue the human rights and equality agenda with the same vigour as their Republican counterparts, they are aware from bitter experience of the coercive power of the state and of its culpability in the production and reproduction of past violence. For example, there is currently considerable political attention regarding the possibility of some form of truth recovery or related mechanism to considering 'dealing with the past' in Northern Ireland (Healing Through Remembering, 2006). Certainly few former prisoners of any hue would countenance that such an effort at reconciliation could be embarked upon without due attention to the culpability of the state.

Second, the intersection between Republican and Loyalist former prisoners is not based upon any artificial representations of 'friendship' but rather an acceptance of the need to respect the rights of the other. While this does not simply resolve conflict it does provide a meaningful discourse around which to frame and operationalise conflict transformation. Such a recognition of the legitimacy of opponents' perspectives is also central to an understanding of reconciliation as a long-term process that is characterised by paradox and contradiction, in which the meaning of reconciliation is itself contested, but involving some kind of common vision as to how pluralism and equality can coexist with political difference Hamber and Kelly, 2004; Barnett and Low, 2004).

Third, the interactions between former prisoners are not premised upon the need to deny or adulterate political identity or to pay lip-service to some synthetic 'middle ground' identity. Certainly the focus groups for this research were proof positive of the strong Republican and Loyalist identities which are retained by former prisoners and combatants. That said, their capacity to engage with each other was founded precisely upon confidence in their own identity. That assuredness was unaffected by engagement with their former enemies.

Finally, many of the interactions between former Loyalist and Republican prisoners are built around how to resolve *real issues* such as marching, rioting, or inter-communal violence, rather than ill-focused explorations of prejudice reduction. Despite high levels of government support, the long-standing tradition within community relations work of 'contact schemes' (usually focused upon children) which brings together individuals from Protestant and Catholic background in order to 'humanise the other' has had little discernable impact on prejudice reduction or levels of violence (McEvoy et al., 2006). The experience of former prisoners suggests that when there is a substantive and practical agenda, a properly structured engagement and identifiable outcomes which are to the benefit of both main communities even the most extreme of former adversaries can engage in real and effective reconciliation work.

We would argue that these are the building blocks of real reconciliation and a more firmly embedded 'shared future' which faces up to the lived realities of intensively divided life in Northern Ireland. It is the best of Northern Ireland's Republican and Loyalist former prisoners who have helped to lay the foundations for such a grounded version of reconciliation.

Notes

INTRODUCTION

1. The reference is to the IRA fire bombing of the La Mon hotel near Belfast in 1978, which killed twelve people in horrific circumstances.
2. For an excellent critique see CAJ (2006).
3. For example, while human rights and the promotion of equality are portrayed as 'an integral part of overall action to promote better relations within the Northern Ireland community' the Chief Executive of the Community Relations Council appears to anticipate the day when equality legislation and human rights protection can be abolished (Morrow, 2006).
4. 'Most Nationalists Willing to Accept Some Kind of Amnesty', *Belfast Telegraph*, 30 September 1996.
5. Mr Parry expressed his position in the following terms: 'Whilst it is offensive to have my son classed as collateral damage, I saw the prisoner release process as part of the Agreement as being absolutely essential. I accepted that the position that both governments were taking, that without prisoner releases there would have been no deal' (Minutes of Evidence to the Northern Ireland Select Committee, 2 March 2005).
6. There is a terminological issue in that some groups prefer the term 'former prisoner', as opposed to 'ex-prisoner' on the grounds that the latter term implies a social, political and legal divide between incarceration and release. Accordingly, 'former prisoner' is employed here although 'ex-prisoner' remains in common usage and is retained below when it is cited in quotations.
7. This included the researchers from the University of Ulster and Queen's University, Belfast, together with representatives from EPIC and Tar Isteach.
8. This was held at the University of Ulster, Belfast, on 24 June 2004.
9. These took place respectively at the LINC Centre, North Belfast, on 1 December 2004 and the Ashton Centre, North Belfast, on 3 December 2004.

CHAPTER 1

1. In April 2006, US military authorities announced a 'rebranding' of the War on Terror as the 'Long War'. See BBC Website, 10 April 2006, 'Planning the US "Long War" on Terror' <http://news.bbc.co.uk/2/hi/americas/4897786.stm>.
2. Von Tangen Page (1998) utilises the even more cumbersome phrase of 'politically motivated violent offenders' to describe the same category of prisoners.

3. These original definitions, replicated in subsequent versions of the Emergency Provisions Act and the Prevention of Terrorism Act, were taken from the legislation which introduced Internment, the Detention of Terrorist (NI) Order 1972, Article 3. The current definition of terrorism, contained in the Terrorism Act 2000, has been modified slightly. It now includes a list of activities (such as serious violence, damage to property, creating a risk to public safety or health, etc.) where 'the use or threat is designed to influence the government or to intimidate the public or a section of the public, and the use or threat is made for the purpose of advancing a political, religious or ideological cause', Terrorism Act 2000, S 1 (1) and (2).

4. Scheduled offences are those normally associated with the commission of terrorist acts (for example, murder, manslaughter, explosions, serious offences against the person, riot, collecting information likely to be of use to terrorists, etc.) and are listed as an appendix to the Emergency legislation. The Act also empowers the Attorney General to decree that certain acts of murder, manslaughter, etc. should not be treated as 'scheduled' offences and should therefore be tried by jury, normally in a case where there is no suspected paramilitary involvement.

5. It is important to note that Irish governments also responded in largely the same manner.

6. See, for example, Richards (2001) with regard to the Spanish Civil War.

7. See, for example, the prominence of discussions on the failure of internment in Palestine and Northern Ireland with regard to contemporary discussion on the tactic in the War on Terror (Newsinger, 2002).

8. For example, Gerry Adams (then an interned suspected IRA leader) was released from prison in July 1972 to be part of a Republican delegation which was flown by the RAF to meet with the British government for negotiations in London (Adams, 1990).

9. The other obvious international example of a 'criminalisation'-style response to political violence has been the Spanish government's policy towards ETA since the late 1980s. After a number of failed efforts at negotiations in the 1980s, and the perceived failure of previously pragmatic approaches to ETA prisoners (Aguilar 2001), Spanish government policy hardened considerably. A 'dirty war' of assassinations was conducted by the security forces and their proxy agents (Woodworth, 2001) and in 2003 the Spanish government eventually banned Herri Batusuna (the political wing of ETA), in effect criminalising extreme Basque nationalist politics (Sawyer, 2003). In the prisons, since 1989, the Spanish authorities have pursued a policy designed to minimise the potential for collective organisation by ETA prisoners. They have refused to negotiate formally with such inmates, dispersed ETA prisoners around different Spanish prisons thus isolating prisoners and causing huge difficulties for their families (United Nations, 2004) and have (publicly at least) largely refused to countenance early releases in the event of a cessation of violence (Mees, 2003; Barros and Luis Gil-Alana, 2006).

10. 'Mrs Thatcher Pledges No Sellout on Ulster', *The Times*, 6 March 1981, p. 1.

11. There are similar traits in other prison systems long used to managing political prisoners. For example, the Israeli prison system has long been the subject of justified criticism by human rights and other groups for its widespread use of torture, humiliation and the administrative detention of large numbers of political prisoners – more in keeping with a reactive containment model of political imprisonment (see, for example, Human Rights Watch, 1994, 2000; B'Tselem, 1992, 2006). However, even in a prison system rightly characterised as repressive in the extreme, one detects a similar weary pragmatism amongst Israeli prison management to that which prefigured the dramatic changes in Northern Ireland. This perspective is apparently informed by a cold-eyed approach to the dangers posed by such prisoners, an acknowledgement of their motivation and the qualities of their leadership and an understanding of the relationship between prison conditions and the conflict outside (Israeli Prison Service, 2004: 1–2).

12. For example, in 1998 Her Majesty's Chief Inspector of Prisons, Sir David Ramsbotham, was asked to carry out a review of the Maze prison following the murder of two prisoners and an escape by IRA prisoner Liam Averill, dressed as a woman. His report concluded that the level of self-determination and self-regulation afforded to the prisoners could not be withdrawn without serious repercussions in the prison and in the community. He recommended that protocols be drawn up by the paramilitary leaders in the prisons and the authorities, specifying the responsibilities and obligations of all parties and the consequences for non-compliance (Ramsbotham, 1998: 17.07). In effect, he afforded a formal seal of approval to practices which had been done informally for a number of years.

13. For these reasons, prisoner control over space is generally resisted strongly by the prison system which holds such prisoners. Thus, for example, hunger strikes by members of the Kurdistan Workers' Party in Turkish prisons were precipitated by the decision to move prisoners from large cells of up to a hundred prisoners (which were effectively controlled by prisoners themselves) to isolation or small cells of two or three prisoners (Human Rights Watch, 2000; Anderson, 2004). This move was designed to crush the prison collective which had been formed in the large cells. Similarly, detention practices by the US administration of those held in places such as Camp Delta, Guantánamo Bay and elsewhere have been designed specifically to control the space, minimise the potential for prisoner mobilisation and maximise guard surveillance (Ratner, 2005; Rhem, 2005).

14. Again the Northern Ireland experience resonates with other international contexts of political imprisonment. Similarly, on Robben Island, the lives of South African political prisoners were significantly transformed by a legal ruling on disciplinary processes (Buntman, 2003). In the post-9/11 period, judicial intervention in the UK and the US has been a prominent check on attempted executive consolidation of power, denial of prisoners' due process rights and efforts to restrict information on such prisoners. Prisoners, their lawyers, NGOs and others concerned at the conditions

of their detention have perhaps made law the key strategy of resistance to the abuses perpetrated in these sites.

15. It should be acknowledged that Loyalist prisoners too can point to a history of both hunger strike and dirty protest during the conflict, albeit less sustained, less strategic and less well known than their Republican counterparts. For example, in 1972, UVF Brigadier (Officer Commanding) Gusty Spence went on hunger strike at the same time as IRA prisoners in support of the demand for political status, lasting a total of 35 days. A few Loyalist prisoners also took part in a 'clean protest' while Republicans were on the dirty protest in the late 1970s, refusing to do prison work or wear a uniform but keeping their cells clean and using the prison toilets as normal. In the 1980s, Loyalist prisoners also engaged in a no-wash and dirty protest (including smearing their cells with excrement) in support of segregation from Republicans at the Maze and sporadic hunger strikes at Magilligan prison. See McEvoy (2001: 100–5) for further discussion.

16. The five demands were the right to wear their own clothes, to be exempt from prison work, to have freedom of association with fellow Republican prisoners, the right to organise educational and recreational facilities, and the restoration of remission lost as a result of the protest.

17. Even after more than a decade since the first IRA ceasefire, the Northern Ireland Prison Service remains an overwhelmingly Protestant organisation. Figures for the year 2005 suggest that 80 per cent of prison service grades staff are Protestant, 9 per cent are Catholic and 11 per cent are undetermined (CAJ, 2006: 28).

18. For a useful account on how armed groups 'think' see Crenshaw (1990), Irvin (1999) and Tilly (2003).

CHAPTER 2

1. In February 1976, Secretary of State Merlyn Rees introduced the Treatment of Offenders (Northern Ireland) Order which set remission rates at 50 per cent for all fixed-term sentences in Northern Ireland. This remission rate was reduced from 50 per cent to 33 per cent for politically motivated prisoners under the Prevention of Terrorism (Temporary Provisions) Act 1989 as part of a series of measures introduced in response to an IRA bomb which killed eight British soldiers. Fifty per cent remission was restored by John Major's government in August 1995 in a belated and ultimately unsuccessful attempt to demonstrate movement in response to the first IRA ceasefire.

2. 'Prison Issues', paper by the British Government, Liaison Sub-committee on Confidence Building Measures Meeting, 4 February 1998 (confidential source).

3. Although Additional Protocol II to the Geneva Convention provides for states to grant 'the broadest possible amnesty' at the end of hostilities in non-international conflict, in practice the breadth of amnesties has been narrowed by the courts over recent years at the national and international level. For example, blanket amnesties 'for all crimes committed between x date and y date' or 'for all offences committed by x group or y group'

have been found to be unlawful (Roht-Arriaza, 1996; Cassese, 2003; Mallinder, 2007). Blanket amnesties of this type in places such as Chile and Argentina have been consistently eroded both by the national courts and international fora such as the Inter-American Court of Human Rights (Chigara, 2002). Often it is because the amnesty provisions (for example, in Peru, Haiti and Uruguay) effectively remove the right to a remedy from those who have been victims of human rights violations, that they are found to be unlawful under international law (Rodley, 2000). Similarly, courts have found unlawful amnesties which included some of the most heinous offences such as genocide, crimes against humanity and other crimes deemed so serious that they are viewed as 'international' in nature, that it is not open to local states to permit the perpetrators of such acts to be amnestied (Bassiouni, 1996).

4. The Commission was co-chaired by South African human rights lawyer Brian Curran, who had also chaired the Amnesty and Indemnity Committee in South Africa, and retired civil servant Sir John Blelloch.

5. The Northern Ireland (Sentences) Act (Sentence Review Commissioners) Rules 1998, Statutory Instrument 1988, No 1859 S 14–15.

6. The Northern Ireland (Sentences) Act 1998, S 4 (1) a.

7. The Northern Ireland (Sentences) Act 1998, S 6 (1) a.

8. The Northern Ireland (Sentences) Act 1998, S 9 (3) b.

9. See, for example, Re Williamson Application for Judicial Review [2000] NI 281, McClean, Re [2005] UKHL 46.

10. Sean Kelly, the man convicted of killing nine civilians in the Shankill bombing in 1993, was released early under the terms of the Northern Ireland (Sentences) Act. He was rearrested and had his licence revoked in June 2005 (some three years after he was alleged to have been involved in riotous behaviour) and was subsequently re-released in July 2005, the day before the widely expected IRA statement calling an end to the unarmed struggle. (See 'Shankill Bomber Back in Prison', *Guardian*, 19 June 2005; 'The Curious Case of Sean Kelly', *Belfast Telegraph*, 6 August 2007.)

11. Four recalled life prisoners were charged with paramilitary type offences, three on the basis of advice from the police and nine because they had been charged with violent (non-paramilitary) offences and were believed to be a danger to the public. Of those revoked, three were Republican and 13 were Loyalist <http://www.niprisonservice. gov.uk/index.cfm/area/information/page/earlyrelease> last accessed 15 May 2007.

12. The prison service website does not detail whether there is such an overlap although it would seem likely. For example, Loyalist prisoner Michael Stone has had his licence revoked and been returned to prison after he attacked the Stormont Assembly in November 2006 armed with an imitation weapon, a knife, an axe, a garrotte and viable nail bombs. It would appear likely, however, that he will be convicted of the charge of attempted murder, notwithstanding his apparent defence that his attack was a piece of 'performance art'. Mr Stone's actions were filmed and he announced his intentions by way of a letter to the press posted before his attack detailing his 'mission to kill' Sinn Féin leaders Gerry Adams and Martin McGuinness. (See 'A Thing of the Past', *Guardian*, 24 November

2006; 'Stone Spelt Out His Murder Plot in Letter to Newspaper', *The Times*, 30 November 2006, p. 30; 'Mission to Kill – Stone's Letter Reveals Targets Were Adams and McGuinness', *Belfast Telegraph*, 30 November 2006.)

13. This is particularly the case when one considers the significant historical overlap amongst Loyalist prisoners in particular between individuals with a record from 'ordinary' criminal convictions, including drug-related offences as well as politically motivated offences. Republican organisations, particularly the IRA, have historically had much fewer prisoners who had also been convicted of non-political offences (see Bruce, 1992; Stevenson, 1997).

14. Previously known as the Northern Ireland Voluntary Trust (NIVT).

15. The Community Foundation has a well-developed national and international reputation for its integrity and political judgement in funding in difficult circumstances.

16. For example, as one prominent civil society funder told one of the authors: 'It was pretty surreal in the early days. You would have a be-suited senior civil servant from the NIO coming down with me to meet say a group of ex-INLA prisoners in ... [name], talking about former prisoner discrimination on one side and financial probity on the other and it was like they were from different planets – totally surreal', confidential source.

17. See, for example, 'Fury Over £6M for Prisoner Groups', *Belfast Telegraph*, 2 December 2000; 'Fury at EU Former Prisoners Cash', *Belfast Telegraph*, 24 April 2002; 'NIVT Ordered to Recover Peace Money', *Belfast Telegraph*, 14 March 2003.

18. 'Group Loses Peace Cash', *Belfast Telegraph*, 19 September 2000.

19. For example, in 2004, CFNI was awarded the prestigious Raymond Georis Prize for Innovative Philanthropy in Europe from the Network of European Foundations. In giving the award Mr Georis made specific mention of their work on distributing the EU monies: 'By giving small, well-targeted grants in risky territory as well as providing policy and development support, the Foundation [CFNI] has proven the essential role of philanthropy: recognising its unique contribution, the European Union has used the Foundation as an intermediary funder for its Peace Building Programme ... Through their work, the Community Foundation for Northern Ireland, led by Avila Kilmurray, has demonstrated how, with courage and innovation, the worst of the legacy of conflict can be used to shape the best in providing hope and peace for the future.' Speech by Raymond Georis at the 15th Annual General Assembly of the European Foundation Centre, Athens, 1 June 2004.

CHAPTER 3

1. Although the decision to end Special Category Status was announced in 1975, the policy was not introduced until the following year. Those convicted after 1 March 1976 were to be treated as 'Ordinary Decent Criminals' (ODCs) and would serve their sentences in the new Maze Prison H-Blocks.

2. The correct quote is 'Will anyone here object if, with a ballot paper in one hand and the Armalite in the other, we take power in Ireland?', and is attributed to Danny Morrison addressing a Sinn Féin Ard Fheis in June 1981 (Taylor, 1997: 281).

3. Because there is very little documentation in public circulation in relation to PROPP before 1994, this section is informed mainly by material made available for the study and by interviews conducted with three Republican and two Loyalist members of PROPP.

4. See, for example, 'Fury Over £6m for Prisoners' Groups: Contrast with Funds for Victim Support', *Belfast Telegraph*, 2 December 2000. Between 1998 and 2001, the British government committed over £18 million to victims' issues. This figure does not include individual awards made under the Criminal Injuries Compensation Scheme (CICS) or the estimated £120 million costs of the Bloody Sunday Inquiry. Funding for trauma services has continued since 2001. Victims-related money has also come from other sources including over £3 million of the EU Peace and Reconciliation Programme in the first wave of funding and almost £5 million under Peace II. Funding for victims issues has also come from a range of different charitable sources. CFNI provides an assessment of how Peace I was reported in the media in their publication, 'Taking "Calculated" Risks for Peace II' (CFNI, 2003).

5. See Wolfsfeld (2004) especially Chapter 6 for a discussion on the role of the media in the Northern Ireland peace process.

6. While these examples may seem somewhat improbable, Republicans in particular often point to South Africa as an exemplar for Northern Ireland and draw (often fanciful) comparisons between the IRA and the African National Congress (ANC).

CHAPTER 4

1. Given the geographical area where the survey was completed, such findings are to be expected bearing in mind the feud that took place between the UDA and UVF during the summer of 2000. The feud started when the UDA showed support for the LVF (a splinter group made up of expelled Mid-Ulster members of the UVF and accused of being heavily involved in the illegal drugs trade) during a UDA parade on the Shankill Road. Over 250 families were displaced before talks to secure an end to the violence succeeded.

CHAPTER 5

1. *McConkey* vs. *Simon Community* NI CASE REF:00452/00FET, January 2007.

2. The working group was chaired by the current head of the Northern Ireland Civil Service Nigel Hamilton, and Sir George Quigley, former permanent secretary and chairman of the Ulsterbank. As well as Loyalist and Republican former prisoner groups, it included representatives from the Confederation of British Industries (CBI), the Irish Congress of Trade Unions (ICTU) and relevant government departments.

3. Sinn Féin's Martin McGuinness was Minister of Education in the Northern Ireland Executive from 2000 until its collapse in October 2002. At the time of writing, he is now Deputy First Minister.
4. Re McComb [2003], NIQB 47.
5. As is discussed further below, the Independent Monitoring Commission, set up by the British and Irish governments on 7 January 2004, reports on certain matters that include activity by paramilitary groups and the normalisation of security measures in Northern Ireland.

CHAPTER 6

1. Nine people were killed in 1972 by the succession of IRA bombings in Belfast (including Oxford Street bus station) that became known as 'Bloody Friday'.
2. The reference is to the 1987 'Poppy Day' bombing in Enniskillen, Co. Fermanagh, when an IRA bomb planted at the town's war memorial killed eleven civilians attending a Remembrance Day service.
3. Shankill Road chip-shop bomb in 1993, which killed nine Protestants (and a IRA bomber); the UDA leader, Johnny Adair, was the target.

CHAPTER 7

1. We are persuaded by the notion of leadership developed by former US Army War College Instructor Colonel Christopher Paparone: 'Leadership is holistic. Leadership means leading laterally or collaboratively, and not just from upper echelons. Leadership entails leading the people, the structure, the process ... Leadership is symbolic. Leadership is about the influence of meanings and interpretations that important constituencies give to the organisation's function' (Paparone, 2004: 9).
2. 'This consultation document is an attempt to provide opportunities for our constituencies to begin debating the issues around truth recovery. We acknowledge that people may experience this document as being inward looking and self reflective. It is. It needs to be. It has to reflect the reality of where our constituency is in its current process of conflict transformation. Our intent is not to alienate others: our intent is to encourage honest and challenging thinking with a constituency and to allow others to respond critically to that thinking' (EPIC, 2004: 3).
3. For an account that suggests considerable veracity in that claim see Office of the Police Ombudsman (2007) *Report on the Police Ombudsman's Investigation into Matters Surrounding the Death of Raymond McCord Junior* (Belfast : OPONI).

CHAPTER 8

1. More recently there are clear indications within the UDA/UFF constituency of similar leadership-centred efforts at conflict transformation. See Gribbin et al. (2005).

2. Bruce (2004) argues that the later collapse of the UDP was partly due to the leadership containing non-militarists and few former prisoners.
3. Video clip available at <http://news.bbc.co.uk/1/hi/northern_ireland/4724599.stm>.
4. The IMC is a highly controversial organisation in Northern Ireland. Under pressure from Unionists in particular, it was established by the British and Irish governments in 2004 to monitor the activities of paramilitary organisations, security normalisation and 'the activities of Assembly Parties'. Its members are a former leader of the moderate Unionist Alliance Party of Northern Ireland, a former Deputy Director of the Central Intelligence Agency, a former Deputy Assistant Commissioner of the Metropolitan Police Service and a former Director General of the Department of Justice in Dublin. Sinn Féin lodged an unsuccessful legal challenge to the legality of the commission wherein they claimed, *inter alia*, that it was biased and failed to offer any evidence to support its conclusions. The IMC is regularly lambasted for its uncritical reliance upon and publicising of security force briefings, unsourced intelligence information and 'rumours' by Nationalist, Republican, Loyalist and other seasoned commentators on Northern Ireland. See, for example, D. Morrison, 'IMC Land', *Andersontown News*, 5 May 2004; 'Progressive Unionist Party Rebuttal of the First IMC Report', *The Blanket*, April 2004; 'IMC Needs to Make Amends', editorial, *Irish News*, 27 April 2004.
5. 'DUP Rocked by Dissension', *Sunday Tribune*, 3 December 2006.
6. 'UVF Statement in Full', 3 May 2007 <http://news.bbc.co.uk/1/hi/northern_ireland/6618365.stm>.
7. 'UVF meets Decommissioning Body', 3 May 2007 <http://news.bbc.co.uk/2/hi/uk_news/northern_ireland/6618475.stm>. Hutchinson, who had served in this liaison role previously between 1997 and 2003 (before contacts were suspended by the UVF) was accompanied at this meeting by a number of individuals identified as 'senior UVF leaders'.
8. The one notable exception was the appointment of Mike Ritchie as Director of Coiste. From a Scottish Christian socialist background, Ritchie is a vastly experienced human rights and voluntary sector activist who had previously worked for a range of organisations including NIACRO and the Committee on the Administration of Justice. Although as one former prisoners told the authors, the appointment of someone who was not an former prisoner 'raised a few eyebrows' amongst some Republicans, few would now dispute that he has contributed significantly to the professionalism which has characterised much of the work of that organisation (see Gormally et al., 2007).

Bibliography

Adams, G. (1990) *Cage Eleven*. Dingle: Brandon Books.

Adams, G. (1997) *Before the Dawn: An Autobiography*. London: Mandarin.

Adams, G. (2000) 'Lock the Door and Throw Away the Key', *Irish News*, 29 July <http://info-nordirland.de/new_55.htm>.

Adams, K. (1992) 'Adjusting to Prison Life', *Crime and Justice: A Review of Research*, 16: 275–359.

Aguilar, P. (2001) 'Justice, Politics and Memory in the Spanish Civil War', in A. Brito, G. Enríquez and A. Fernández (eds), *Politics of Memory: Transitional Justice in Democratizing Societies*. Oxford: Oxford University Press.

Alison, M. (2004) 'Women as Agents of Political Violence: Gendering Society', *Security Dialogue*, 35 (4): 447–63.

An Tus Nua (1998) *The Cost of Imprisonment*. Belfast: Upper Springfield Development Trust.

Anderson, P. (2004) '"To Lie Down to Death for Days": The Turkish Hungerstrike 2000–2003', *Cultural Studies* 18 (6): 816–46.

Annan, K. (2004) 'Learning the Lessons of Peace Building'. The Tip O' Neill Lecture. Magee Campus, University of Ulster, 18 October 2004.

Applebaum, A. (2003) *Gulag: A History*. New York: Random House.

Ardoyne Commemoration Project (2002) *Ardoyne: The Untold Truth*. Belfast: Beyond the Pale.

Arendt, H. (1990) *On Revolution*. London: Penguin.

Aretxaga, B. (1995) 'Dirty Protest: Symbolic Over-determination and Gender in Northern Ireland Ethnic Violence', *Ethos*, 23 (2): 123–49.

Aughey, A. (2005) *The Politics of Northern Ireland: Beyond the Belfast Agreement*. London: Routledge.

Auld, J., Gormally, B., McEvoy, K. and M. Ritchie (1997) *'The Blue Book': Designing a System of Restorative Justice in Northern Ireland*. Belfast: The authors.

B'Tselem (1992) *Detained Without Trial: Administrative Detention in the Occupied Territories Since the Beginning of the Intifada*. Jerusalem: B'Tselem.

B'Tselem (2006) *Barred From Contact: Violation of the Right to Visit Palestinians Held by Israel*. Jerusalem: B'Tselem.

Baaré, A. (2001) *Demobilization and Reintegration: Revisiting the Uganda Experience* <http//www.certi.org/news_events/demobilization2/ppts/usaid_drp_uganda_presentation_anton_baar.htm>.

Babo-Soares, D. (2004) '*Nahe Biti*: The Philosophy and Process of Grassroots Reconciliation (and Justice) in East Timor', *Asia Pacific Journal of Anthropology*, 5 (1): 15–33.

Bairner, P. and P. Shirlow (2003) 'When Leisure Turns to Fear: Understanding the Reproduction of Ethno-Sectarianism in Belfast', *Leisure Studies*, 22 (3): 247–76.

Bar-Siman-Tov, Y. (2007) *The Israeli–Palestinian Conflict: From Conflict Resolution to Conflict Management*. Basingstoke: Palgrave.

Barnett, C. and M. Low (2004) (eds) *Spaces of Democracy: Geographical Perspectives on Citizenship, Participation and Representation*. London. Sage Publications.

Barros, C., Caporale, G. and A. Gil-Alana (2006) 'ETA Terrorism: Police Action, Political Measures and the Influence of Violence on Economic Activity in the Basque Country', Economics and Finance Discussion Papers 06–03, Brunel: Brunel Business School.

Bassiouni, M. (1996) 'Searching for Peace and Achieving Justice: The Need for Accountability', *Law and Contemporary Problems*, 59 (4): 9–28.

Bean, K. (2002) 'Defining Republicanism', in Elliot, M. (ed.) *The Long Road to Peace in Northern Ireland*. Liverpool: Liverpool University Press.

Becker, J. (1989) (3rd edn) *Hitler's Children: The Story of the Baader-Meinhoff Terrorist Gang*. London: Pickwick.

Belfast Agreement (1998) *The Belfast Agreement* <archive.ofmdfmni.gov.uk/publications/ba.htm>.

Bell, C. (2001) *Human Rights and Peace Agreements*. Oxford: Oxford University Press.

Bell, C. (2006) *Negotiating Justice? Human Rights and Peace Agreements*. Geneva: International Council on Human Rights Policy.

Bennett, S. (2003) '"Free American Political Prisoners": Pacifist Activism and Civil Liberties, 1945–48', *Journal of Peace Research*, 40 (4): 413–33.

Benson, M. (ed.) (1981) *The Sun Will Rise: Statements from the dock by Southern African political prisoners*. Cape Town: International Defence and Aid Fund for Southern Africa.

Berdal, M. (2005) *Disarmament and Demobilisation After Civil Wars*. London: Routledge.

Beresford, D. (1987) *Ten Men Dead: The Story of the 1981 Irish Hunger Strike*. London: Grafton.

Bishop, P. and E. Mallie (1987) *The Provisional IRA*. London: Heinemann.

Blondel, J. (1987) *Political Leadership: Towards a General Analysis*. London: Sage.

Bloomfield, D. and B. Reilly (1998) 'The Changing Nature of Conflict and Conflict Management', in P. Harris and B. Reilly (eds) *Democracy and Deep-rooted Conflict*. Stockholm: Institute for Democracy and Electoral Assistance.

Borneman, J. (1997) *Settling Accounts: Violence, Justice and Accountability in Post Socialist Europe*. Princeton, NJ: Princeton University Press.

Bornstein, A. (2001) *Crossing the Green Line between the West Bank and Israel*. Philadelphia: University of Pennsylvania Press.

Braithwaite, J. (1989) *Crime, Shame and Reintegration*. Cambridge: Cambridge University Press.

Braithwaite, J. (2002) 'Setting Standards for Restorative Justice', *British Journal of Criminology*, 42 (3): 563–77.

Bresler, F. (1965) *Reprieve: A Study of a System*. London: George G. Harrap Publishing.

Bruce, S. (1992) *The Red Hand: Loyalist Paramilitaries in Northern Ireland*. Oxford: Oxford University Press.

Bruce, S. (2004) 'Turf War and Peace: Loyalist Paramilitaries Since 1994', *Terrorism and Political Violence*, 16 (3): 501–21.

Buck, M. (2000) 'Prison, Social Control and Political Prisoners', *Social Justice*, 27 (3): 25–8.

Bukstel, L. and P. Kilman (1980) 'Psychological Effects of Imprisonment on Confined Individuals', *Psychological Bulletin*, 88 (2): 469–93.

Buntman, F. (1998) 'Categorical and Strategic Resistance and the Making of Political Prisoner Identity in Apartheid's Robben Island Prison', *Social Identities*, 4 (3): 417–40.

Buntman, F. (2003) *Robben Island and Prisoner Resistance to Apartheid*. Cambridge: Cambridge University Press.

Burnett, R. and S. Maruna (2006) 'The Kindness of Prisoners: Strength-based Resettlement in Theory and in Action', *Criminology and Criminal Justice*, 6: 83–106.

Burns, J.M. (1978) *Leadership*. New York: Harper and Row.

Burton, J. (1993) 'Conflict Resolution as a Political Philosophy', in D. Sandole and H. van der Merwe (eds) *Conflict Resolution Theory and Practice: Integration and Application*. Manchester: Manchester University Press.

Burton, J. (1997) *Violence Explained: The Sources of Conflict, Violence and Crime and Their Prevention*. Manchester: Manchester University Press.

CAJ (2006) *Equality in Northern Ireland: The Rhetoric and the Reality*. Belfast: Committee on the Administration of Justice.

Campbell, B., McKeown, L. and P. O'Hagan (1994) *Nor Meekly Serve My Time: The H Block Struggle, 1976–1981*. Belfast: Beyond the Pale Publications.

Campbell, C. (1989) 'Extradition to Northern Ireland: Prospects and Problems', *Modern Law Review*, 52 (5): 585–621.

Carlos, B. and L. Gil-Alana (2006) 'ETA: A Persistent Phenomenon', *Defence and Peace Economics*, 17 (2): 95–116.

Carrabine, E. (2005) 'Prison Riots, Social Order and the Problem of Legitimacy', *British Journal of Criminology*, 45: 896–913.

Cassese, A. (2003) *International Criminal Law*. New York: Oxford University Press.

Center for Constitutional Rights (2005) *The Guantánamo Prisoner Hunger Strikes and Protests: February 2002–August 2005*. New York: Center for Constitutional Rights.

Center for Constitutional Rights (2006), *Report on Torture and Cruel, Inhuman, and Degrading Treatment of Prisoners at Guantánamo Bay, Cuba*. New York: Center for Constitutional Rights.

CFNI (2003) *Taking 'Calculated' Risks for Peace II*. Belfast: The Community Foundation for Northern Ireland.

Chambliss, W. (1976) *Criminal Law in Action*. Indianapolis, IN: John Wiley and Sons.

Chigara, B. (2002) *Amnesty in International Law*. London: Longman.

Christensen-Nelson, C. (ed.) (2004) *Literature of the Women's Suffrage Campaign in England*. Ontario: Broadview Press.

Clarke, L. (1987) *Broadening the Battlefield: The H Blocks and the Rise of Sinn Féin*. Dublin: Gill and Macmillan.

Clemmer, D. (1940) *The Prison Community*. New York: Rinehart and Winston (later edn 1958).

Cochrane, F. (1997) *Unionist Politics and the Politics of Unionism Since the Anglo-Irish Agreement*. Cork: Cork University Press.

Cohen, S. (1996) 'Crime and Politics: Spot the Difference', *British Journal of Sociology*, 47 (1): 1–21.

Coiste (2003a) *A Nation Once Again? People, Territory and Institutions, Transcripts of Summer School*. Belfast: Coiste na n-Iarchimí.

Coiste (2003b) *Submission on Shared Future Consultation Document*. Belfast: Coiste na n-Iarchimí.

Coiste (2003c) *Processes of Nation Building, Models of Governance: The Good Friday Agreement and Beyond*. Belfast: Coiste na n-Iarchimí.

Coiste (2003d) *Processes of Nation Building, Responses to Government Consultations on Community Relations and Resettlement of Ex-Prisoners*. Belfast: Coiste na n-Iarchimí.

Coiste (2003e) *Processes of Nation Building: Cultural Diversity*. Belfast: Coiste na n-Iarchimí.

Coiste (2004) 'Coiste Political Tours Project', 6 (March–May 2004). Belfast: Coiste na n-Iarchimí.

Collins, T. (1986) *The Irish Hunger Strike*. Dublin: White Island Book Company.

Community Foundation for Northern Ireland (2003) *Taking 'Calculated' Risks for Peace*. Belfast: Community Foundation for Northern Ireland.

Connolly, P. and J. Healy (2002) 'The Development of Children's Attitudes Toward "The Troubles" in Northern Ireland, in O. Hargie and D. Dickson (eds), *Researching the Troubles*. Edinburgh: Mainstream Publishing.

Coogan, T.P. (1980) *On the Blanket: The H Block Story*. Dublin: Ward River Press.

Coogan, T.P. (1987) *Disillusioned Decades*. Dublin: Gill and Macmillan.

Corcoran, M. (2006) *Out of Order: The Political Imprisonment of Women in Northern Ireland, 1972–1999*. Cullompton: Willan.

Corcoran, M. (2007) 'Normalization and its Discontents: Constructing the "Irreconcilable" Female Political Prisoner in Northern Ireland', *British Journal of Criminology*, 47 (3): 405–22.

Cox, M., Guelke, A., and F. Stephen (eds) (2006) (2nd edn) *A Farewell to Arms: Beyond the Good Friday Agreement*. Manchester: Manchester University Press.

Crawford, C. (1979) 'Long Kesh: An Alternative Perspective', M.Sc. Thesis, Cranfield Institute of Technology.

Crawford, C. (1999) *Defenders or Criminals? Loyalist Prisoners and Criminalisation*. Belfast: Blackstaff Press.

Crenshaw, M. (1990) *Theories of Terrorism: Instrumental and Organizational Approaches*. University Park: Pennsylvania State Press.

Criminal Justice Inspection (2007) *Northern Ireland Alternatives: Report of an Inspection with a View to Accreditation Under the Government's Protocol for Community Based Restorative Justice*. Belfast: Criminal Justice Inspection Northern Ireland.

Crothers, J. (1998) *EPIC Research Document No. 2: Reintegration – the Problems and the Issues*. Belfast: EPIC.

Della Porta, D. (2006) *Social Movements, Political Violence, and the State: A Comparative Analysis of Italy and Germany*. Cambridge: Cambridge University Press.

Deutsch, M., Coleman, P. and E. Marcus (eds) (2006) *A Handbook of Conflict Resolution: Theory and Practice*. Hoboken, NJ: Jossey Bass Publishing.

Dewar, M. (1985) *The British Army in Northern Ireland*. London: Arms and Armour Press.

Dickson, B. (1992) 'Northern Ireland's Emergency Legislation: The Wrong Medicine?', *Public Law*, 26 (2): 592–624.

Dilulio, J. (1987) *Governing Prisons: A Comparative Study of Correctional Management*. New York: Free Press.

Ditchfield, J.A. (1990) *Control in Prisons: A Review of the Literature*. London: HMSO.

Dixon, P. (2001) *Northern Ireland: The Politics of War and Peace*. Basingstoke: Palgrave Macmillan.

Dowler, L. (2001) 'No Man's Land: Gender and the Geopolitics of Mobility in West Belfast', *Geopolitics*, 6 (3): 158–76.

DTZ (2005) *Report on Labour Market Dynamics, Phase Four: Equality of Opportunity Considerations*. Belfast: DTZ Pieda Consulting (on behalf of the Office of the First Minister and Deputy First Minister).

Duguid, G. (2000) *Can Prisons Work? The Prisoner as Object and Subject in Modern Corrections*. Toronto: University of Toronto Press.

Dunne, D. (1988) *Out of the Maze: The True Story of the Biggest Jail Escape Since the War*. Dublin: Gill and Macmillan.

DUP (1998) *DUP Manifesto: Northern Ireland Assembly Election*. Belfast: DUP.

DUP (2003) *A Voice for Victims*. Belfast: DUP.

Dwyer, C. (2007) 'Risk, Politics and the "Scientification" of Political Judgement', *British Journal of Criminology*, 47 (5): 1–19.

Dyzenhaus, D. (1991) *Hard Cases in Wicked Legal Systems: South African Law in the Perspective Of Legal Philosophy*. Oxford: Oxford University Press.

Edgar, K., O'Donnell, I. and C. Martin (2003) *Prison Violence: The Dynamics of Conflict, Fear and Power*. Cullompton: Willan.

Elcock, H. (2001) *Political Leadership*. Northampton, MA: Edward Elgar Publishing.

English, R. (2004) *Armed Struggle: The History of the IRA*. London: Pan.

Eolas Project (2003) *Consultation Paper on Truth and Justice*. Belfast: Relatives for Justice.

EPIC (2004) *Information Leaflet*. Belfast: EPIC.

EPIC (2005) *Truth Recovery: A Contribution from Loyalism*. Belfast: EPIC.

Equality Commission for Northern Ireland (2002) *The Single Equality Bill: Further Considerations, February 2002*. Belfast: Equality Commission for Northern Ireland.

Farrell, M. (1976) *The Orange State*. London: Pluto Press.

Fay, M.T., Morrissey, M. and M. Smith (1999) *Northern Ireland's Troubles: The Human Costs*. London: Pluto Press.

Fealy, G. (1995) 'The Release of Indonesia's Political Prisoners: Domestic Versus Foreign Policy, 1975–1979', Working Paper No. 94. Melbourne: Centre of Southeast Asian Studies.

Feeley, M. and J. Simon (1992) 'The New Penology: Notes on the Emerging Strategy of Corrections and its Implications', *Criminology*, 30 (4): 449–74.

Feldman, A. (1991) *Formations of Violence: The Narrative of the Body and Political Terror in Northern Ireland*. Chicago, IL: University of Chicago Press.

Fields, R. (1973) *A Society on the Run: A Psychology of Northern Ireland.* Harmondsworth: Penguin.

Fisher, R. and L. Keashly (1991) 'The Potential Complementarity of Mediation and Consultation Within a Contingency Model of Third-Party Intervention', *Journal of Peace Research,* 28: 29–42.

Foucault, M, (1983) 'The Subject and Power', in H. Dreyfus and P. Rabinow (eds), *Michel Foucault: Beyond Structuralism and Hermeneutics.* Chicago, IL: University of Chicago Press.

Francis, D. (2002) *People, Peace and Power: Conflict Transformation in Action.* London: Pluto Press.

Freeman, R. (1999) *Correctional Organization and Management: Public Policies, Challenges, Behaviour and Structure.* Boston, MA: Butterworth Heinemann.

Freedland, J. (2000) 'Man Shot Dead in Belfast', *Guardian Unlimited,* 21 August.

Fuller, L. (1958) 'Positivism and Fidelity to Law – A Reply to Professor Hart', *Harvard Law Review,* 71: 630–72.

Gallaher, C. and P. Shirlow (2006) 'The Geography of Loyalist Paramilitary Feuding in Belfast', *Space and Polity,* 10 (2): 149–69.

Gardiner, Lord (1975) *The Report of a Committee to Consider in the Context of Civil Liberties and Human Rights, Measures to Deal with Terrorism in Northern Ireland.* Cmnd 5847. Belfast: HMSO.

Gardner, H. (1995) *Leading Minds: An Anatomy of Leadership.* New York: Basic Books.

Garland, R. (2001) *Gusty Spence.* Belfast: Blackstaff Press.

Gear, S. (2002) *Wishing Us Away: Challenges Facing Ex-combatants in the 'New' South Africa.* Johannesburg: Centre for the Study of Violence and Reconciliation.

Gearty, C. (ed.) (1996) *Terrorism.* Aldershot: Ashgate.

Gearty, C. and A. Tomkins (1996) *Understanding Human Rights.* London and New York: Mansell.

Gibbs, J. (1991) 'Environmental Congruence and Symptoms of Psychopathology: A Further Exploration of the Effects of Exposure to the Jail Environment', *Criminal Justice and Behavior,* 18 (1): 351–74.

Goffman, E. (1961) *Asylums: Essays on the Social Situation of Mental Patients and Other Inmates.* Garden City, NJ: Anchor.

Goodwin, J. (2006) 'Understanding Revolutionary Terrorism'. Paper presented at 'Revolution, Class and Modernity' conference, King's College, Cambridge, 1–2 April <http://www.crassh.cam.ac.uk/events/abstracts/revolution/JGoodwin.pdf>.

Gormally, B. (2001) *Conversion from War to Peace: Reintegration of Ex-Prisoners in Northern Ireland.* Derry: INCORE.

Gormally, B., McEvoy, K. and D. Wall (1993) 'Criminal Justice in a Divided Society: Northern Ireland Prisons', *Crime and Justice: A Review of Research,* 17: 51–135.

Gormally, B. and K. McEvoy (1993) 'Vacations for Terrorists: Home Leave in Northern Ireland', *Overcrowded Times* (October) 1: 14–18.

Gormally, B. and K. McEvoy (1995) *Release and Reintegration of Politically Motivated Prisoners in Northern Ireland: A Comparative Study of South Africa,*

Israel/Palestine, Italy, Spain, the Republic of Ireland and Northern Ireland. Belfast: NIACRO.

Gormally, B., Maruna, S. and K. McEvoy (2007) *Thematic Evaluation of Funded Projects: Politically-motivated Former Prisoners and their Families.* Monaghan: Border Action.

Graham, B. (ed.) (1997) *In Search of Ireland: A Cultural Geography.* London: Routledge.

Graham, B. (2004) 'The Past in the Present: The Shaping of Identity in Loyalist Ulster', *Terrorism and Political Violence,* 16 (3): 483–500.

Graham, B. and P. Shirlow (1998) 'An Elusive Agenda: The Development of a Middle Ground in Northern Ireland', *Area,* 30 (3): 245–54.

Graham, B. and P. Shirlow (2002) 'The Battle of the Somme in Ulster Memory and Identity', *Political Geography,* 21 (2): 881–904.

Green, M. (1998) *EPIC Research Document No. 1: The Prison Experience: A Loyalist Perspective.* Belfast: EPIC.

Greenberg, K., Dratel, L. and A. Lewis (2005) *The Torture Papers: The Road to Abu Ghraib.* Cambridge: Cambridge University Press.

Greenwood, C. (1989) 'Terrorism and Humanitarian Law: The Debate Over Additional Protocol 1', *Israel Yearbook on Human Rights,* 19: 187–207.

Greer, S. (1995) *Supergrasses: A Study in Anti-terrorist Law Enforcement in Northern Ireland.* Oxford: Clarendon Press.

Gribbin, V., Kelly, R. and C. Mitchell (2005) *Loyalist Conflict Transformation Initiatives* <http://www.ofmdfmni.gov.uk/conflict.pdf>. Research report funded by OFM/DFM.

Grounds, A. and R. Jamieson (2003) 'No Sense of an Ending: Researching the Experience of Imprisonment and Release Among Republican Ex-prisoners', *Theoretical Criminology,* 7 (3): 347–62.

Guillaume, G. (2004) 'Terrorism and International Law', *International and Comparative Law Quarterly,* 53: 537–48.

Gunter, M. (1997) *The Kurds and the Future of Turkey.* Basingstoke: Palgrave Macmillan.

Habermas, J. (1975) *Legitimation Crisis.* Boston, MA: Beacon Press.

Hadfield, B. and E. Weaver (1994) 'Trends in Judicial Review in Northern Ireland', *Public Law,* 12: 12–16.

Hagan, F. (1997) *Political Crime: Ideology and Criminality.* Needham Heights: Allyn and Bacon.

Hain, P. (1984) *Political Trials in Britain: From the Past to the Present Day.* Harmondsworth: Penguin.

Hall, M. (2005) *Loyalism in Transition 2: Learning from Others in Conflict.* Belfast: Island Publications.

Hamber, B. (2003) 'Rights and Reasons: Challenges for Truth Recovery in South Africa and Northern Ireland', *Fordham International Law Journal,* 26 (4): 1074–94.

Hamber, B. (2005) *Blocks to the Future: An Independent Report into the Psychological Impact of the 'No Wash/Blanket' Prisoner Protest.* Derry: Cunamh.

Hamber, B. and G. Kelly (2004) *A Place for Reconciliation? Conflict and Locality in Northern Ireland Report 18.* Belfast: Democratic Dialogue.

Harbinson, J. (2002) *Review of Community Relations Policy* <http://www.ofmdfmni.gov.uk/communityrelationsunit/harbisonreport.pdf>.

Hargie, O. and D. Dickson (eds) (2003) *Researching the Troubles*. Edinburgh: Mainstream Publishing.

Harris, J. (1991) 'Judicial Review and the Prerogative of Mercy', *Public Law*, 31: 389–401.

Hart, H. (1983) 'Positivism and the Separation of Law and Morals', reprinted in H. Hart, *Essays in Jurisprudence and Philosophy*. Oxford: Clarendon Press.

Healing Through Remembering (2006) *Making Peace with the Past*. Belfast: Healing Through Remembering.

Healy, J. (1984) 'Hungerstrikes Around the World', *Social Studies*, 8: 81–108.

Henderson, D. (2000) 'Adair Left Isolated as Allies End Feud Links', *Irish Examiner*, 21 July, p. 3.

Hennessey, J. (1984) *A Report of an Inquiry by HM Chief Inspector of Prisons into the Security Arrangement at HMP Maze*, Cmnd 203. London: HMSO.

Hogan, G. and C. Walker (1989) *Political Violence and the Law in Ireland*. Manchester: Manchester University Press.

Home Office (2001) *Through the Prison Gate: A Joint Thematic Review by HM Inspectorates of Prisons and Probation*. London: Home Office.

Howe, S. (2005) *Mad Dogs and Ulstermen: The Crisis of Loyalism* (part 2) <http://www.opendemocracy.net/democracy–protest/loyalism_2885.jsp>.

Human Rights Watch (1994) *Torture and Ill-Treatment: Israel's Interrogation of Palestinians from the Occupied Territories*. New York: Human Rights Watch.

Human Rights Watch (2000) *Turkey: Small Group Isolation in Turkish Prisons: An Avoidable Disaster*. New York: Human Rights Watch.

Ignatieff, M. (1999) *The Warrior's Honour: Ethnic War and the Modern Conscience*. London: Vintage.

Independent Monitoring Commission (2004) *Third Report of the Independent Monitoring Commission*. London: The Stationery Office.

IMC (2007a) *Fourteenth Report of the Independent Monitoring Commission*. London: The Stationery Office.

IMC (2007b) *Fifteenth Report of the Independent Monitoring Commission*. London: The Stationery Office.

Irvin, C. (1999) *Militant Nationalism: Between Movement and Party in Ireland and the Basque Country*. Minneapolis: University of Minnesota Press.

Israeli Prison Service (2004) *Security Prisoners in Israel Prison Service Facilities*. Tel Aviv: Israeli Prison Service.

Jackson, J. and S. Doran (1995) *Judge Without Jury: Diplock Trials in the Adversary System*. Oxford: Clarendon Press.

Jamieson, R. and K. McEvoy (2005) 'State Crime by Proxy and Juridical Othering', *British Journal of Criminology*, 45: 504–27

Jarman, N. (2002) *Human Rights and Community Relations: Competing or Complementary Approaches in Responding to Conflict?* Belfast: Institute for Conflict Research.

Jarman, N. (2004) 'From War to Peace? Changing Patterns of Violence in Northern Ireland, 1990–2003', *Terrorism and Political Violence*, 16 (3): 420–38.

Jeong, H.W. (1999) *Conflict Resolution: Dynamics, Process and Structure*. Aldershot: Ashgate.

Justice Oversight Commissioner (2004) *Second Report of the Justice Oversight Commissioner*. Belfast: JOC.

Kaminski, M. (2004), *Games Prisoners Play: The Tragicomic Worlds of Polish Prison*. Princeton, NJ: Princeton University Press.

Keightley, R. (1993) 'Political Offences and Indemnity in South Africa', *South African Journal of Human Rights*, 9 (3): 334–57.

Kenway, P., MacInnes, T., Kelly, A. and G. Palmer (2006) *Monitoring Poverty And Social Exclusion in Northern Ireland*. London: Joseph Rowntree Trust.

Kenyon, G. (1999) 'Australian Hunger Strike Doctors Urged to Stop', *British Medical Journal*, 31 (8): 894–6.

Kigma, K. (2001) *Demobilisation and Reintegration of Ex-Combatants in Post-war and Transition Countries*. Eschborn: Deutsche Gesellschaft für Technische Zusammenarbeit.

Kirchheimer, O. (1961) *Political Justice: The Use of Legal Procedure for Political Ends*. Princeton, NJ: Princeton University Press.

Kitson, F. (1991) *Directing Operations*. London: Faber and Faber.

Kleiboer, M. (1994) 'Ripeness of Conflict: A Fruitful Notion?', *Journal of Peace Research*, 3 (1): 109–16.

Lane, A. (1979) *Nuremberg: A Nation on Trial*. London: Penguin.

Lederach, J.P. (1995) *Preparing for Peace: Conflict Transformation Across Cultures*. Syracuse, NY: Syracuse University Press.

Lederach, J.P. (1997) *Building Peace: Sustainable Reconciliation in Divided Societies*. Washington, DC: United States Institute of Peace Press.

Liebling, A. and S. Maruna (eds) (2005) *The Effects of Imprisonment*. Cullompton: Willan.

Livingstone, S. (2000) 'Prisoners' Rights in the Context of the European Convention on Human Rights', *Punishment and Society*, 2 (3): 309–24.

Livingstone, S., Owen, T., and A. MacDonald (2003) *Prison Law*. Oxford: Oxford University Press.

Livingstone, S. (1995) 'Legal Options and Obstacles Regarding the Early Release of Prisoners in Northern Ireland'. Belfast: NIACRO (unpublished).

Lundy, P. and M. McGovern (2005) *Community, 'Truth-Telling' and Conflict Resolution*. Belfast: Peace II Funds Community Relations Council.

Maguire, S. and P. Shirlow (2004) 'Rural Identities and Sectarian Attitudes among Young People in Northern Ireland', *Children's Geographies*, 2 (1): 12–26.

Mallinder, L. (2007) 'Can Amnesties and Internation Justice be Reconciled?', *International Journal of Transitional Justice*, 1(2): 208–30.

Mandela, N. (1994) *The Long Walk to Freedom: The Autobiography of Nelson Mandela*. Boston, MA: Little Brown.

Maran, R. (1989) *Torture: The Role of Ideology in the French Algerian War*. Oxford: Greenwood.

Marks, S. (2000) *Watching the Wind: Conflict Resolution During South Africa's Transition to Democracy*. Washington, DC: United States Institute of Peace Press.

Maruna, S. and R. Immarigeon (eds) (2004) *After Crime and Punishment: Pathways to Offender Reintegration*. Cullompton: Willan.

Maruna, S. and T. LeBel (2003). 'Welcome Home?: Examining the "Reentry Court" Concept from a Strengths-based Perspective', *Western Criminology Review*, 4 (2): 91–107.

Mathews, J. (ed.) (2002) *The Future of the Army Profession*. Boston, MA: McGraw Hill Primis.

Mathiesen, T. (1965) *Defences of the Weak*. London: Tavistock.

Matthews, R. (1999) *Doing Time: An Introduction to the Sociology of Imprisonment*. London: Macmillan.

Maze Consultation Panel (2006) 'A New Future for the Maze/Long Kesh' <http://www.newfuturemazelongkesh.com/panel.htm>.

McBride, A. (2004) 'The Northern Ireland Victim Experience'. Address delivered at the Catalan Parliament Conference on Lessons from Northern Ireland for the Basque Peace Process.

McDonald, H. and J. Cusack (2000) *UVF*. Dublin: Poolbeg.

McDonald, H., and J. Cusack (2005) *UDA: Inside the Heart of Loyalist Terror*. Dublin: Penguin Ireland.

McEvoy, K. (1998) 'Prisoner Release and Conflict Resolution: International Lessons for Northern Ireland', *International Criminal Justice Review*, 8: 33–61.

McEvoy, K. (1999) 'The Agreement, Prisoner Release and the Political Character of the Conflict', *Fordham International Law Journal*, 26 (1): 145–81.

McEvoy, K. (2000) 'Law, Struggle and Political Transformation in Northern Ireland', *Journal of Law and Society*, 27 (4): 542–71.

McEvoy, K. (2001) *Paramilitary Imprisonment in Northern Ireland: Resistance, Management and Release*. Oxford: Oxford University Press.

McEvoy, K. (2003) 'Beyond the Metaphor: Political Violence, Human Rights and "New" Peacemaking Criminology', *Theoretical Criminology*, 7 (3): 319–46.

McEvoy, K. and A. Eriksson (2006) 'Restorative Justice in Transition: Ownership, Leadership and "Bottom Up" Human Rights', in D. Sullivan and L. Tift (eds), *A Handbook of Restorative Justice*. London: Routledge.

McEvoy, K. and A. Eriksson (2007) 'Who Owns Justice?: Community, State and the Northern Ireland Transition', in J. Shapland (ed.), *Justice, Community and Civil Society*. Cullompton: Willan.

McEvoy, K. and H. Mika (2001) 'Policing, Punishment and Praxis: Restorative Justice and Non-Violent Alternatives to Paramilitary Punishments in Northern Ireland', *Policing and Society*, 11 (3/4): 259–382.

McEvoy, K. and H. Mika (2002) 'Restorative Justice and the Critique of Informalism in Northern Ireland', *British Journal of Criminology*, 43 (3): 534–63.

McEvoy, K. and T. Newburn (eds) (2003) *Criminology, Conflict Resolution and Restorative Justice*. London: Palgrave.

McEvoy, L., McEvoy, K. and K. McConnachie (2006) 'Reconciliation as a Dirty Word: Education in Northern Ireland', *Journal of International Affairs* 60 (1): 81–107.

McEvoy, K., McConnachie, K. and R. Jamieson (2007) 'Political imprisonment and the "War on Terror"', in Y. Jewkes (ed.), *Handbook of Prisons*. Cullompton: Willan.

McEvoy, K., Mika, H., and K. McConnachie (2008) *Reconstructing Justice After Conflict: The View from Below*. Cambridge: Cambridge University Press.

McEvoy, K., O'Mahony, D., Horner, C. and O. Lyner (1999) 'The Home Front: The Families of Politically Motivated Prisoners in Northern Ireland', *British Journal of Criminology*, 39 (2): 175–97.

McEvoy, K., Shirlow, P. and K. McElrath (2004) 'Resistance, Transition and Exclusion: Politically Motivated Ex-prisoners and Conflict Transformation in Northern Ireland', *Terrorism and Political Violence*, 16 (3): 646–70.

McGarry, J. (1998) 'Political Settlements in Northern Ireland and South Africa', *Political Studies*, XLVI: 853–70.

McGuffin, J. (1973) *Internment*. Tralee: Anvil Books.

McKeown, L. (2001) *Out of Time: Irish Republican Prisoners 1970–2000*. Belfast: Beyond the Pale Press.

McKittrick, D., Kelters, S., Feeney, B., Thornton, C. and D. McVea (2004) *Lost Lives: The Stories of the Men, Women and Children Who Died Through the Northern Ireland Troubles*. London: Mainstream Publishing.

McShane, L. (1998) *Northern Ireland Voluntary Trust – Interim Report: Politically Motivated Ex-Prisoner Self-Help Projects*. Belfast: NIVT.

McVeigh, R. (2002) 'Between Reconciliation and Pacification: The British State and Community Relations', *Community Development Journal*, 37: 47–59.

Meade, R.C. (1990) *Red Brigades: The Story of Italian Terrorism*. London: Macmillan.

Mees, L. (2003) *Nationalism, Violence and Democracy: The Basque Clash of Identities*. Basingstoke and New York: Macmillan.

Mertus, J. and J. Helsing (eds) (2006) *Human Rights and Conflict: Exploring the Links Between Rights, Law, and Peacebuilding*. Washington, DC: United States Institute of Peace Press.

Mika, H. (2004) 'Evaluation of Community Restorative Justice Ireland and Northern Ireland Alternatives' (unpublished).

Mika, H. (2006) *Community Based Restorative Justice in Northern Ireland*. Belfast: Institute of Criminology and Criminal Justice.

Mika, H. and K. McEvoy (2001) 'Restorative Justice in Conflict: Paramilitarism, Community and the Construction of Legitimacy in Northern Ireland', *Contemporary Justice Review*, 4: 7–35.

Mitchell, G. (2000) *Making Peace: The Inside Story of the Making of the Good Friday Agreement*. London: Heinemann.

Moloney, E. (2003) *A Sercet History of the IRA*. London: Penguin.

Moore, K. (1989) *Pardons: Justice, Mercy and the Public Interest*. Oxford: Oxford University Press.

Morgan, A. (2000) *The Belfast Agreement: A Practical Legal Analysis*. London: The Belfast Press.

Morrow, D. (2006) 'Sustainability in a Divided Society: Applying social capital theory to Northern Ireland', *Shared Space*, 2: 63–79 <http://www.community-elations.org.uk/document uploads/Chapter_5.pdf>.

Morrison, D. (1999) *Then the Walls Came Down: A Prison Journal*. Cork: Mercier Press.

Moss, D. (1989) *The Politics of Left-Wing Violence in Italy, 1969–85*. London: Macmillan.

Mowlam, M. (2003) *Momentum: The Struggle for Peace, Politics and the People*. Philadelphia, PA: Coronet Books.

Mulcahy, A. (1995) 'Claims-Making and the Construction of Legitimacy: Press Coverage of the 1981 Northern Irish Hunger Strikes', *Social Problems*, 42 (4): 449–67.

Mullan, M. (1995) 'Pardon and Amnesty in Ireland to 1937' (unpublished report). Belfast: NIACRO.

Muller, E.N. and E. Weede (1990) 'Cross-national Variation in Political Violence: A Rational Action Approach', *Journal of Conflict Resolution*, 34 (4): 624–51.

Narey, M. (1998) *Report of an Inquiry into the Escape of a Prisoner from HMP Maze on 10th December 1997 and the Shooting of a Prisoner on 27th December 1997*, London: HMSO. Cmnd 658.

Neir, A. (1995) 'Confining Dissent: The Political Prison', in N. Morris and D. Rothman (eds), *The Oxford History of the Prison: The Practice of Punishment in Western Society*. Oxford: Oxford University Press.

Nelken, D. (1994) 'Whom Can You trust? The Future of Comparative Criminology', in D. Nelken (ed.), *The Futures of Criminology*. London: Sage, 220–44.

Neuman, P. (2002) 'The Imperfect Peace: Explaining Paramilitary Violence in Northern Ireland', *Low Intensity Conflict and Law*, 11 (1): 116–38.

Newburn, T. (2003) *Crime and Criminal Justice Policy*. London: Pearson Longman.

Newsinger, J. (2001) *British Counterinsurgency: From Palestine to Northern Ireland*. London: Palgrave.

NIACRO (1984) *Detained at the Secretary of State's Pleasure*. Belfast: Northern Ireland Association for the Care and Resettlement of Offenders.

NIACRO (2006) *Working with Convictions: A Guide to Good Practice in the Employment of People with a Criminal Record*. Belfast: Northern Ireland Association for the Care and Resettlement of Offenders.

Nicosia, G. (2004) *Home to War: A History of the Vietnam Veterans' Movement*. New York: Carroll and Graf Publishers.

NIPS (1985). *Annual Report of the Northern Ireland Prison Service*. Belfast: HMSO.

NIPS (1987) *Annual Report of the Northern Ireland Prison Service*. Belfast: HMSO.

NIPS (2003) *Northern Ireland Prison Service Strategy for Prisoner Resettlement*. Belfast: HMSO.

NIVT (2001) *A Level Playing Field: The Final Evaluation Report of the Work of Politically Motivated Ex-prisoner Self-help Projects Funded by the Peace Programme*. Belfast: NIVT.

Northern Ireland Human Rights Commission (2002) *Annual Report*. Belfast: Northern Ireland Human Rights Commission.

Nueman, P. (2002) 'The Imperfect Peace: Explaining Paramilitary Violence in Northern Ireland', *Low Intensity Conflict and Law Enforcement*, 11 (1): 116–38.

Office of the Police Ombudsman Northern Ireland (2007) *Report on the Police Ombudsman's Investigation into Matters Surrounding the Death of Raymond McCord Junior*. Belfast: OPONI.

OFM/DFM (2003) *A Shared Future: A Consultation Paper on Improving Relations in Northern Ireland*. Belfast: OFM/DFM.

OFM/DFM (2005) 'A Shared Future' <http://www.ofmdfmni.gov.uk/finalversion020506.pdf>. Belfast: OFM/DFM.

OFM/DFM (2007) *Recruiting People with Conflict-Related Convictions: Employers' Guidance* <http://www.ofmdfmni.gov.uk/1.05.07_exprisoners_final_guidance>. Belfast: OFM/DFM.

Ó hAdhmaill, F. (2001) *Equal Citizenship for a New Society? An Analysis of the Training and Employment Opportunities for Republican Ex-prisoners.* Belfast: Coiste na n-Iarchimí.

O'Kane, E. (2007) 'Decommissioning and the Peace Process: Where Did It Come From and Why Did It Stay So Long?', *Irish Political Studies*, 22 (1): 81–101.

O'Leary, B. (1999) 'The nature of the Agreement', *Fordham Journal of International Law*, 22 (4): 1628–67.

O'Malley, P. (1990) *Biting at the Grave: The Irish Hunger Strikes and the Politics of Despair.* Belfast: Blackstaff Press.

Paparone, C. (2004) 'Deconstructing Army Leadership', *Military Review*, January–February: 2–10.

Philips, R.L. and C.R. McConnell (2004) (2nd edn) *The Effective Corrections Manager: Correctional Supervision for the Future.* Boston, MA: Jones and Bartlett.

Pile, S. (1997) *Geographies of Resistance.* London: Routledge.

Porter, N. (2003) *The Elusive Quest: Reconciliation in Northern Ireland.* Belfast: The Blackstaff Press.

Primoratz, I. (1990) 'What is Terrorism?', *Journal of Applied Philosophy*, 7: 129–38.

Progressive Unionist Party (2004) *Statement on IMC Report.* Belfast: Progressive Unionist Party.

Quinney, R. (1970) *The Social Reality of Crime.* Boston, MA: Little Brown and Co.

Radzinowicz, L. and R. Hood (1979) 'The Status of Political Prisoners in England: The Struggle for Recognition', *Virginia Law Review*, 65: 1421–81.

Ramsbotham, D. (1998*) Report of an Inspection by Her Majesty's Chief Inspector of Prisons of HMP Maze.* Belfast: Northern Ireland Office.

Ramsbotham, O., Woodhouse, T., and H. Miall (2005) (2nd edn) *Contemporary Conflict Resolution.* Cambridge: Polity Press.

Ratner, M. (2005) 'The Guantánamo Prisoners', in R. Meeropol (ed.), *America's Disappeared: Secret Imprisonment, Detainees and the 'War on Terror',* London and New York: Seven Stories Press.

Rhem, K. (2005) 'Guantánamo Detainees Still Yielding Valuable Intelligence', American Forces Press Service, 4 March.

Richards, M. (2001) *A Time of Silence: Civil War and the Culture of Repression in Franco's Spain, 1936–45.* Cambridge: Cambridge University Press.

Robinson, P. (1980) *Self Inflicted: An Exposure of the H Blocks Issue.* Belfast: Democratic Unionist Party.

Rodley, N. (2000) (2nd edn) *The Treatment of Prisoners under International Law.* Oxford: Oxford University Press.

Rodriguez, D. (2006) *Forced Passages: Imprisoned Radical Intellectuals and the U.S. Prison Regime.* Minneapolis: University of Minnesota Press.

Roht-Arriaza, N. (1996) 'Combating Impunity: Some Thoughts on the Way Forward', *Law and Contemporary Problems*, 59 (4): 93–107.

Rolston, B. and Tomlinson, M. (1986) 'Long Term Imprisonment in Northern Ireland: Psychological or Political Survival?', in B. Rolston and M. Tomlinson (eds), *The Expansion of European Prison Systems: Working Papers in European Criminology*. Belfast: European Group for the Study of Deviance and Social Control.

Rolston, B. (2007) 'Demobilization and Reintegration of Ex-Combatants: The Irish Case in International Perspective', *Social and Legal Studies*, 16 (2): 259–80.

Routledge, P. (1997) 'A Spatiality of Resistances: Theory and Practice in Nepal's Revolution of 1990', in S. Pile and M. Keith (eds), *Geographies Of Resistance*. London: Routledge.

Ryan, S. (2007) *The Transformation of Violent Intercommunal Conflict*. Aldershot: Ashgate.

Sappington, A. (1996) 'Relationship Among Prison Adjustment, Beliefs and Cognitive Coping Style', *International Journal of Offender Therapy and Comparative Criminology*, 40 (1): 54–62.

Sawyer, K. (2003) 'Rejection of Weimarian Politics or Betrayal of Democracy: Spain's Proscription of Batasuna under the European Convention on Human Rights', *American University Law Review*, 52: 1531–81.

Schafer, S. (1974) *The Political Criminal: The Problem of Morality and Crime*. New York: The Free Press.

Schubert, M. (1986) 'Political Prisoners in West Germany: Their Situation and Some Consequences Concerning their Rights in Respect of the Treatment of Political Prisoners in International Law', in B. Rolston and M. Tomlinson (eds), *The Expansion of European Prison Systems. Working Papers in European Criminology*, No. 7. Belfast: The European Group for the Study of Deviance and Control.

Schulze, K. (2004) *The Free Aceh Movement (GAM): Anatomy of a Separatist Organization*. Washington, DC: East-West Centre.

Schmid, A., Jongman, A. and M. Stohl (1990) *Political Terrorism: A New Guide to Actors, Authors, Concepts, Databases, Theorists, and Literature*. Amsterdam: North Holland Publishing Company.

Scott, J.C. (1985) *Weapons of the Weak: Everyday Forms of Peasant Resistance*. New Haven, CT: Yale University Press.

Scott, J.C. (1990) *Domination and the Arts of Resistance: Hidden Transcripts*. New Haven, CT: Yale University Press.

Sentence Review Commission (2004) *Annual Report of the Northern Ireland Sentence Review Commission*. Belfast: HMSO.

Sentence Review Commission (2006) *Annual Report of the Northern Ireland Sentence Review Commission*. Belfast: HMSO.

Sheffer, G. (ed.) (1993) *Innovative Leaders in International Politics*. Albany: State University of New York Press.

Shirlow, P. (2001a) *The State They Are In: An Independent Evaluation*. Belfast: University of Ulster Social Exclusion Research Unit.

Shirlow, P. (2001b) 'Devolution in Northern Ireland/Ulster/the North/the Six Counties: Delete as Appropriate', *Regional Studies*, 35 (2): 743–52.

Shirlow, P. (2003a) 'Ethno-sectarianism and the Reproduction of Fear in Belfast', *Capital and Class*, 80 (2): 77–94.

Shirlow, P. (2003b) '"Who Fears to Speak": Fear, Mobility, and Ethno-sectarianism in the Two "Ardoynes"', *Global Review of Ethnopolitics*, 3 (1): 76–91.

Shirlow, P. and M. McGovern (1996) 'Sectarianism, Socio-Economic Competition and the Political Economy of Ulster Loyalism', *Antipode*, 28 (4): 377–96.

Shirlow, P. and M. McGovern (1998) 'Language, Discourse and Dialogue: Sinn Fein and the Irish Peace Process', *Political Geography*, 17 (2): 171–86.

Shirlow, P. and R. Monaghan (2004) 'Northern Ireland: Ten Years On', *Terrorism and Political Violence*, 15 (3): 397–400.

Shirlow, P. and R. Monaghan (2006) *Ulster Loyalism? Forwards to the Past*. Swindon: ESRC (RES-000–22–1013).

Shirlow, P. and B. Murtagh (2004) 'Capacity Building, Representation and Intra-Community Conflict', *Urban Studies*, 41 (1): 57–70.

Shirlow, P. and B. Murtagh (2006) *Belfast: Segregation and the City*. London: Pluto Press, and Ann Arbor: University of Michigan Press.

Shirlow, P., Graham, B., Murtagh, B., Robinson, G. and N. Southern (2005) *Negotiating Change: Sharing and Conflict Amelioration in Derry/Londonderry*. Belfast: OFM/DFM, Equality Unit/Joseph Rowntree Charitable Trust.

Sinn Féin (2003) 'A Shared Future: Response' <http://www.sinnfein.ie/policies/document/128>.

Sinn Féin Prisoner of War Department (1986) *Lifers*. Belfast: Republican Publications.

Sinnerton, H. (2003) *David Ervine: Uncharted Waters*. Cork: Brandon.

Sluka, J. (1995) 'Domination, Resistance and Political-Culture in Northern-Ireland Catholic-Nationalist Ghettos', *Critique Of Anthropology*, 1: 71–102.

Smith, A. (1983) 'The Prerogative of Mercy, the Power of Pardon and Criminal Justice', *Public Law*, 28: 398–439.

Sparks, R., Bottoms, A. and W. Hay (1996) *Prisons and the Problem of Order*. Oxford: Clarendon Press.

Spujt, R. (1986) 'Internment and Detention without Trial in Northern Ireland (1971–1975)', *Modern Law Review*, 49: 712–39.

Stevenson, J. (1996) *We Wrecked the Place: Contemplating the End to the Northern Irish Troubles*. New York: The Free Press.

Sullivan, D. and L. Tifft (eds) (2006) *The Handbook of Restorative Justice: Global Perspectives*. London: Routledge.

Sykes, G. (1958) *The Society of Captives*. Princeton, NJ: Princeton University Press.

Sykes, G. and S. Messinger (1960) 'The Inmate Social System', in R. Cloward et al. (eds), *Theoretical Studies in the Social Organization of the Prison*. New York: Social Science Research Council.

Tar Anall (2000) *Employment, Training and Further Education Opportunities Facing Republican Prisoners Released Before 1990*. Belfast: Tar Anall.

Tar Isteach (2004) *Annual Report*. Belfast: Tar Isteach.

Tarrow, S. (1989) *Democracy and Disorder: Protest Politics in Italy, 1965–1975*. Oxford: Oxford University Press.

Taylor, P. (1980) *Beating the Terrorists? Interrogations at Omagh, Gough and Castlereagh*. Harmondsworth: Penguin.

Taylor, P. (1997) *Provo: The IRA and Sinn Féin*. London: Bloomsbury.

Teichman J. (1996) 'How to Define Terrorism', in C. Gearty (ed.), *Terrorism*. Aldershot: Ashgate, 3–17.

The Captive Voice/An Glor Gafa (1989), 'Prison News', *The Captive Voice/An Glor Gafa*, 1 (1). Belfast: Republican Publications.

Tidwell, A. (1998) *Conflict Resolved?: A Critical Assessment of Conflict Resolution*. London: Continuum International Publishing Group Ltd.

Tilly, C. (2003) *The Politics of Collective Violence*. Cambridge: Cambridge University Press.

Tonge, J. (2004) '"They Haven't Gone Away, You Know": Irish Republican "Dissidents" and "Armed Struggle"', *Terrorism and Political Violence*, 16 (3): 671–93.

Tonge, J. (2005) *Northern Ireland: Conflict and Change*. Harlow: Longman.

United Nations (2004) *Report of the UN Special Rapporteur on Torture on Spain*. New York: United Nations.

Van Den Wyngaert, C. (1980) *The Political Offence Exception to Extradition: The Delicate Problem of Balancing the Rights of the Individual and the International Public Order*. Boston, MA: Kluwer.

Verwimp, P. and M. Verpoorten (2004) 'What are All the Soldiers Going to Do? Demobilisation, Reintegration And Employment in Rwanda', *Conflict, Security and Development*, 4 (1): 39–57.

Von Tangen Page, M. (1998) *Prisons, Peace and Terrorism*. London: Macmillan.

Von Tangen Page, M. (2006) 'A "Most Difficult and Unpalatable Part" – The Release of Politically Motivated Violent Offenders', in M. Cox, A. Guelke and F. Stephen (eds), *A Farewell to Arms: Beyond the Good Friday Agreement*. Manchester: Manchester University Press.

Ward, T. and T. Gannon (2006) 'Rehabilitation, Etiology and Self-Regulation: The Good Lives Model of Sexual Offender Treatment', *Aggression and Violent Behaviour*, 11: 77–94.

Ward, T. and S. Maruna (2007) *Rehabilitation: Beyond the Risk Paradigm*. London: Routledge.

Weber, M. (1958) *From Max Weber: Essays in Sociology*. Oxford: Oxford University Press.

Westlake, M. (2000) *Leaders of Transition*. New York: St. Martin's Press.

Whyte, B. (1984) *John Hume: Statesman of the Troubles*. Belfast: Blackstaff Press.

White, J. (1998) *Loyalist Political Prisoners in Context: An Action Research Assessment*. Belfast: Prisoners' Aid and Post Conflict Resettlement Group.

Wilkinson, P. (1986) *Terrorism and the Liberal State*. London: Macmillan.

Williams, J. (2001) 'Hunger-Strikes: A Prisoner's Right or a "Wicked Folly"?', *Howard Journal of Criminal Justice*, 40 (3): 285–96.

Winston, T. (1997) 'Alternatives to Punishment Beatings and Shootings in a Loyalist Community in Belfast', *Critical Criminology*, 8 (1): 122–8.

Wolfsfeld, G. (2004) *Media and the Path to Peace*. Cambridge: Cambridge University Press.

Woodworth, P. (2001) *Dirty War, Clean Hands: ETA, GAL and Spanish Democracy*. Cork: Cork University Press.

Woodworth, P. (2004) 'The War against Terrorism: The Spanish Experience from ETA to Al Qaeda', *International Journal of Iberian Studies*, 17 (3): 169–82.

World Bank (2002) *Greater Great Lakes Regional Strategy for Demobilization and Reintegration*. Report No. 23869-AFR. New York: World Bank.

Yiftachel, O. (2002) 'Territory as the Kernel of Nationalism', *Geopolitics*, 7 (3): 215–48.

Zamble, E. and S. Porporino (1988) *Coping, Behaviour and Adaptation in Prison Inmates*. New York: Springer-Verlag.

Zartman, I. (2007) *Negotiation and Conflict Management: Essays on Theory and Practice*. London: Routledge.

Zhao, D. (2004) *The Power of Tiananmen: State-Society Relations and the 1989 Beijing Student Movement*. Chicago, IL: University of Chicago Press.

Index

Compiled by Sue Carlton